PRAISE FOR *THE HO*

MW00620698

With its scriptural alertness, its generous appropriation of elements of classical Christian thought, and its dogmatic intelligence and scope, this is a rewarding study of the lordly and life-giving Spirit.

—*John Webster,* Professor of Divinity, St Mary's College, University of St Andrews

This is a thorough and novel approach to the doctrine of the Holy Spirit, which takes an historical approach to dogmatic questions while still making normative judgments. Especially welcome is its attention to the Spirit's priestly work as centered in the cross of Christ, a topic often neglected. This is a worthy contribution that enriches our understanding of the Holy Spirit's person and work by upholding the centrality of Christ.

—*George Hunsinger,* Hazel Thompson McCord Professor of Systematic Theology, Princeton Theological Seminary

One of the church's best young theologians, Chris Holmes, takes us into some deep theological waters. We could have no better guide than Holmes. In this masterful, groundbreaking work, he enters into informed conversation with Augustine, Aquinas, and Barth and comes forth with a fresh, engaging celebration of the Holy Spirit. Here is adventuresome dogmatic theology at its best. Holmes's vibrantly Christological, exuberantly Trinitarian engagement with the Holy Spirit is demanding, invigorating theological engagement.

—*Will Willimon,* Professor of the Practice of Christian Ministry, Duke Divinity School, Durham, NC, and United Methodist bishop, retired

Guided by such luminaries as John Webster and Kevin Vanhoozer, Reformed dogmatic theology has been powerfully revitalized in recent years. Professor Holmes's exploration of the glorious mystery of the Holy Spirit is a fruit of this renewal and a most welcome fruit indeed. The interplay of the Spirit and the church is here not only exposited but also reflected in Holmes's deft integration of piety and scholarship.

—*Matthew Levering,* Perry Family Foundation Professor of Theology, Mundelein Seminary

An excellent companion for those who would like to accompany Barth and Aquinas through their rigorous and biblical accounts of the Holy Spirit.

—*Eugene F. Rogers Jr., Professor of Religious Studies,*
The University of North Carolina, Greensboro

Ours is an age in which things "spiritual" have broken free from things "religious" or "theological." Christopher Holmes, in this clear and forceful book, knits back together the spiritual and the theological, insisting on the proper priority of the triune God over all our attempts to worship, obey, know, and follow him. Holmes offers a doctrine of the Third Person anchored in a fresh vision of the Spirit as One who is Other-directed: the Holy Spirit manifests, exalts, and leads us to the Son, who is the express Image of the Father. Here is a book that begins—and does not depart from—Holy Scripture. To read this book is to breathe the air of one who loves theology and loves the Love that is the Eternal Gift and End of all things.

—*Katherine Sonderegger, William Meade Professor*
of Theology, Virginia Theological Seminary

NEW STUDIES IN DOGMATICS

THE HOLY SPIRIT

NEW STUDIES IN DOGMATICS

THE HOLY SPIRIT

CHRISTOPHER R. J. HOLMES

MICHAEL ALLEN AND SCOTT R. SWAIN,
GENERAL EDITORS

ZONDERVAN

The Holy Spirit

Copyright © 2015 by Christopher R. J. Holmes

This title is also available as a Zondervan ebook. Visit www.zondervan.com/ebooks.

Requests for information should be addressed to:
Zondervan, 3900 *Sparks Dr. SE, Grand Rapids, Michigan 49546*

Library of Congress Cataloging-in-Publication Data

The Holy Spirit / Christopher R. J. Holmes, Michael Allen, and Scott R. Swain, general editors.
    pages cm. — (New studies in dogmatics)
    Includes bibliographical references and index.
    ISBN 978-0-310-49170-5 (softcover)
    1. Holy Spirit — History of doctrines. I. Title.
BT119.H64 2015
231'.3 — dc23   2015007229

Cover design: Micah Kandros
Interior design: Kait Lamphere

Printed in the United States of America

15 16 17 18 19 20 21 22 23 24 /DCI/ 20 19 18 17 16 15 14 13 12 11 10 9 8 7 6 5 4 3 2

To Christina

CONTENTS

DETAILED CONTENTS

SERIES PREFACE

New Studies in Dogmatics follows in the tradition of G. C. Berkouwer's classic series, Studies in Dogmatics, in seeking to offer concise, focused treatments of major topics in dogmatic theology that fill the gap between introductory theology textbooks and advanced theological monographs. Dogmatic theology, as understood by editors and contributors to the series, is a conceptual representation of scriptural teaching about God and all things in relation to God. The source of dogmatics is Holy Scripture; its scope is the summing up of all things in Jesus Christ; its setting is the communion of the saints; and its end is the conversion, consolation, and instruction of creaturely wayfarers in the knowledge and love of the triune God until that knowledge and love is consummated in the beatific vision.

The series wagers that the way forward in constructive theology lies in a program of renewal through retrieval. This wager follows upon the judgment that much modern theology exhibits "a stubborn tendency to grow not higher but to the side," to borrow Alexander Solzhenitsyn's words from another context. Though modern theology continues to grow in a number of areas of technical expertise and interdisciplinary facility (especially in both the exegetical and historical domains), this growth too often displays a sideways drift rather than an upward progression in relation to theology's subject matter, scope, and source, and in fulfilling theology's end. We believe the path toward theological renewal in such a situation lies in drawing more deeply upon the resources of Holy Scripture in conversation with the church's most trusted teachers (ancient, medieval, and modern) who have sought to fathom Christ's unsearchable riches. In keeping with this belief, authors from a broad evangelical constituency will seek in this series to retrieve the riches of Scripture and tradition for constructive dogmatics. The purpose of retrieval is neither simple repetition of past theologians nor repristination of an earlier phase in church history; Christianity, at any rate, has no golden age east of Eden and short of the kingdom of God.

Properly understood, retrieval is an inclusive and enlarging venture, a matter of tapping into a vital root and, in some cases, of relearning a lost grammar of theological discourse, all for the sake of equipping the church in its contemporary vocation to think and speak faithfully and fruitfully about God and God's works.

While the specific emphases of individual volumes will vary, each volume will display (1) awareness of the "state of the question" pertaining to the doctrine under discussion; (2) attention to the patterns of biblical reasoning (exegetical, biblical-theological, etc.) from which the doctrine emerges; (3) engagement with relevant ecclesiastical statements of the doctrine (creedal, conciliar, confessional), as well as with leading theologians of the church; and (4) appreciation of the doctrine's location within the larger system of theology, as well as of its contribution to Christian piety and practice.

Our prayer is that by drawing upon the best resources of the past and with an awareness of both perennial and proximate challenges to Christian thought and practice in the present, New Studies in Dogmatics will contribute to a flourishing theological culture in the church today. Soli Deo Gloria.

Michael Allen and Scott R. Swain

ACKNOWLEDGMENTS

I received a great deal of help in writing this book. My sincere gratitude goes out to many. I would especially like to thank the Humanities Division of the University of Otago for a research leave during the second half of 2013. The leave gave me the time to write a draft of the text. Otago is a generous employer; the Department of Theology and Religion, a wonderful place in which to do systematic theology. I am continually amazed by the kindness and dedication of my colleagues. The department has been nothing but a collegial and friendly environment in which to work.

Many people commented on the text at various stages of its development. Six acknowledgments must be made. First, I appreciate the wisdom of my colleague Professor Murray Rae. Murray helped me to discern whether this project was an appropriate one to take on.

Second, Dr. Mark Gingerich, a newly minted Otago systematics PhD, read through the entirety of the first, rather clunky, draft, offering numerous comments along the way.

Third, Professor Eugene Rogers helped me to see what is at stake in Augustine's and Thomas's Trinitarian treatises. Eugene's thorough and incisive comments on the first five chapters of an early draft were profoundly useful. One of the great privileges of living in Dunedin, a beautiful university town at the bottom of the world, is just how many distinguished theological voices visit on a regular basis. Eugene's trip to Dunedin in December 2013 was one of those. I do not always agree with him, but I am better for knowing one as sharp as Gene with whom to disagree.

Fourth, Professor John Webster has always been generous with his time and consistently encouraging. His forthright comments on the penultimate draft made for a better and much more readable book. I owe him many favours.

Fifth, the Rev. Dr. Jonathan Hicks, also a newly minted Otago systematics PhD, read through the final draft, eliminating the last (I hope) of the stylistic infelicities and offering careful comments along the way. I pray that Jonathan's teaching ministry in the Anglican province of Melanesia will bear much fruit in the coming years.

Sixth, Mike Allen, Scott Swain, and Katya Covrett are, quite simply, extraordinary editors. It is rather humbling to have one's work taken so seriously and with so much grace and humour. Katya's patience with some of my stylistic quirks and infelicities deserves a gold medal.

My thanks also goes out to Matthew Levering, Philip Ziegler, and Katherine Sonderegger for many helpful conversations along the way; also to the Christian Thought and History Seminar of the Department of Theology and Religion at Otago, and those who responded to my paper at the colloquium "Beyond Sacrifice" with Professor Sarah Coakley in Auckland in December 2013.

The people of St. John's Anglican Church are our family. My wife (Christina) and I are most grateful for the generosity shown to our family, especially to our three young children: Lillian, Fiona, and Markus. The vicar, the Rev. Eric Kyte, preaches the gospel without shame and is a wonderful conversation partner. I am grateful for the body of Christ.

Last, I dedicate this text to Christina. Her support and patience, her willingness to move to the opposite end of the world, and her embrace of our new home and church community have been beyond what one could ask or imagine.

CHAPTER 1

INTRODUCTION: ON LEARNING THE HOLY SPIRIT

This is a book about the being, identity, and activity of the Holy Spirit. What is the Holy Spirit? Who is the Holy Spirit? How does the Spirit do things? And what does the Spirit do? These are the central questions. The Spirit's abiding interest is to bind us to Christ and to his Father, our Father, thereby leading everyone back to the Father through the Son. But why is this? Why does the Spirit act in this way? This book answers these deep questions. My contention is that God's being is reliably expressed in God's acts, given God's covenant faithfulness. However, Holy Scripture teaches us that God's acts cannot contain God's being any more than Israel's temple could contain the immense majesty of God. The being of God is what grounds the missions of Son and Spirit. God's great acts of creation, reconciliation, and perfection have a source. That source is God's being, complete in itself. This book is an unfolding of that life and of how we share in that life through the gift of the Holy Spirit.

SPEAKING OF GOD

The church confesses that it believes in one God, Father, Son, and Holy Spirit. In so doing, it has never denied that the description of God will take us to the very limits of speech, indeed beyond them. This is not to say, however, that we are simply reduced to silence before God the Holy Trinity. The Trinity is a mystery that wills to be known, loved, served, and spoken of as that mystery truly *is*. The Trinity is a knowable mystery. The Trinity would have us talk of the Trinity as the Trinity truly is.

Karl Barth—about whom you will hear much in this study—spoke eloquently of how the God of the gospel "commandeers" our speech.[1] Rather than letting us think we know in advance the content of the name "Holy Spirit," the biblical testimony teaches us to speak faithfully and truthfully with respect to the being and identity of the "Holy Spirit." In other words, Scripture commandeers the names "Father" or "Holy Spirit," teaching us how to speak of the name of God with proper reverence. Just so, the name "Holy Spirit" is a revealed name; the same is true of "Father." These names are given their content by Scripture. This study is an exercise in how sacred Scripture teaches us to speak of the Spirit's person and work in a way that would honour Thomas F. Torrance's statement that "the Spirit is not just something divine or something akin to God emanating from him, not some sort of action at a distance or some kind of gift detachable from himself, for in the Holy Spirit God acts directly upon us himself, and in giving us his Holy Spirit God gives us nothing less than himself."[2]

This volume is also concerned with mapping the being of the God whom Scripture gives us to know and love. The God of the Bible—as scandalous as this may seem—really is "actually and unreservedly as we encounter him in his revelation."[3] That is why it is appropriate and necessary to speak with confidence about God's life on the basis of the missions of Son and Spirit. God's inner life is encountered, revealed, and disclosed in God's outward life, God's saving acts. It is these acts that point us to their origin, that teach us of a profound unity of being between the Father, Son, and Spirit. Our joyful task ahead is to recognize in the idiom of Scripture rich metaphysical teaching about the one being of the triune God. In other words, the Old and New Testaments encourage us to talk with sobriety not only about what God does but also about what and how God is. The Testaments taken together promote reflection on the shape of God's inner life as revealed in Israel and Jesus.

---

1. See Karl Barth, *Church Dogmatics*, ed. G. W. Bromiley and T. F. Torrance (Edinburgh: T&T Clark, 1957–1975), I/1, 136 (hereafter *CD*).

2. Thomas F. Torrance, *The Trinitarian Faith: The Evangelical Theology of the Ancient Catholic Church* (Edinburgh: T&T Clark, 1988), 191.

3. Barth, *CD* II/1, 58.

THE SPIRIT'S BEING AND NATURE

When Christians call on the Spirit, we are calling on the Spirit of the risen Jesus. Rather than being directed away from Jesus Christ, the Spirit deepens our fellowship with him and his people, all to the glory of the Father. The Spirit does not replace Christ or take over from him. Rather, the Spirit's work "is to carry forward the divine philanthropy begun in the incarnation."[4] The Spirit does not detract from Christ, supersede Christ, or act as his substitute. As we will see, the Spirit is primarily at work in relation to the Word (incarnate, written, and proclaimed), strengthening baptized children of God to remain true to Christ. Indeed, the mission of the Holy Spirit is coextensive with the mission of the Word (the Lord Jesus Christ).

But why does the Spirit act this way? Why is the Spirit other-directed? Herein lies the key idea of the volume. There are basic reasons the three do what they do in creating and, in turn, reconciling and perfecting humankind for a life of blessedness. Those reasons have to do with how the three are. Such talk of how the three are is necessary if we are to understand why God's work toward the outside has the shape that it does.

THE SPIRIT'S ECONOMY

God's work toward the outside—what I will call the economy— has assumed disproportionate significance in contemporary theology. Talk of God's inner life (*in se*) is assumed to be abstract, lacking any kind of immediate theological or pastoral purchase. Does not such talk discourage us from taking seriously Luther's advice to seek God where "true theology and recognition of God" is to be found, that is, "in the crucified Christ"?[5] I do not think so. In this book, I offer a calm statement of the deity and identity of the God who wills to be found there. This is important because of the reality that God is. In God essence and existence are one. This is what it means to speak of God as one who lives from himself. God does not need anyone or anything outside of God in order to be God. Explanation of this life that is utterly complete

---

4. H. B. Swete, *The Holy Catholic Church* (New York: Macmillan, 1915), 183, cited in Yves Congar, *I Believe in the Holy Spirit*, trans. David Smith (New York: Seabury, 1983), 2:17.

5. Timothy F. Lull, ed. *Martin Luther's Basic Theological Writings* (Minneapolis: Fortress, 1989), 43–44.

in itself requires first principles. First principles describe the reality that God is, that this life exists from itself. Without talk of first principles, we miss out on understanding the rationale for why the Son is sent and the Father is the one who sends. Scripture's content is metaphysical. We also do not know why it is the Spirit who is breathed by the Son, poured out by the Father. We do not learn the principles of intelligibility for why the saving economy of God has the shape that it does. Many contemporary thinkers are indebted to Luther for urging us to take seriously the cross as key to knowing God. Much contemporary theology has heard Luther on this point, understanding him to eschew Trinitarian metaphysics. I think that there is some good in that, but it is not a path that I take.

The present text seeks to make a contribution to the contemporary discussion around the divinity, nature, identity, and acts of God the Holy Trinity and specifically of God's Spirit. God's outward work has the shape that it does because it reveals the life of one who is wholly complete from eternity. God's life is perfect in itself. God's life is pure act, a life in which the Son is begotten of the Father in a perpetual eternity, the Spirit comes forth or proceeds as the Love of the Father for the Son and the Son for the Father from eternity. Talk of what God does, which is the basis for how God is known, has a foundation. That foundation has to do with the being of God.

THE OTHER-DIRECTED SPIRIT

In this volume, I talk about the Holy Spirit as the Spirit *of* Christ. That is not to reduce the Spirit to an appendage of Christ or to collapse the Spirit into him. Rather, it is to say that the Spirit demonstrates profound boldness in promoting another, Jesus Christ. The Spirit's actions are directed to Christ to the glory of the Father. This is what it means to talk about the Spirit as the Spirit *of* Jesus. Whether it be the Spirit's casting down of Saul on the road to Damascus or the conceiving of Jesus in Mary's womb, the Spirit is other-directed, Christ-directed.

The "of" makes all the difference for the approach that I champion. The Spirit never departs from the Son. The Spirit works tirelessly in the economy of grace to expand the community of those baptized into the Son, the living Lord Jesus. Emphasizing this point makes it far more difficult to think of the Spirit apart from Jesus Christ and his Father,

our Father. In keeping the Spirit tethered to the Son
biblical testimony encourages, the Spirit does not float
and his Father. The indissoluble bond that exists betwee
and the Holy Spirit, between the Father who sends him
who breathes him, is thereby honoured.

The Holy Spirit is the other-directed third person ... Holy
Trinity. We know the Spirit, Yves Congar writes, "not directly in
himself, but through what he brings about in us."[6] The "us" in whom
the Spirit brings about the Spirit's gifts is the Christian community.
The Spirit who gathers to Christ is constantly working to grow the
community of Christ. The Spirit sends out those gathered to Jesus to
witness to Jesus' work of promoting his own environment. The "environment of Jesus Christ," to use Barth's language, is not static.[7] The
Spirit is in the process of drawing people everywhere to Christ and his
community. This is good news because the community of Christ to
whom the Spirit leads is always in process. The community's dynamism
is proper to Christ and the Spirit.

It is important to consider this at the beginning of the book.
Because the Spirit is a person, the Spirit has unique work to do. Perhaps
the most radical and far-reaching biblical example is that of the inclu-
sion of the Gentiles. The Spirit bears witness to Christ by drastically
expanding the parameters of his mission. No longer is Jesus the one
who is "sent only to the lost sheep of Israel" (Matt 15:24). The Spirit
whom Christ breathes and who is poured out onto many at Pentecost
completely reconfigures expectations. The dimensions of the church's
sphere become "very different from what we know them to be."[8] In
Luke-Acts, for example, but also in Romans and Galatians, the good
news of Jesus Christ is understood not only to be for the Jew but also
for the Gentile. In ways that the disciples prior to Jesus' resurrection
could not understand, Moses and the prophets testify anew to him in
whom salvation for the Jew and for the Gentile is to be found.

The Spirit is ever extending the borders of the Word's sovereignty.
The Spirit is other-directed, that is, Christ-directed, but the Spirit is
not simply a principle in relationship to Christ. The remarkable inde-
pendence of the Spirit—the Spirit's blowing where he wills (cf. John

---

6. Congar, *Holy Spirit*, 1:viii.
7. Barth, *CD* II/2, 196.
8. Barth, *CD* I/1, 54.

—is a function of the remarkable interdependence of the two. The Spirit works tirelessly to declare the "I" of another, Jesus Christ. Therein we receive a glimpse of the Spirit's hypostatic uniqueness in God. We see a person who is so secure in himself that he can be entirely given over to declaration of another. The Spirit's actions encourage us to contemplate their rationale. This is the work of Trinitarian metaphysics.[9]

THE THIRD PERSON

We might think that the designation "third person" suggests that the Spirit is of a rank below the first and second persons, Father and Son, respectively. Nothing could be further from the truth: the Spirit is consubstantial with Father and Son, of one essence with the Father and Son. There is unity of being between the three, from eternity. The Spirit points us to Jesus Christ, knits us into life with him and his people, all to the glory of his Father in order that we might share in their life to all eternity. The Spirit has no interest in pointing us to the Spirit's self. That is not because the Spirit does not have a self. Rather, the personhood of the Spirit—the Spirit's hypostatic uniqueness—is expressed in the Spirit's binding us to Christ and in him to the Father. This work does not constitute the Spirit. Instead, the Spirit's work displays the Spirit's hypostatic uniqueness that is in fact constituted by his eternal procession.

I do not approach such a presentation of the Holy Spirit from an objective or neutral vantage point. Knowledge of the God of the gospel is unlike any other kind of knowledge. It is radically self-involving. In other words, to know the God of the Bible is to be transformed. Knowledge of the one who encounters us in Israel (the Old Testament) and Jesus (the New Testament) through the prophets and apostles is self-authenticating knowledge. The God the Bible attests to us creates hearers of his Word *ex nihilo*. Therefore, the tone of this work is one of confidence: confidence that this God works with "clay jars" such as ourselves (2 Cor 4:7) in order that we might be made to testify to the one who is the Alpha and Omega, the Beginning and the End.

---

9. Note that in this study I will occasionally refer to the Spirit with the personal pronoun "he" or possessive pronoun "his." In so doing, I do not intend to suggest that the Spirit is masculine or male in gender or sexuality. The Spirit is beyond gender. Rather, because the Latin and German grammatical gender of the word "Spirit" is masculine, and because my sources (Augustine, Thomas, and Barth) happen to come from those languages, despite the fact that the Spirit is feminine in Hebrew and is neuter in New Testament Greek, I chose to use "he" and "his."

Let us consider for a moment Paul's famous statement in Galatians 4:6: "And because you are children, God has sent the Spirit of his Son into our hearts, crying, 'Abba! Father!'" The cry of "the Spirit of his Son" is a cry to the Father, the God of Israel. The pattern here is Trinitarian. Paul recognizes that the Old Testament—the only Bible he had to go by—is Trinitarian. Paul receives the Hebrew Scriptures *in* the Spirit. Accordingly, he hears their testimony as radically Trinitarian. The Spirit uncovers what is there, although his doing so may appear to be rather surprising. The Spirit, as with Jesus' encounter with his disciples on the road to Emmaus in Luke 24, directs us anew to the testimony of Moses and the prophets in order to receive it as testimony to Christ. The Spirit of the Son generates a cry, the "Abba! Father!" that Jews and Gentiles alike cry out in Christ. Through the Spirit do we receive the fullness of the biblical testimony to God.

I write from within the faith of Christ and his universal church so as to nourish and edify. Faith's content is of course Christ, his Father, and their Spirit. Faith is not a human capacity but rather something that God the Spirit creates through the hearing of the written and pro-claimed Word, and renews within the hearts of the baptized through the celebration of the sacred supper. Works of theology such as this are indeed life-giving to the extent that they evoke a fresh hearing of those Scriptures and a life of grateful obedience to their message. It is not for nothing that the Spirit is noted to be the one who evokes gratitude.

THE KEY IDEA: THEOLOGY AND ECONOMY

In terms of the key idea, two points need to be secured above all else. The first concerns "processions," the latter "missions." The Greek Fathers of the church "called [them] 'theology and economy.' To talk about theology is to talk about 'the mystery of the Trinitarian God.' To discuss the economy is to discuss 'the mystery of incarnation and redemption.'"[10] An account of the Holy Spirit has its basis in the eternal

---

10. Felix Heinzer, "L'explication trinitaire de l'économie chez Maxime le Confesseur," in *Maximus Confessor: Actes du Symposium sur Maxime le Confesseur Fribourg, 2–5 September 1980*, ed. Felix Heinzer and Christoph von Schönborn (Fribourg-en-Suisse: Éditions Universitarires, 1982), 159, quoted in A. Edward Siecienski, *The Filioque: History of a Doctrinal Controversy* (New York: Oxford University Press, 2010), 75. Gregory Nazianzen, in his discussion of the character of the Spirit's procession as a kind of "midway between ingeneracy and generacy," refers to those who resist his account as beating "a retreat from theology." See Frederick W. Norris, *Faith Gives Fullness to Reasoning: The Five Theological Orations of Gregory of Nazianzen*, trans. Lionel Wickham

(or immanent) life of God—theology—as revealed in the economy of salvation. Our knowledge of the Spirit follows up the Spirit's being. To speak of the immanent life of God—who God is in himself (*in se*)—is to describe the way in which the three persons of the Godhead, Father, Son, and Holy Spirit, are eternally united in essence and yet personally distinct from one another. It is to speak of a life that has an order. This involves us in a description of the processions of the Son and Spirit. To describe their processions is to unfold their relations of origin. Talk of the various relations of origin is in the service of describing how these three are. This may sound dull. That theologians as astute and intelligent as Augustine, Thomas, and Barth had many interesting things to say on this topic makes it worth considering.

Contemporary theology's reticence to go where Augustine, Thomas, and Barth were happy to go, especially in their scriptural commentaries, is problematic. Talk of processions is clumsy, but such talk is necessary not only to ward off false teaching but also to accentuate how God is. Theology should be grateful to talk about the being of God and how the one being of God is. This is not to violate the mystery of the triune God but to honour the extent to which God wants his people to know and love him as he truly is.

THE PROCESSIONS

In God, as we will discover, there are two processions: the generation of the Son and the procession of the Holy Spirit. The two processions are the foundation for discussion of the three persons, Father, Son, and Spirit. The three are who they are, and indeed ordered to each in the way that they are, by virtue of their relations of origin one to another. The Father is paternity. The Father is the one who begets the Son. The Son is sonship, the one who is begotten by the Father. The Spirit is the

and Frederick Williams (Leiden: Brill, 1991), 31.7. Similarly, Boris Bobrinskoy, a leading twentieth-century Orthodox theologian, writes, "Reflecting the thought of the Church Fathers, Orthodox theology rightly distinguishes between Trinitarian 'theology' and Trinitarian 'economy.' Trinitarian *theology* deals with the mystery of the Trinity in its eternal 'immanence,' the infinite, blessed communion of the divine Persons among themselves, *without reference to creation.* Trinitarian *economy*, on the other hand, refers to the concerted activity of the three Persons *ad extra*, in creation, as they maintain and restore the created world to a state of well-being and communion with God. The distinction between Trinitarian theology and Trinitarian economy is both *fundamental* and *relative*." The approach to the Spirit undertaken in this volume assumes and unfolds Bobrinskoy's articulation of the distinction as "both *fundamental* and *relative*." See his *The Mystery of the Trinity: Trinitarian Experience and Vision in the Biblical and Patristic Tradition*, trans. Anthony P. Gythiel (Crestwood, NY: St. Vladimir's Seminary Press, 1999), 2–3.

one who proceeds "'from the Father as the absolute source' and 'from the Father through the Son.'"[11]

In the great acts of creation, reconciliation, and redemption, we see the three doing different things. The fact that they do different things attests their different origins. What renders the persons and their actions distinct from one another are their different characteristics. Why is the Son and not the Father or the Spirit the one who becomes incarnate? Why is the Son the sent one rather than the sender? The respective characteristics of the three are expressed in their acts. That they have different characteristics and act differently from one to another has to do with their origins. Again, the Father begets and therefore in the fullness of time sends; the Son is begotten and therefore sent in the fullness of time; and the Spirit proceeds from the Father and Son as their love and gift and is therefore poured out in the fullness of time by the Father through the breath of the Son.[12]

God is pure act, and so these originating relations are never static. Indeed, they describe something of *how* God is. This insight explains the biblical testimony, why the three act as they do. If I come to believe that Jesus is the Way, it is because the Spirit is working in me. The Spirit who proceeds through Christ leads to Christ. In like manner, since I cannot come to God except by God, then the Spirit must be God. The acts of the three press us to ask *how* each is, how the Spirit is God as the Father and the Son but God in a different way. Augustine, Thomas, and Barth have found talk of originating relations revealing of *how* the God of our salvation is also God and remains God in all that he does for us and for our salvation. Several chapters will show why they think talk of originating relations is helpful.

THE MISSIONS

From the beginning, the Holy Trinity creates with a view to being our God and us being God's people (Ezek 37:27). The fulfillment of this eternal determination centres on the life, death, and resurrection of

---

11. Yves Congar argues persuasively that East and West do not disagree at the level of faith, for they share the same faith. Rather, they disagree at the level of the expression of that faith. See *Holy Spirit*, 3:206, xiii.

12. Whether the Spirit is said to proceed from the Father and the Son or from the Father alone through the Son will be discussed in much greater detail throughout the volume. The issue with respect to the *filioque* concerns the role of the Son in the Spirit's origins and the matter of who changed the Creed.

Jesus Christ in fulfillment of the promises made to Israel. Jesus' obedience unto death, his laying down of his life, indicates *who* he is, namely, God's beloved Son. Similarly, the Spirit's empowering of the Hebrew prophets, his filling of Jesus, and his indwelling of Jesus' people says much about *who* he eternally is in relation to the Father and the Son as their love and gift.[13] In this study, I undertake description of *how* each (especially the Spirit) is. Without such description, we do not really know whether salvation goes all the way down in God, whether there is some other God behind the one who loves us. Indeed, the processions help us to articulate the *how* of the three. The *how*, in turn, is expressed in their life toward the outside, the mission of the Son and the Spirit.

The mission of the Spirit among us extends the procession of the Spirit as the love of the Father for the Son and the Son for the Father. Thomas calls the Spirit their *"love proceeding."*[14] The Spirit's activity encourages us to ask about and to reflect on the Spirit's being and identity in God. The Spirit's divinity grounds the Spirit's work among us. We only ask about relations *ad intra* because we know about God's unity *ad extra*. We only ask about God's inner life, because we wonder where God's goodness toward us comes from. The basic reason one cannot concentrate exclusively on the economy of the Trinity, as much contemporary theology does, is that God's self-revelation encourages us to speak of its source in God's life. It is God's life that must govern any account of what God does.

IS THE SPIRIT THE GRANDSON OF THE FATHER?

To drive the volume's key idea home, ask, Why is the Spirit not the grandson of the Father? If the Son is the second of the three and the Spirit the third, why would we not call the Spirit the son of the Son and the grandson of the Father? Trinitarian metaphysics or, to put it another way, antecedent first principles, answer these questions. The Spirit conceives the Son (Luke 1:35). The origins of the three are circular. The persons of the Trinity all share in the same reality, and equally; they are united in essence. But that essence or nature exists only in a tripersonal way. What distinguishes the three from each other are, therefore, not

---

13. "Love" and "Gift," as names of the Holy Spirit, will only be capitalized when discussing them in terms of Augustine and Thomas.

14. Saint Thomas Aquinas, *Summa Theologica* I, q. 37, a. 1, ad 4 (hereafter *ST*).

degrees of divinity. Rather, what distinguishes them is their originating relations. In the words of Augustine, "the Holy Spirit is not begotten, as they assert of the Son, from the Father, for Christ is the only-begotten Son, nor is he begotten from the Son, the grandson, as it were of the almighty Father."[15] The Spirit proceeds from a single principle (the Father and Son). But the Spirit does not proceed from each in the same way. Augustine reminds us that the Son "has this faculty of being the co-principle of the Spirit entirely from the Father."[16]

THE STRUCTURE OF THE VOLUME

Now that I have outlined the significance of the key idea, let me introduce the volume's structure. The volume unfolds the divinity of the Spirit in relationship to the Father and the Son in the inner life of God. The works of God and of God's Spirit, to which we will also give our attention, come forth from that life. Three classical thinkers help us to understand God's life and what that life achieves for us and for our salvation: the greatest of all Latin-speaking theologians, Saint Augustine; the austere medieval genius Saint Thomas Aquinas; and the most able modern theologian of all, Karl Barth. Each of these thinkers appreciates first principles and the function of these principles in describing God's being and activity. My account will honour the different emphases between Augustine, Thomas, and Barth, while arguing that they largely speak with one voice. We see this in their exegesis of the Fourth Gospel. Indeed, it is their exegetical works that interpret and ground their synthetic works. The exegesis of each is in its own way alert to the text's claims regarding first principles in governing an account of the economy of grace. In other words, each thinks that Scripture makes metaphysical claims about God's being as the ground from which his works originate.

In chapters 2 and 3, I answer the "What is the Spirit?" question. The Spirit is God. Chapter 2 focuses upon the being of the Holy Spirit as enacted in the Spirit's work. We will see the Spirit as one who gathers people to the Son, begetting them from above for new life. John

---

15. Saint Augustine, *On Christian Belief*, part 1, vol. 8 of *The Works of Saint Augustine*, ed. Boniface Ramsey, trans. Edmund Hill et al. (Hyde Park, NY: New City, 2005), quoted in Siecienski, *Filioque*, 60.

16. Congar, *Holy Spirit*, 3:86. Congar is commenting on Augustine.

2:23–3:21 will be the exegetical basis for this exploration in dialogue with Augustine's homilies and, to a lesser extent, Thomas's lectures on the same.

By attending to the Spirit's work in relation to the Son, we have opportunity to reflect in chapter 3 on the Spirit as "the principle of our return to the Father through the Son," and on the metaphysical dimension and basis of the Spirit's work in the life of the one God.[17] We ask (again), "What is the Spirit?" The focus of chapter 3 is to answer the question—"One what?" The Spirit is God, of the essence of God. That is what the Spirit is: God. To unfold the contours of the unity of essence, and the Spirit's prevenient deity therein, is the task. The contours of the Spirit's deity will be taken up in conversation with selections from Augustine's *On the Trinity* in a way that demonstrates its indebtedness to his *Homilies on the Gospel of John*.

In chapters 4 and 5, we answer the question "Who is the Spirit?" We will first recourse to Thomas's *Commentary on the Gospel of John*, especially John 14–16. Thomas's comment on this text helps us to see that the Spirit's activity in relationship to Christ reflects the immanent life of the Son and Spirit, specifically the Spirit as the love and gift of God. Thomas's exegesis is alert to their personal distinctions—what may be said to distinguish each from the other and the Father within God's life. He is also mindful of how those distinctions manifest themselves in the different acts of the three.

In chapter 5, I again address the question of "Who is the Spirit?" and do so in a way that draws on Thomas's Trinitarian treatise in the *Summa Theologica* I (qq. 27–43) inasmuch as it illuminates exegetical conclusions reached in his *Commentary on the Gospel of John*. I describe what makes, for Thomas, the Spirit God in a way that is different from Father and Son. Thomas teaches us about relations of relative opposition whereby the Spirit is distinguished from the other two and constituted wholly God. The Spirit proceeds as the impulse of the Lover (the Father) toward the Beloved (the Son) and the Beloved (the Son) to the Lover (the Father). Accordingly, Thomas's treatise on the Trinity illuminates the Spirit's procession in the Godhead whereby the Spirit is one of the three *hypostases*.[18]

In chapters 6 and 7, we ask "How does the Spirit do things?" The

---

17. Congar, *Holy Spirit*, 1:81.
18. Congar, *Holy Spirit*, 3:118.

Spirit does things, not surprisingly, in relation to the Son and to his community. I expound the Son's prophetic office—his speech—and the Spirit's economy of gathering in reference to Christ. This treatment will yield insight into the pattern of the Spirit's life-giving acts. The focus is in part on Barth's lectures on the Fourth Gospel from the 1920s.

In chapter 7, I explore the prevenient basis of the Spirit's gathering, upbuilding, and sending of the Christian community in obedience to the eloquent Son. I unfold how what the Spirit does is grounded on the Spirit's origin as one breathed by the Father and Son, the very inner term or ground of the Spirit's mission. The Spirit's being "breathed" in the inner life of God functions as the principle of intelligibility for explaining how the Spirit achieves things. This inquiry takes place in conversation with relevant paragraphs from Barth's *Church Dogmatics*, namely, §62, §67, and §72.

In chapters 8 and 9, I answer the question "What does the Spirit do?" I take up corollaries to the doctrine of the Spirit, specifically regeneration and its concomitant sight (chapter 8) and the theology of church and tradition (chapter 9). Pneumatological teaching informs, demands, and functions as the basic foundation for these doctrinal themes.

In chapter 10, the final chapter, I conclude the study by tying together the different strands with a view to unfolding how pneumatology informs a contemplative account of theology and indeed of Christian existence. To contemplate God is to love God, and to see God the Holy Trinity as the Trinity is, is to fulfill the end for which we were created. I argue that the contemplative life is not a passive life. It is a matter of prayer, of the hearing of God and of all things in God. Theology's contemplative vocation is one of continually being arrested by the sublime truth of John 3:35: "The Father loves the Son and has placed all things in his hands."

THEOLOGY'S VOCATION

Theology's vocation is to learn to hear that "all things" have indeed been given into the Son's hands. Included in the "all things" is the Spirit whose witness is true. The Spirit is the subject and agent of the spiritual life. Increase of the spiritual life is theology's goal. Indeed, theology—or better, sacred doctrine—is "sapiential contemplation of God."[19] Such contemplation "aims not merely at understanding Scripture *per se*, but at an intellectual (and affective) union with realities taught by Scripture, so as to attain a foretaste of beatific contemplation."[20]

"Beatific contemplation" is the goal and essence of the spiritual life. Thomas, commenting on John 3:8, writes that "you [Nicodemus] do not know where it [the Spirit] goes, because the Spirit leads one to a hidden end, that is, eternal happiness."[21] "Beatific contemplation" is "eternal happiness." Scripture teaches us of the Spirit so as to point to Christ, who unites us with that same Spirit. The Spirit makes us happy, here in this life and without interruption or end in the life of the world to come. The regenerated life, the spiritual life, is the happy life. May this volume facilitate a spiritual vision whereby one is reborn into such happiness.

---

19. Saint Thomas Aquinas, *Commentary on the Gospel of John*, trans. Fabian Larcher and James A. Weisheipf, with introduction and notes by Daniel Keating and Matthew Levering (Washington, D.C.: Catholic University of America Press, 2010), 1:x.

20. Keating and Levering, introduction to Aquinas, *Commentary on John*, 1:x.

21. Aquinas, *Commentary on John*, 455, 173. The number "455" denotes the paragraph number, "173" the page number.

An Alternative Approach to the Holy Spirit in Contemporary Theological Discourse

An alternative approach to pneumatology that is fitting to engage briefly at the outset of the volume is Sarah Coakley's. She is certainly one of the most important voices in Anglo-American divinity today, and also a fellow priest of the Anglican Church. She is one of only a handful of theologians in the English-speaking world writing a multi-volume systematic theology.[1] In the comments below, I engage with a few key essays of hers, as well as with the first volume of her systematic theology — *God, Sexuality, and the Self: An Essay "On the Trinity."* I consider her doctrine of the Spirit, which she locates and treats, rightly so, within the doctrine of the Trinity. I also engage her findings not to demonstrate that she is wrong and I am right — notwithstanding my reservations about some aspects of her project — but rather to demonstrate from the start what an alternative approach to the one I take in this volume looks like. Indeed, in this excursus, I will describe what makes her approach — what she calls a *théologie totale* — an alternative, offer some comments on the extent to which I think that alternative profitable and edifying, and explain why at points I depart from it.

A "SPIRIT-LEADING APPROACH"

What Coakley argues for is a "Spirit-leading approach to the Trinity."[2] Taking her cues from Romans 8:9–30, she argues that there

---

1. The others, to my knowledge, are Douglas F. Kelly (Reformed Theological Seminary), R. Kendall Soulen (Wesley Theological Seminary), Kathryn Sonderegger (Virginia Theological Seminary), Kathryn Tanner (Yale Divinity School), Kevin J. Vanhoozer (Trinity Evangelical Divinity School), and John Webster (University of St Andrews). Volumes from the latter three have yet to appear.

2. Sarah Coakley, "Why Three?" in *The Making and Remaking of Christian Doctrine:*

is "mystical evidence" present therein that supplies the "rational, and experientially based, grounds for 'hypostatizing' the Spirit."[3] Coakley's concern is that "linear accounts"—principally but not exclusively those of the early Karl Barth and Karl Rahner—"*assume* the hypostatization of the Spirit. And in both one senses a slightly desperate search for something distinctive for the Spirit to do."[4] What she means by a "linear" vision of the economy is that of "(first the Father, then the Son, then the Spirit) in which it remains for the Spirit only to recapitulate, unfold, or at best enable the recognition of what has already been achieved in the Son ... For all that these authors [Barth and Rahner] retrieve the 'immanent' trinity from obscurantism, then, it is somewhat at the expense of a convincing doctrine of the Spirit."[5] The issue for Coakley is on what grounds one can offer "a convincing doctrine of the Spirit" that involves more than the Spirit's awakening us to what the Son has done. The matter at hand, in other words, is "rightly locating the *intrinsic* role of the Spirit in the Father-Son relationship."[6] Significant voices such as Barth and Rahner do not offer us, Coakley argues, sufficient grounds on which to articulate the Spirit's distinct existence given the presumption of "a privileged dyad" already established into which the Spirit has to be somehow fit.[7]

Coakley adjudges that the best way toward solving this lacuna is to recover the role of the Holy Spirit in salvation. Accordingly, the Spirit is more than a metaphor for an aspect of the Father's or Son's action in the world. She draws attention to the "*the Holy Spirit as a means of incorporation into the Trinitarian life of God* ... actually catching up and incorporating the created realm into the life of God (or rather the 'redeemed life of sonship' to use Pauline terminology)."[8] In short, what Coakley is after is "a developed Trinitarian metaphysic true to the cardinal insights of Romans 8 from which our analysis began."[9] This is the best place from which to fund an account of the Spirit's hypostatic uniqueness.

Essays in Honour of Maurice Wiles, ed. Sarah Coakley and David A. Pailin (Oxford: Clarendon, 1993), 44; idem, *God, Sexuality, and the Self: An Essay "On the Trinity"* (Cambridge: Cambridge University Press, 2013), 104.

   3. Coakley, "Why Three?" in *Making and Remaking*, 48.
   4. Ibid., 33. The italics are original to any citations throughout.
   5. Ibid., 33.
   6. Coakley, *God, Sexuality, and the Self*, 333.
   7. Ibid., 330.
   8. Coakley, "Why Three?" in *Making and Remaking*, 36.
   9. Coakley, *God, Sexuality, and the Self*, 313.

AN INCORPORATIVE MODEL

Coakley's incorporative model funds a recovery of more robust language about how the New Testament appropriates the indivisible work of the Trinity in saving humankind not to the Father or the Son alone but also to the Holy Spirit. Coakley draws attention to Romans 8:9–30,

> with its description of the co-operative action of the praying Christian with the energizing promptings of the "indwelling" Holy Spirit. On this view, what the "Trinity" *is* is the graced ways of God with creation, alluring and conforming that creation into the life of the "Son." But note that the priority here, experientially speaking, is given to the Spirit: the "Spirit" is that which, whilst being nothing less than "God," cannot quite be reduced to a metaphorical naming of the Father's outreach … a sort of answering of God to God in and through the one who prays (see Rom. 8:26–7). Here, if I am right, is the only valid *experiential* pressure towards *hypostatizing the Spirit* [emphasis mine]. It is the sense (admittedly obscure) of an irreducibly bipolar divine activity into which the pray-er is drawn and incorporated.[10]

Coakley is arguing that Paul's text gives us sound reasons — often unappreciated — for personalising or hypostatizing the Spirit. Our task is to talk about the Spirit in a manner that is more like Romans 8. Accordingly, only inasmuch as we are "being radically transformed by ecstatic participation in the Spirit," are we able to develop an account of the Trinity true to such participation.[11] Experience is a matter of recognizing that the pray-er is "pressured" in such a way that hypostatic existence must be ascribed to the one who pressures thus — "a sort of answering of God to God in and through the one who prays."[12] Accordingly, to conceptualize the Trinity in a linear way is to shortchange the riches of an "experientially-rooted" and therewith "Spirit-leading approach to the Trinity through prayer."[13] In sum, one best explains the hypostatic particularity and uniqueness of the Spirit

---

10. Coakley, "Why Three?" in *Making and Remaking*, 37.
11. Coakley, *God, Sexuality, and the Self*, 322.
12. Coakley, "Why Three?" in *Making and Remaking*, 37.
13. Sarah Coakley, "Trinity, Prayer and Sexuality: A Neglected Nexus in the Fathers and Beyond," *Centro Pro Unione* 58 (2000): 13.

by highlighting Romans 8:26–27. Only then can one appreciate the extent to which the eternal, ontological life of the Trinity is articulated on the basis of its impingement in relation to the life of the believer.[14]

PRAYER AND RIGHT DESIRE

Coakley's emphasis on prayer is crucial for understanding her project. Prayer indicates, so Coakley argues, "an acutely revealing matrix for explaining the origins of Trinitarian reflection."[15] Put again, in more "ineluctably tri-faceted" terms, "The 'Father' is both source and ultimate object of divine desire; the 'Spirit' is that (irreducibly distinct) enabler and incorporator of that desire in creation—that which *makes* the creation divine; the 'Son' *is* that divine and perfected creation."[16] This, argues Coakley, "prayer-based argument for the Spirit's 'hypostatic' (or distinct) existence" was "never wielded by the early Fathers."[17] Indeed, the Nicene tradition does not push its own best insights far enough. The "one radical conclusion" necessary is absent: "that there can be in God's Trinitarian ontology no Sonship which is not eternally 'sourced' by 'Father' *in the Spirit* (in such a way, in fact, as to query even the usual and exclusive meanings of Fatherly 'source,' as already indicated)."[18] This is disappointing, "granted the suggestive basis for this in Romans 8."[19] We are hamstrung by the tradition at just this point, as it is unable to appreciate the intrinsic role of the Spirit in the Father-Son relationship. Hence Coakley's constructive proposal, an "incorporative Trinitarianism," becomes the kind of Trinitarianism that licenses the giving of "experiential priority to the Spirit ... in prayer." Unfortunately, this was discouraged by the Fathers not only because of Montanism but also because of "possible confusion between loss of control to that Spirit and loss of *sexual* control."[20]

It is important to pause here. What makes Coakley's argument

---

14. See Coakley, *God, Sexuality, and the Self*, 230.

15. Coakley, "Trinity, Prayer and Sexuality," 14.

16. Coakley, "Why Three?" in *Making and Remaking*, 38.

17. Ibid., 39.

18. Coakley, *God, Sexuality, and the Self*, 332. Interestingly, Coakley notes her broad sympathies with Thomas Weinandy's proposals regarding a Spirit Christology. See ibid., 338, and my excursus on the same in chapter 5.

19. Coakley, "Why Three?" in *Making and Remaking*, 39.

20. Ibid., 45, 47; "Trinity, Prayer and Sexuality," 15; *God, Sexuality, and the Self*, 153. The Montanists "discouraged explicitly or apologetic use of a Trinitarianism giving experiential priority to the Spirit." See Coakley, *God, Sexuality, and the Self*, 126.

idiosyncratic, especially in regard to possible confusion between Spirit and sex, is her championing a genealogy of Trinitarian doctrine that is to my knowledge not argued elsewhere: "'gender' and 'sex' (as we now call them) are much more intrinsically connected to Trinitarian thinking in the classic period than one might assume."[21] Coakley is well aware of the "false divisions" in the textbooks between "theology" and "spirituality," of the underprivileging of discourse in the latter for explaining Trinitarian origins. Just so, the textbooks, she argues, need to be more aware of Trinitarian language's "sexual, political, and ecclesiastical overtones and implications."[22] While it is beyond the scope of my expertise and concern to debate the merits of her readings of, for example, Origen, it is crucial to note the constructive upshot of her argument. There lies "an argument in the church's mystic armoury which it has never adequately brought into doctrinal play, but [for which] the time may now be ripe."[23] If the church would be able to be less squeamish about the language of "desire," especially "the lure" of the Spirit's groanings, then it might be in a better position to articulate "an adequately-rich Trinitarian theology of sexuality to confront the ecclesiastical ructions on matters of sex and gender that now so profoundly exercise us."[24] As well, the church would have more resources with which to speak of the Spirit's hypostatic uniqueness were it to keep on talking the way Romans 8 does.

Another dimension of Paul's language to which Coakley draws attention is that of desire, of groanings (see Rom 8:23). Desire for God, Coakley argues, is "*worn* [emphasis mine] into our existence about the final and ultimate union we seek."[25] However, desire for God is always predicated upon divine desire's purgative reformulation of human desire.[26] Accordingly, "that desire is both transcendent to us and immanent within us. God is kenotically infused (not by divine loss or withdrawal, but by effusive pouring out) into every causal joint of the creative process, yet precisely without overt derangement of apparent randomness ... there seems no *irrationality* in positing the existence of a transcendent (and immanent) divine providence, albeit one that

---

21. Coakley, *God, Sexuality, and the Self*, 300.
22. Ibid., 313.
23. Coakley, "Why Three?" in *Making and Remaking*, 45.
24. Coakley, "Trinity, Prayer and Sexuality," 17.
25. Ibid., 16.
26. See Coakley, *God, Sexuality, and the Self*, 59.

kenotically 'self-hides' in the spirit of incarnational presence."[27] Divine desire is rooted in the Spirit, who "is the vibrant point of contact and entry into the flow of this divine desire, the irreplaceable mode of invitation for the cracking open of the crooked human heart."[28] The Spirit's desiring has a metaphysical ground insofar as "it is what makes God irreducibly *three*, simultaneously distinguishing and binding Father and Son, and so refusing also—by analogous outreach—the mutual narcissism of even the most delighted of human lovers."[29]

We have begun to see by now something of the shape of Coakley's "incorporative Trinitarianism."[30] The register is primarily on Trinitarian effects, on what God the Spirit must be on the basis of what the Spirit does in remaking us in Christ's likeness, which is "in the lure of the Spirit" to invite "the human will ... into an ever-deepening engagement with the implications of the Incarnation—its 'groanings' (Rom 8.23) for the sake of redemption."[31] But more than that, the effects allow us to say something about the how and the who. Thus the question to be asked is how God's ways with us on earth are "now to be thematized eternally and 'ontologically' (as God immanent in Godself)."[32] This is, of course, where the rubber hits the road. Coakley avers, "Even though we stand by the insistence that 'the economic Trinity' *is* the 'immanent (or 'ontological') Trinity', the latter (the 'ontological') clearly cannot simply be *reduced* to the former (the 'economic'): there must be that which God *is* which eternally 'precedes' God's manifestation to us. And hence the speculation that follows here."[33]

That is to say, God is not to be collapsed into what God effects. The "*vestigia* of God's ways ... mirror forth the Trinitarian image."[34] Accordingly, divine revelation leads us to a Trinitarian ontology in which there can be "no Sonship which is not eternally 'sourced' by 'Father' *in the Spirit* (in such a way, in fact, as to query even the usual and exclusive meanings of Fatherly 'source', as already indicated)."[35] This is the speculative dimension to which Coakley refers.

---

27. Sarah Coakley, "Evolution, Cooperation, and Divine Providence," in *Evolution, Games, and God: The Principle of Cooperation*, ed. Martin A. Nowak and Sarah Coakley (Cambridge: Harvard University Press, 2013), 378.
28. Coakley, *God, Sexuality, and the Self*, 24.
29. Ibid., 23.
30. Coakley, "Why Three?" in *Making and Remaking*, 45.
31. Coakley, "Evolution," in *Evolution*, 380.
32. Coakley, *God, Sexuality, and the Self*, 134.
33. Ibid., 332.
34. Coakley, "Trinity, Prayer and Sexuality," 17.
35. Coakley, *God, Sexuality, and the Self*, 332.

To recap so far, the solution to the problem of the tradition's providing inadequate resources for hypostatizing the Spirit and its confusions regarding sexuality is to take far more rigorously the scriptural testimony to God's desiring of us *via* the Spirit. The strength of Coakley's solution is the appeal to Scripture, to the experience Paul speaks of in Romans 8 as being germane to a Trinitarianism that is "incorporative" in nature and true to these "cardinal insights."[36] A *théologie totale* is therefore a scriptural theology insofar as it is committed to thinking with utmost rigour "about the place of the Spirit in the Trinity" by developing a method that "prioritizes the Spirit in prayer," thereby leading to ascetical practice that truly transforms "the approach to the theological task itself."[37] So Coakley: "In short, from the perspective of a *théologie totale*, desire, asceticism, and God as Trinity belong together, all the way down."[38]

SOME SHORTCOMINGS

Where I think there is a shortcoming in Coakley's project is with respect to a lack of reflection on what *qualifies* the Spirit to do what the Spirit does. Where my proposal differs from hers is with regard to the necessity of the language of immanent processions—which of course she would not deny is necessary—being of more material import than she would envisage. Coakley's focus on Trinitarian effects via Romans 8 as the key to providing better grounds for personalizing the Spirit needs yet further supplementation, I would argue, with respect to an account of what qualifies the Spirit to do what the Spirit indeed does in fostering the "groans" for the sake of redemption. Here Thomas is most helpful. He argues that the immanent processions ground and are expressed in the missions of Son and Spirit.[39] The processions are the missions' principle of intelligibility. Accordingly, where my account differs from hers is that I seek to give, at every point, explanation as to the "whence" of what happens in the economy. I am not yet convinced that an "incorporative Trinitarianism" encourages sustained reflection on the main thing, the perfection and prevenience of God.

---

36. Ibid., 332.
37. Ibid., 163, 153, 66.
38. Ibid., 67.
39. This is unfolded at length in chapters 4 and 5.

In sum, Coakley's account asks some salutary questions, namely, what feature(s) of the divine economy would pressure us toward hypostatizing the Spirit? Her argument that experiential pressure via Romans 8 must be incorporated if the Spirit be understood to be more than a metaphor for a dimension of the Father's or Son's action in the world or outreach is a useful counterpoint for the tack that I take in this volume. My volume champions the immanent force—the speculative dimension—of pneumatology. The vision I present is focused on the immanent as the basis of the economic. Accordingly, Coakley's proposals do not seem to generate sustained recourse to a track of Trinitarian teaching—the doctrine of the processions—as that which supplies us with resources for describing what designates why the Spirit acts as he does, thereby giving shape to the Spirit's activity. My account at every juncture seeks to draw attention to just this, the why.

Aside from the fact that this book is a single-volume work and not a multivolume work, I am not pursuing a *théologie totale*, that is to say, "a *complete* inventory of Christian doctrine, ethics, and sacramental practice, and their relation to contemporary philosophical and interreligious discussion."[40] This I do not have the background or expertise to do, and therefore can only defer to Coakley. For example, sustained engagement with feminism(s) and the social sciences, the undertaking of fieldwork, and doctrinally motivated reflections on theological art are beyond the purview of a one-volume study such as this. My focus is on doctrinally motivated readings of the Fourth Gospel and their Trinitarian and pneumatological fruit in the writings of three doctors of the Western church. And so, while I depart from Coakley's assertion that "the more systematic one's intentions, the more necessary the exploration of such dark and neglected corners," I share with her the conviction that "to know God is unlike any other knowledge; indeed, it is more truly to *be* known, and so transformed."[41] Yes, knowledge of the Spirit of Christ is truly deeply participatory knowledge. To be filled with the Spirit is to be known by the Spirit, and to be transformed by that self-knowledge into the likeness of Christ. This I hope to stress as does she.

Knowledge of the Spirit that the Spirit supplies in relationship to Christ and his Father also demands "intended practices of 'un-mastery.'"[42]

---

40. Coakley, *God, Sexuality, and the Self*, 38.
41. Ibid., 48, 45.
42. Ibid., 66.

While I do not understand the correlates I handle in chapters 8 and 9 to be practices—faith, for example, is not a practice but a gift—I am sympathetic to "ascetical demands" being conceived as intrinsic to the theological task of unmaking the idols.[43] To press this point: Peter, for example, will die a death he does not want to die in obedience to Christ.[44] The question Christ poses to Peter is a question he poses to us—"Do you love me?" To love Christ is to know Christ, knowledge that will lead in Peter's case to the ultimate ascetic demand, the laying down of his life for love of the one whose sheep he is to feed. To know God is to live in accordance with the imperative that is God's self-disclosure.

The Spirit brings us into alignment with reality (the indicative), into fellowship with Christ and the Father and their people, and gives us the capacity to obey the imperatives intrinsic to that fellowship. That alignment is awakened contemplatively in relationship to Word and Spirit.[45] But, and here I genuinely do differ, I am not convinced by Coakley that a Spirit-leading approach to the Trinitarian life of God is the best way forward into the doctrine of the Trinity, given that the Spirit is not interested in replacing Christ but in declaring Christ to us.[46] Directly conflicting with my approach as well as with the classical tradition, Coakley states that John's gospel funds an "effective subordinationist tendency in relation to the Spirit" by teaching that the Spirit comes to "*replace*" Christ.[47] To declare is not to replace but to attest. The subject of witness is the Spirit. Does a Spirit-*leading* approach to the Trinitarian life of God honour the whole scriptural counsel of God wherein the Spirit is revealed to *be* one who is given in God and among us?[48] I am not yet convinced.

COMMENDATIONS AND RESERVATIONS

Coakley's systematic endeavors are propelled "inexorably to one radical ontological conclusion: that there can be in God's Trinitarian

---

43. Ibid.
44. See John 21:18.
45. Much more will be said in chapter 9 about two further correlates of a responsible pneumatology, church, and tradition.
46. See Coakley, *God, Sexuality, and the Self*, 102.
47. Ibid., 101, n.1.
48. Ibid., 102.

ontology no Sonship which is not eternally 'sourced' by 'Father' *in the Spirit*."[49] This is where Coakley's Spirit-leading incorporative/reflexive approach leads. My commendation of her project is with respect to her anchoring of it in Scripture, in Romans 8, and thereby her asking the salutary question: What kind of Trinitarian metaphysic is true to this passage? My reservation has to do with the Trinitarian metaphysic not being developed as deeply as one might hope as it concerns the "whence" of the life of the Spirit. The force of Coakley's Trinitarianism remains by and large on the economic level. My view is that the dimension she deems speculative is of absolute material consequence. Hence I take it up at every appropriate point in service of expounding a metaphysic true not only to Romans 8 but also to the witness of the Fourth Gospel and, I hope, to the rest of the scriptural witness. To this task we now turn in conversation with Augustine's homilies on the Fourth Gospel.

---

49. Ibid., 332; see Saint Augustine, *The Trinity*, part 1, vol. 5 of *The Works of Saint Augustine*, ed. John E. Rotelle, trans. Edmund Hill (Hyde Park, NY: New City, 1991), 15.5.36.

ENGAGING AUGUSTINE

THE DIVINITY OF THE HOLY SPIRIT

CHAPTER 2

THE SPIRIT AND THE NEW BIRTH

INTRODUCTION

The focus of this chapter is John 2:23–3:21. Augustine's commentary on this passage will serve as the principle of organization. The passage helps to answer the question, "One what?" The "One what?" of God means, as we will see, the undivided essence of Father, Son, and Spirit. Augustine has much to say on this point. And what he says arises from Scripture itself. Augustine recognizes that Scripture makes claims about God's being. Rather than argue a thesis in this chapter, I unfold Augustine's reading of the Nicodemus story, mindful of how the Spirit interacts with Jesus Christ, and what that interaction teaches regarding the common essence of Father, Son, and Spirit. In so doing, I will demonstrate how alert Augustine is to the text's claims regarding first principles. The purpose of the chapter is to show how easily Augustine moves between Trinitarian first principles and the text itself. The text compels unfolding of first principles; it generates them. I show why I think Augustine is right in reading the text in this way.

Before we actually attend to Augustine's reading, a brief overview of his *Homilies on the Gospel of John*, preached in the midst of the Donatist controversy, is in order. Homily 11 (on John 2:23–25; 3:1–5) was preached on Palm Sunday, April 7, 407, and Homily 12 (on John 3:6–21) on the Tuesday of Holy Week, April 19, 407. The points that Augustine makes circle around a few important themes, one of which is God's prevenience. The Spirit bears anew because he is God. Augustine does not in his homilies unfold this point in as great a depth

45

as in *On the Trinity*. Yet he emphasizes that because the Spirit is God, the Spirit does these things. The Spirit is God without us. The theme is that the Spirit renders us trustable to Christ, gives life, the life that is intrinsic to God's being from eternity. Another point to note in our brief overview is the question of origins. Where does this new birth come from? It comes from God, from eternity. That is its condition of possibility. The Spirit's teaching comes from God because the Spirit is God. What is the Spirit? The response Scripture gives is God.

John 2:23–3:21 describes the contours of the temporal mission of the Spirit in relationship to Christ. As we contemplate Jesus' discourse "*to*" Nicodemus, we notice much that grounds Jesus' priestly or atoning work and the Spirit's action therein.[1] As E. C. Hoskyns notes of this passage, Jesus "lays bare all the fundamental themes of His mission. The whole is in the part, and what follows is not a discourse, but The Discourse, the subject-matter of which is repeated in all subsequent discourses [of the gospel]."[2]

Jesus is our great high priest, the one who atones for sin. His lifting up on the cross achieves the life of the world, in fact, the world's salvation (John 3:14–15, 17). Jesus' discourse to Nicodemus indicates how Jesus' crucifixion functions as the means by which the world's darkness is overcome. However, without the Spirit's convincing us otherwise, we cannot believe the darkness has been overcome. We cannot "believe"—as is the case with Nicodemus—and so we come to the one lifted up in order that we may have "eternal life" (John 3:15). Without the Spirit, we cannot receive what Thomas calls the "spiritual vision" whereby "we are regenerated as sons of God, in the likeness of the true Son."[3] Bereft of the Spirit, Christ's great work of atonement comes to us as but a dead letter. We remain enamored with saving ourselves and indifferent to the kingdom of God.

READING JOHN 2:23–3:21

John qualifies Nicodemus's visit to the Lord by telling us Jesus was unwilling to "entrust himself" to those who "believed in his name" on the basis of "the signs that he was doing" (John 2:24, 23). Why?

---

1. E. C. Hoskyns, *The Fourth Gospel* (London: Faber and Faber, 1942), 1:215.
2. Ibid., 1:216.
3. Saint Thomas Aquinas, *Commentary on the Gospel of John* (Washington, D.C.: Catholic University of America Press, 2010), 432, 1:164; 442, 1:167.

"Because he [Jesus] knew all people and needed no one to testify about anyone; for he himself knew what was in everyone" (John 2:24–25). Augustine comments, "Human beings put their faith in Christ, and Christ does not put his faith in human beings."[4] Augustine's point is that we are rather like Nicodemus. We dwell in the dark, unwilling and unable to see. We only rather superficially believe that this one takes away the sin of the world. Those to whom Christ entrusts himself believe otherwise. They are those who believe in his divinity, who come to him in the day by the powerful wind of the Spirit. Without the knowledge of God that the Spirit effects in us—specifically, knowledge that Jesus is God—we approach Jesus as Nicodemus did, that is, "by night" (John 3:3). The "night" or "darkness" has its grip on all people. This grip manifests itself in the fact that "his own people did not accept him" (John 1:11). Nicodemus represents not just his own people, however, but us (Gentiles) too. We too come to the Lord at night, in the dark; just so, we go looking for "the day in the dark."[5]

Augustine shows us that darkness is our natural habitat on this side of the fall. In Saint Paul's words, we respond to Jesus not "as spiritual people, but rather as people of the flesh" (1 Cor 3:1). With Nicodemus, we respond with incredulity to Jesus' discourse. "How can anyone be born after having grown old?" (John 3:4). That we talk this way tells us why Jesus refuses to entrust himself to us. Only when we take up the eucharistic mysteries, argues Augustine, do we truly "savor the flesh of Christ," and therefore receive the Spirit who enables us to hear and to see the one who stands before us.[6] "Let them cross through the Red Sea, let them eat manna, in order that just as they have trusted in the name of Jesus, Jesus may entrust himself to them."[7]

To cross through the Red Sea is to submit to the waters of baptism; to be "born of water" (John 3:5) and to eat manna are to heed Jesus' counsel in John 6:56–57: "Those who eat my flesh and drink my blood abide in me, and I in them ... so whoever eats me will live because of me." Accordingly, to feast upon Christ's flesh "as the place of revelation and of faith" is a function of one's being "born of the Spirit" (John

---

4. Saint Augustine, *Homilies on the Gospel of John 1–40*, part 3, vol. 12 of *The Works of Saint Augustine*, ed. Boniface Ramsey, trans. Edmund Hill (Hyde Park, NY: New City, 2009), 11, 211. Note that the number "11" indicates the number of the homily, and the number "211" the page.

5. Ibid., 11, 213.

6. Ibid., 11, 215.

7. Ibid.

3:8). This is the Spirit who produces children for life. Such work is evidence of the Spirit's divinity, the Godhead of the Spirit. Only by being born again can we truly receive Christ, indeed Christ as God. Eating and drinking of him is the way to receive him as he is, the one who comes from the Father and who is one with the Father.

Children of the Spirit bear many fruits, one of which is a spirit free to worship and to love God. In Augustine's words, those born of the Spirit are "lovers of the kingdom of heaven, admirers of Christ who long for eternal life, worshiping God freely."[8] Those baptized by water and the Spirit "come to the light," for they come to love Christ (John 3:21). We see here something of a pneumatological and ecclesiological epistemology arising. Jesus entrusts himself to those who have been humbled by him, those who by his grace are learning to free themselves from ruling over him in favour of being ruled by him. However, only those who receive him in the water as well as in the sacred supper of the believing community truly receive him.[9] Augustine would not have his hearers believe the nonsense that their coming to Christ takes place on their own terms. Instead, he would have them—like Nicodemus—to be born of the Spirit, who bears us for life in the waters of baptism and seals us in the life that is Christ through the eucharistic mysteries.

Thomas says similar things. If one is to come to the light, one must be reformed by grace. Thomas describes this as "spiritual generation": "Reformation by grace comes about through spiritual generation and by the conferring of benefits on those regenerated."[10] Spiritual generation is God's cleansing of "the soul from the stain of sin." Jesus accomplishes this through the Holy Spirit. Spiritual generation also concerns another dimension, namely, vision. Thomas has in mind the receiving of the vision that Jesus is divine, and not just Jesus but also the Spirit from whom such spiritual generation comes. "It is clear that the Holy Spirit is God, since he [Jesus] says, **unless one is born again of water and the Holy Spirit** (*ex aqua et Spiritu Sancto*)."[11] Being born of water and Spirit is a

---

8. Ibid., 11, 223.
9. There are, of course, many diverse viewpoints regarding the sacraments in general and baptism and Eucharist in particular. As a theologian in the Anglican tradition, I resonate deeply with the Book of Common Prayer. I take there to be two sacraments, baptism and Eucharist. When the Word is present and received in faith, the bread and wine function in the Spirit as effective signs whereby the Christian community is sealed in the promises of the gospel and renewed in its baptism into Jesus Christ.
10. Aquinas, *Commentary on John*, 423, 1:161.
11. Ibid., 444, 1:169.

matter of being "reborn as sons of God through the grace of the Holy Spirit."[12] The Holy Spirit makes persons "spiritual" because the Spirit is God.[13] The Spirit bears us for love of God because the Spirit is Love, the Love internal to God's undivided essence—the one "what" of God. Indeed, Thomas is also alert to what the text teaches regarding first principles. The Spirit's work reveals the Spirit's antecedent divinity, that the Spirit is essentially God together with Father and Son.[14]

WHAT MAKES AUGUSTINE'S HOMILIES INSTRUCTIVE

Augustine's homilies are profoundly instructive in these matters. Although Augustine does not unfold the Spirit's divinity, he assumes it. Scripture teaches it. Unfolding what is taught by Scripture is Augustine's task in *On the Trinity*. The Spirit's work expresses the Spirit's divinity. The Spirit is—together with Father and Son—identical with the one being of God. Further to this, Augustine has a rich sense of how Jesus' discourse to Nicodemus transcends its occasion. Through Nicodemus, we, the readers of the gospel of John, are accosted as those to whom Jesus also speaks. Nicodemus soon disappears "in the darkness he had selected for his visit," Augustine comments, and through the Spirit, Jesus directs the words issued to Nicodemus to us.[15] The reading of Augustine's (and Thomas's) homilies is edifying because he does not allow his hearers—you and me—to flee unscathed. We too are confronted by Jesus' interrogation of Nicodemus. Just so, Augustine hears the text in accord with what it is: the risen Jesus' address to and claim upon his people. Jesus' address and claim have power in and through the Spirit, who effects in us an obedient response to his proclamation.

Augustine also points to the ecclesial dimension of the Spirit's work. Intertwining language about water and the Spirit with that of the church, Augustine states: "Let the Church make known those to whom she has given birth."[16] His point is that "*God* [emphasis mine]

---

12. Ibid., 448, 1:170.

13. Ibid.

14. In relation to Augustine, Lewis Ayres comments, "Father, Son and Spirit have an essence that is their own, which is eternally one, and also which is the Spirit." See *Augustine and the Trinity* (Cambridge: Cambridge University Press, 2010), 259.

15. Hoskyns, *Fourth Gospel*, 1:215.

16. Augustine, *Homilies on John*, 12, 230.

bears sons by the Church."[17] To be born spiritually is to be born "by word and sacrament." It is to be born through the waters of baptism and, most importantly, by the Word through the eucharistic mysteries. Accordingly, Augustine is mindful of how God the Spirit does not generally work without appointed means. The chief instrument through which the Spirit works is Scripture. When "the divine word is read," Augustine writes, "it is the voice of the Spirit."[18] Scripture is read in the church as "the voice of the Spirit." Scripture draws us to the Table where we are sealed in the promises of baptism. The Spirit's voice is a gift, the gift that gives us the life of the One from whom the Spirit proceeds (the Father) and by whom the Spirit is given (the Son). Khaled Anatolios comments, "His [Augustine's] response is that the Spirit eternally exists as 'the Giveable God' (*Deus donabilis*)."[19] The Spirit is God. Part of the burden of Augustine's *Homilies on the Gospel of John* is to highlight this.

Nicodemus does "not know where it [the Spirit] comes from or where it goes" precisely because he has not been spiritually reborn (John 3:8). "Nobody" Augustine comments, "can be born of the Spirit without being humble, because humility is what brings us to birth by the Spirit; because *the Lord is close to those whose hearts are bruised* (Ps 33:19)."[20] Here we see Augustine exhorting the catechumenate, not of course in a Pelagian sense, but rather with the understanding that those "born of the Spirit ... will keep to God's paths, so as to follow Christ's humility."[21] Augustine cannot conceive of preaching a text such as this without hearing it as a text that makes metaphysical claims. Indeed, Augustine's hearers—and we in turn—are exhorted to "come to the light" (John 3:21) in order "to follow Christ's humility."[22] We see that the Spirit bears us in Christ, thereby bearing us anew in the Father's love. The Spirit baptizes us in Christ's humility, making us into his disciples. The Spirit does this because the Spirit is God.

---

17. Ibid., 12, 232.
18. Ibid.
19. Khaled Anatolios, *Retrieving Nicaea: The Development and Meaning of the Trinitarian Doctrine* (Grand Rapids: Baker Academic, 2011), 143.
20. Augustine, *Homilies on John*, 12, 233.
21. Ibid.
22. Ibid.; John 3:21.

THE SOURCE OF THE NEW BIRTH

The exhortation to humility is rooted in the humility of God. The things of which Jesus speaks to Nicodemus are matters best described as "heavenly things" and not "earthly things" (John 3:12). The works of God, in this case of "the Son of Man" who "descended from heaven," indicate something rather remarkable about their source, their antecedent first principles. So Augustine: "There you are, he was here and he was in heaven, he was here in the flesh, he was in heaven in his divinity—or rather, everywhere in his divinity. Born of a mother without departing from his Father."[23] This heavenly thing of which Augustine speaks is the revealed humility of one who, even as he died, "cut death down."[24] What enables the Son to be "born of a mother without departing from his Father," to set us free from death by his own death, is, Augustine argues, his relation of origin with respect to the Father. It is Jesus' abiding union with the Father that qualifies him to cut death down. First principles govern, in Augustine's mind, the Son's atoning work. Never departing from his Father, he cuts death down. Herein we see again one of the main Trinitarian teachings Augustine assumes. There is oneness or unity of being between the Father and the Son. Not only does the text point to the Spirit's divinity; it points to the consubstantiality of Father, Son, and Spirit.

Jesus' descent, his incarnation, his ministry, and his proclamation of the kingdom all rest on his filial relationship with the Father. The Son of God became a mortal; even more, he became a mortal who did not depart from his Father. Even in the midst of his cutting death down, he manifests *who* he is as one who co-owns, together with the Father, the divine nature—the one "what" common to them: "But Jesus—Son of God, Word of God through which all things were made, the only Son, equal to the Father—became a mortal, for *the Word became flesh and took up residence among us* (Jn 1:14)."[25] Augustine helps us to see that the Word was not changed into flesh but rather became flesh. Jesus the Son does not change but rather does something new that manifests

---

23. Ibid., 12, 235. The latent "extra" present here will subsequently become known as the *extra Calvinisticum*.

24. Augustine, *Homilies on John*, 12, 236.

25. Ibid., 12, 237. That Thomas and Augustine appear to be saying quite similar things is indeed true. However, this is not to homogenize them. Thomas is more willing than Augustine to describe "the structure of the Trinity [with] a complex metaphysical terminology." See further Ayres, *Augustine*, 270.

what he has always been—"the only Son, equal to the Father." What *qualifies* Christ for incarnation as well as passion and atonement is— once again—his being "the only Son, equal to the Father." This is the incarnation's antecedent first principle. Because Jesus is equal to God the Father, he can be "in heaven and earth at the same time" and can "cut death down."[26]

Thomas says similar things in his commentary on John 3:13. Let us briefly turn to it. The Son of Man "descended only according to his divine nature. For since in Christ there is one *suppositum* [self-subsistent thing], or *hypostasis,* or person of the two natures, the divine and human natures."[27] What qualifies Jesus Christ, for Thomas, to take up the priestly office is his *divine* person. Jesus is a divine person; as the Son of God, he is not external to God. The Son "who descended from heaven" does divine things—like overcome death—*and* human things—like suffer death (John 3:13). Christ is one person in two natures, argues Thomas. The task of the Christian theologian is to speak truthfully about what acts may be attributed to what nature: "The Son of God was crucified, not according to his divine nature, but according to human nature; and the Son of Man created the stars according to his divine nature."[28] So, when we think of the Son of Man being lifted up, we are to think according to his human nature. If we think according to both in regard to his crucifixion, then he ceases to be the one he is, the one who ascends into heaven. Again Thomas: "For he came down from heaven without ceasing to be above, yet assuming a nature which is from below."[29] The key is the language of "without ceasing." Thomas affirms that at no time does Christ cease to be the one eternally born of the Father. He remains the one born of the Father even as he assumes a nature from below. What qualifies Christ to bear us in life eternal is his person. He does this because he is God. The fruit that Jesus in his divine humanity bears is life. The life Jesus possesses from the being of the Father is the life that he shares with us in the Spirit, the "giveable" God.[30]

---

26. Augustine, *Homilies on John,* 12, 235, 236.
27. Aquinas, *Commentary on John,* 468, 1:177.
28. Ibid.
29. Ibid., 469, 1:177–78.
30. Saint Augustine, *The Trinity,* part 1, vol. 5 of *The Works of Saint Augustine* (Hyde Park, NY: New City, 1991), 5.15.16.

THE BEING OF THE THREE

Jesus' humility is anchored in his *being*. It is Jesus' being, his oneness with the Father, that enables him to do what he does. It is Jesus' "having equally radical ontological status" with the Father that qualifies him to suffer our death and thus to destroy it.[31] It would not do any saving good if you or I were to die: we cannot destroy death. But Christ is *different* from us. Augustine writes, "Death died" when he died, precisely because the Word who became flesh is life itself: "the fullness of life swallowed death, death was devoured in the body of Christ."[32]

The focal point of Jesus' priesthood is his death from which innumerable benefits flow. "Those who gaze in faith on the death of Christ are healed of the bite of sins."[33] Jesus' death is a reconciling death because he is one with the Father. It is important to note that the coextensive character of the Father and Son's action indicates, Augustine argues, their oneness of being. The fact that one begets (produces) and one is begotten (produced) implies no gradation of being but rather is constitutive of the one being of God. The same is true of the Spirit. That the Spirit has a different origin than Father and Son in God's life does not imply any diminution of divinity on the Spirit's part.

THE NEW BIRTH OF THE SPIRIT

Without the new birth of the Spirit, these heavenly truths—such as the oneness of Father and Son—remain unknown and unseen. We remain unable to receive this "testimony" (John 3:11). Without the scriptural word, we cannot hear the voice of the Spirit; without the birthing activity of the Spirit, we cannot be humbled and so receive teaching about the Lord Jesus, who is "born of a mother without departing from his Father."[34] To talk about Jesus Christ as high priest and the atonement as the principal fruit of this office is to describe a work that includes the power to achieve our participation in it. Christ never ceases—even in death—to breathe the Spirit, who proceeds from the Father through him as their Love.

---

31. Anatolios, *Retrieving Nicaea*, 24.
32. Augustine, *Homilies on John*, 12, 238.
33. Ibid.
34. Ibid., 12, 235. I would argue that this birthing is to be accompanied by water baptism but not necessarily coterminous with water baptism itself.

Jesus' insistence that the wind of the Spirit "blows where it chooses" (John 3:8) reminds us that Jesus does not give the Spirit away. "He [the Spirit] is not man's own spirit and he will never be," Barth comments.[35] The Spirit's identity is secured via his proceeding from the Father and the Son. The Spirit is constituted by that procession. The Spirit's identity as God remains intact by virtue of those relations of origin by which the Spirit originates in God. The Spirit is God in his work of realizing the filial love of Father and Son in us. That is (again) what the Spirit is: God. The reason Nicodemus's knowledge of Jesus remains unprofitable and deadening is that he has not been made alive by the Spirit; Nicodemus cannot quite believe that the one who believes in the Son of Man "lifted up … may have eternal life" (John 3:14–15). Nicodemus can only become a true "teacher of Israel" by being "born from above," by learning to love his subject (John 3:7, 10). Without that analogy, Nicodemus (and we ourselves) could too easily domesticate things. We could think that the new birth is ours to effect, rather than God's.

Augustine's reading of John 2:23–3:21 is careful to honour the "visible" dimension of the work of the Spirit. The Spirit, together with Christ, is the light who exposes the darkness and the deeds done therein. The darkness, which manifests itself in unbelief, remains invisible; whereas Christ's form takes up space as that of "deeds [that] have been done in God" (John 3:21). Deeds done in God, such as the fruit of being born of water and the Spirit, are a function of the invisible work of the Holy Spirit becoming visible.

The triune God creates a people who sing his praises. Praise comes forth from those who are learning by the subject and object of their praise to "come to the light" (John 3:20). Such praise assumes the Spirit's regenerative work. Nicodemus cannot hear that he is actually deaf and blind because he has not been born again by the Spirit, who would give him ears to hear and eyes to see and a voice with which to sing. Bound by the darkness in which he approaches Jesus, Nicodemus is unable to comprehend. Although in terms of John's narrative Jesus' crucifixion is some distance away, the ministry, passion, and crucifixion of Jesus seem to overlap. Christ the high priest's work is effective even now in its confrontation with darkness. The light has come into the world and condemned the darkness. Christ overcomes the darkness,

---

35. Barth, *CD* IV/1, 646.

giving the Spirit "without measure" in the fullness of his resurrected life (John 3:34). The Spirit that Nicodemus must receive is indeed the principal benefit of the Son of Man's crucifixion, his atoning work as high priest. Without the water and the Spirit, the work of Jesus remains unheeded, a kind of dead letter.

RECEIVING THE SPIRIT

What Jesus is offering Nicodemus (and us) is a new history. There is an enormous gulf between what Nicodemus knows and what Jesus teaches him. Jesus' history is a baptismal history: "No one can enter the kingdom of God without being born of water and Spirit" (John 3:5). The rule of Jesus eludes all attempts to enter it that are not baptismal and pneumatological in nature. Into the Son's hands the Father has placed everything, including the Spirit "without measure" (John 3:34). The Spirit is of the Father's Son from eternity. The Son baptizes us in the Spirit and frees us for life in the Spirit, who is from him and the Father. Christ interprets himself to Nicodemus through the water of baptism and the Spirit into whom he baptizes. Without water and Spirit, Jesus' words, indeed his passion and death, cannot be met with faith. Without water and the Spirit, the Spirit cannot be received as God.

Nicodemus's "belief"—to which Jesus will not entrust himself—is the occasion by which Jesus' self-witness enters the stream of history. Even Nicodemus's obduracy functions as an occasion for Christ to interpret himself to us as one whose kingdom cannot be entered without spiritual rebirth. Nicodemus's witness is negative, to be sure, and yet Christ uses it to speak of the need of the Spirit's illumination. This is the heart of John's gospel. John teaches us that to receive Christ is to receive the Spirit. Even at one of the earliest junctures in John's narrative—John 1:33—Jesus is filled with the Spirit he receives and gives "without measure." Those who receive Jesus receive his Spirit "without measure" and are not condemned (John 3:34). Rather, by the Spirit they receive the gift of living water. But those who disobey Christ will not "see the kingdom of God" and will not be baptized with his Spirit (John 3:3). Accordingly, they will not receive purification from sin and birth from above.

Receiving the Spirit as he did at his baptism by John means that Jesus' life is entirely permeable to the kingdom of God, to which he seeks to introduce Nicodemus and us. This is only fitting given that Jesus' life and ministry reveal an eternal order. The Father in generating him does so in the Spirit, who proceeds from him (and the Father). Augustine does not develop this point here. And yet he thinks John's gospel teaches it. Augustine recognizes that this is the Spirit who is breathed by Father and Son as their love and gift. Jesus shares this Spirit with us. In order to appreciate this, Augustine directs us to 1 Corinthians 12:8–10, 29–30. These verses describe "a measuring out, a division of gifts … But Christ, who gives these things, does not himself receive by measure."[36] Augustine argues that this is because the Father "loves him [Jesus] as his only Son, not as an adopted son. And so he placed all things in his hand. What does *all things* mean? That the Son should be as great as the Father … In sending the Son, the Father sends his other self."[37] The Father places his other self into the hands of the Son, who gives us the Spirit "without measure" (John 3:34). Unlike us, then, the Son "has" the Spirit antecedently. The Spirit is of the Son, proceeding from him (secondarily) as from the Father (primarily). The Father is the *principium* (principle) and the Son is from the *principium* without there being a difference or division of nature. The same is true of the Spirit, who is from them. Together, the Father and the Son are "that blessed bliss, in that eternity of being," which by the grace of God the Spirit we share.[38]

CONCLUSION

In sum, Augustine's reading of John 2:23–3:21 to which we have briefly referred is metaphysically motivated. Augustine is keen to highlight some of the first principles of Trinitarian theology and of pneumatology in particular because he thinks the text encourages such talk. It is only natural to talk about the Spirit's divinity, given that the Spirit is the agent of the new birth. Through this text, as with so many in the Fourth Gospel, we come to see something of the fecundity of the Spirit as the Spirit of *life* and of *light* who draws us to the Father through the Son, the Spirit whom we receive from the Father through the Son. If such is the case, then, Augustine does not import metaphysical

---

36. Augustine, *Homilies on John*, 14, 271.
37. Ibid., 14, 271–72.
38. Ibid., 6, 121.

categories onto the text. Rather, he understands them to function in a modest way. They help us to talk as John's gospel talks of God.

The Spirit communicates the fertile and lively life and light of God to us, enabling us to return to the Father through the Son who gives the Spirit with whom he baptizes "without measure" (John 3:34). The Spirit does so because the Spirit is God. That is what the Spirit is. Augustine's exegesis of 2:23–3:21 contains highly suggestive albeit scattered remarks that encourage reflection on the Spirit's full divinity. The Spirit equally shares in what is common to the Father and Son. Equality of divinity is what grounds the Spirit's mission and work. Equality of divinity is the principle of intelligibility for the Spirit's bearing "from above."

Nicodemus cannot commune with Christ. His heart has not yet been pierced by the baptism of the Spirit, who descended on the one whom John baptized. Expressed metaphysically, Nicodemus cannot conceive of continuity between theology and economy. Congar writes, "The only immanence of God to which we have access is God's self-economized immanence."[39] "How can these things be?" (John 3:9). Augustine's reading of this passage is profitable because of the natural way in which he unfolds this continuity. Theology is present in the text. Better yet, the text is theological. Theology expounds what we receive in these Scriptures. Might Jesus not only be "from God," as Nicodemus avers, but also one who is also God, the Father's "other self" (John 3:2)?[40] Might not the Spirit be God? Might not theology be present here? Might not the Trinity in itself be expressed? Might not the mission of the Son to bear us "from above" by his Spirit (John 3:7) disclose theology? Augustine of course says yes to all this. The text encourages and promotes such a yes; it is intrinsic to the text.

> The Holy Spirit is, after all, God, just as the Son of God is God and the Father is God. Three times I have said "God," but I have not said three gods, because Father and Son and Holy Spirit are one God; you know that perfectly well. So then the Holy Spirit does not groan within on his own account in that Trinity, in that blessed bliss, in that eternity of being; but he groans in us, because he makes us groan.[41]

---

39. Yves Congar speaks of Augustine as one who appreciated this very point. See *I Believe in the Holy Spirit* (New York: Seabury, 1983), 1:79; Anatolios, *Retrieving Nicaea*, 230.

40. Augustine, *Homilies on John*, 14, 272.

41. Ibid., 6, 121.

The Spirit makes us groan with longing in order that God be our true happiness. It is the Spirit, that "blessed bliss," that champions unfettered openness to the full vision and contemplation of the one, true God. The Spirit does this as one who is God.

Before we move to Augustine's great synthetic work, *On the Trinity*, let us sum up the two things that stand out. First, there is equality of being between the three. Each is God; each is fully what God is. Second, the Spirit is no less God than the Father and Son but is God in a different way. In treating Augustine's *On the Trinity*, we will see these great motifs unfolded. Moreover, we will see them described as a natural extension of Scripture itself. Attention must be paid to the divinity of the Spirit. In *On the Trinity*, he keeps talking as John's gospel talks about the Spirit's divinity, and of how that divinity anchors the Spirit's mission of revealing and regenerating.

CHAPTER 3

"HEAVENLY THINGS"

INTRODUCTION

In the previous chapter, we noted Augustine's comments on John 2:23–3:21 as but one of many Johannine samples of Trinitarian talk. Augustine's comments helped us to answer the question "What is the Spirit?" Throughout John's gospel and the New Testament as a whole, we are privileged to see the Spirit who is God at work with Father and Son making all things new. Their activity gives us an extraordinary glimpse into the life of the one God. In this chapter, we explore in a more systematic fashion the kinds of rules Augustine derives from New Testament (especially Johannine) Trinitarian talk with respect to the Son's divinity. Two points emerge. First, there is the oneness of God, the one being of God. Second, there is the matter of the Father as the source of the Son and Spirit. Augustine's *On the Trinity* is a powerful example of how to talk about the three who are one and the Father as the source of Son and Spirit in a way that endeavors not to prove false to the biblical witness.

To think "Trinitarianly" is to move in harmony with the biblical testimony. Thus Augustine's counsel to "fix our thoughts on the grandeur that was clothed in the flesh and not weighed down by the flesh" in order that we may become "such a one as can grasp God."[1] Our thinking will be but through a glass darkly. We speak of things that we do not understand. Yet press ahead we must. Contemplation of the blessed Trinity, or what Calvin calls "spiritual doctrine," has as its goal

---

1. Saint Augustine, *Homilies on the Gospel of John 1–40*, part 3, vol. 12 of *The Works of Saint Augustine* (Hyde Park, NY: New City, 2009), 14, 272, 273,

a "seeing" — "no one can see the kingdom of God without being born from above" (John 3:3).[2]

Learning the inexhaustible richness of Trinitarian teaching is about "making progress in heavenly doctrine."[3] The kind of discipleship of the mind and affections envisaged by Augustine takes place by our becoming new and holy people. The quest for knowledge of God is accordingly the quest for the Holy Spirit, who fashions us so that we "may begin to be spiritual."[4] This is the basic epistemological principle that needs to be stated outright. Our inquiry into theology proper — God *in se* — is an act of devotional obedience. We subject ourselves to the regenerating Spirit, who ensures that our entrance into the school of the Trinity does not become "choked with many noxious weeds."[5] Knowledge of God the Spirit is teaching that makes one spiritual.

The focus of this chapter is on books 4–7 of Augustine's great work, *On the Trinity*, and, secondarily, his *Homilies on the Gospel of John*. We will see the extent to which Augustine's great work derives from his exegesis of the Fourth Gospel. The resonances between the treatise and the sermons are clear. In fidelity to the New Testament witness, Augustine discusses a kind of oneness that is not prior to the three. There exists an ineffable unity between them. It is a unity of three who are irreducible, and are no less one because of that. Moreover, reading Augustine's seminal work is helpful for understanding New Testament talk of the Spirit's leading into the relationship of the Son to the Father.

THE ONE BEING OF GOD

Father, Son, and Spirit are one "what," that is, substance (*substantia*) or essence (*essentia*). God is, Augustine writes, "an essence."[6] Essence or substance is not a biblical term. To be sure, the language is cumbersome, but it can be taken captive in such a way as to say something true

---

2. Calvin comments that the kingdom of God does not mean in this instance "Heaven" but "rather the spiritual life." See John Calvin, *The Gospel According to St John 1–10*, trans. T. H. L. Parker; Calvin's Commentaries (Grand Rapids: Eerdmans, 1995), 63.

3. Ibid., 60.

4. Ibid., 67.

5. Ibid., 63.

6. Saint Augustine, *The Trinity*, part 1, vol. 5 of *The Works of Saint Augustine* (Hyde Park, NY: New City, 1991), 5.1.3. Augustine prefers *essentia* to *substantia*, as he understands substance to exist in something else and so encourages a notion of changeability that sits rather uneasily with his account of simplicity. See also Lewis Ayres, *Augustine and the Trinity* (Cambridge: Cambridge University Press, 2010), 201.

about what God is. For God, "BEING itself, whence comes the name of essence, most especially and most truly belongs."[7] Being itself is not something extrinsic to God. God does not need anyone or anything else in order to be. God is a God whose being is ineffably God's. In his homily on John 5:19, Augustine, in commenting on *"the Son can do nothing on his own, but only what he sees the Father doing,"* puts it this way: "[with God] there is not one thing, substance, by which he is, and another, power, by which he can, but whatever he has, it is all consubstantial with his very self, and he is whatever he is, because God simply is."[8] Augustine's point is twofold. The first point, as was mentioned earlier, is that God is not God because of anything outside of God, including "substance" or "essence." Second, with God, being (the "is") and power (the "can") are identical. God contains all that it is possible for God to do.

If one is to ascend to a faithful understanding of this mystery, according to Augustine, one cannot proceed in accordance with a "materialistic understanding."[9] A "materialistic understanding" assumes that talk of the three—note that Augustine does not use "person" language in his *Homilies*, as he would rather remain silent—necessarily implies three natures or substances between the persons. Such a way of thinking is false to the New Testament. Thinking that is true to the New Testament, however, recognizes that there is "no difference of nature or substance between" the three.[10] The three are not different things. Rather, the three are the same thing in relation to themselves: God. Augustine writes, "Father and Son and Holy Spirit, one God, one Almighty. Therefore one Beginning."[11] The three are one and of "one Beginning."

God is one insofar as there is no ontological hierarchy in God. The Father is not said to be more "God" than the Son and Spirit by virtue of being their beginning. In God's acts toward the outside, we are given a glimpse of a God whose essence or nature is tripersonal. Each one of the three is the fullness of God: God the Father, God the Son, and God the Spirit. The three do not participate in a reality that is prior to them. Let me unfold this. A person—a *hypostasis*—is the subject of an

---

7. Ibid.
8. Augustine, *Homilies on John*, 20, 361.
9. Ibid., 362.
10. Ibid.
11. Ibid., 589.

61

action in a sentence. If I have a set of qualities (woofs, wags tail, bears puppies, etc.), I have a "what," a "nature," a canine nature. But the set of qualities cannot do anything: the set cannot woof or bear puppies. To bear puppies, you need a concrete bearer of the nature, a *who*. You actually need an existing Fido or Lassie in the room. The three are the way in which the one God, the what, exists. The three persons *bear* the divine nature. That nature is not prior to them but coterminous. God is not Trinity one moment and a monad at another. Talk along these lines is, for Augustine, a matter of "not think[ing] God is something different from what he really is."[12] Thus we believe that the New Testament not only helps us to identify what God is not, namely, three different things or beings; it also teaches something true about how God is. God is one whose being is common to the three. Each possesses the fullness of what it is to be God—and that, no less, without measure.

In Book 5 of *On the Trinity*, Augustine makes an important statement. He writes, "We will find it easier to excuse one another if we know, or at least firmly believe and maintain, that whatever we say about that unchanging and invisible nature, that supreme and all-sufficient life, cannot be measured by the standard of things visible, changeable, mortal and deficient."[13] Augustine thinks that God's nature or substance—the terms here are interchangeable—is "unchangeable." Why does Augustine place so much weight on this particular attribute? Changeability would imply lack on God's part. Remember, however, that God does not need another in order to be. God is life *in se*; God is self-originating. Were God changeable, God would be said to be lacking in something. One of the consequences of such lack is that God would be untrustworthy. God could very well become other than the one revealed. Similarly, if God's nature were visible, such would be a "mortal way of thinking."[14] A mortal way of thinking attempts to secure God's nature in advance of the saving self-disclosure of God. Inasmuch as our thinking is actually determined by how God acts toward us, however, we get a glimpse of one whose nature and very divinity are absolute life and sufficient to itself. Augustine recognizes that God has no competitors, needs no one or nothing outside of God in order to be. God is self-sufficient. God exists out of and solely in relationship to himself.

12. Ibid., 414.
13. Augustine, *Trinity*, 5.prologue.2.
14. Augustine, *Homilies on John*, 21, 372.

It follows that if God is "a nature, unchangeable, invisible, and having life absolutely and sufficient to itself," God is without passion.[15] To our ears this suggests anything but a dynamic and lively God, a God whose being is pure act; indeed, it connotes a God who is inert. In like manner, it suggests an account of God that is "metaphysically driven," pejoratively speaking. By arguing as Augustine does that God is not "liable to passions as far as belongs to that substance whereby He is God," Augustine is (again) stating that God lacks nothing.[16] Put in more Trinitarian terms, "Both the being called the Father, and the being called the Son, is eternal and unchangeable to them."[17] Were not their being from which substance or essence language derives eternal to the three, God would be subject to passion and thus change. Threeness would be something that happens to God. On the contrary, Augustine argues that threeness is coextensive with the one nature or substance of God. In exegeting the *my teaching is not mine* of John 7:16, Augustine emphasizes that there is "no difference of nature or substance between them."[18] There is absolute substantial oneness with respect to the three.

THE ARIAN HERESY

The Arian target—or what Lewis Ayres, in accordance with "new canon" research on Augustine, describes as Latin Homoians—is important to understand if what Augustine argues about the one substance common to the three is to be appreciated.[19] That God be thought as unchangeable, without passion, indeed, one of whom nothing is said "according to accident," is, in part, Augustine's way of warding off heresy. Augustine forecloses the notion that some things may be said of God accidentally: "therefore there is nothing accidental in God, because there is nothing changeable that may be lost."[20] This secures a basic but absolutely fundamental point: the three are with respect to themselves God. God could not and never will become otherwise. In

---

15. Augustine, *Trinity*, 5.5.2.

16. Ibid., 5.2.9.

17. Ibid., 5.1.6.

18. Augustine, *Homilies on John*, 29, 492.

19. "The Arians very firmly did say, that all accident words, when predicated of God, turn into substance words." Edmund Hill, foreword to books 5, 6, and 7, Augustine, *Trinity*, 186. By "new canon" research, I mean those—chiefly Lewis Ayres and René Michel Barnes—who quite self-consciously distance themselves from Theodore de Régnon's paradigm, namely, that Augustine is "overly strongly committed to the divine unity." See Ayres, *Augustine*, 1.

20. Augustine, *Trinity*, 5.1.5.

God there is nothing accidental. God is Father, Son, and Holy Spirit. Each of the three is divine in and of himself.

The Latin Homoians—the Arians—understand the Son to be accidentally related to the substance of God. They embraced the notion that the substance of God is somehow behind or prior to the Son. Augustine's "consciously dynamic vocabulary for God," however, moves beyond the polarities suggested by the Latin Homoians. Although it is true that substance is said to be true of the three, and unchangeably so, not everything that is said of the three is "said according to substance."[21] This is an important move. Following Augustine, the Son's begottenness or the Spirit's proceeding is a relation of origin that has a relative quality. A relative quality is not an accidental quality, however. Instead, it is a quality that is always said in relationship to another: talk of the Father as begetter implicates us in talk of the Son, who is begotten.

The main point to recognize is that Augustine does not conceive of an essence in itself. Truthful talk of the essence of God requires that the relations of the persons one to another be not accidental to the one essence of God. Augustine always maintains that the three are united by something absolute, namely, "the being called one essence, but also Trinity from the being called three substances or persons."[22] In other words, Godhead is neither an abstraction nor an *a priori* with respect to the three; likewise, the three are not subsequent to the being of God. The one essence of God is Trinity, threefold.[23]

As Augustine contemplates God's work, he understands that work to have come from somewhere. He understands God's work of creation, reconciliation, and perfection arises from the one being of God himself. This is a rule derived from the New Testament, as Augustine's comments on John 10:30 unfold it: "'are one' means 'What he is, that I am too by way of being (*esse*), not by way of relationship.'" The

---

21. Ayres, *Augustine*, 207; Augustine, *Trinity*, 5.1.6.

22. Augustine, *Trinity*, 7.3.9. Note that *persona* denotes "irreducible individual"; it does not mean mask. See Ayres, *Augustine*, 77, n. 25. It is not difficult to fault Western Christians for thinking that Eastern Christians' invocation of three *hypostases* with reference to God sponsored tritheism, that is, three separate divine substances. "For him [Augustine] the distinction between 'substance' and 'person' in the Latin terminology is purely and simply one of arbitrary linguistic convention." See Hill, foreword to books 5, 6, and 7, 188.

23. For a technical discussion of *genus*, see Richard A. Muller, *Dictionary of Latin and Greek Theological Terms: Drawn Principally from Protestant Scholastic Theology* (Grand Rapids: Baker, 1985), 128; for a technical discussion of person and nature in books 5 and 7 of *On the Trinity*, see Ayres, *Augustine*, 217–18. Augustine argues that "neither is essence the genus of which the persons are a species, nor is essence a genus and persons individuals" (ibid., 219).

"one" signifies the substance of the three, their essence, their absolute simplicity whereby they are one and for whom "there is no possibility of … perfection growing."[24] Or, to make the same point differently, "So they are each in each and all in each, and each in all and all in all, and all are one."[25] All three are by way of being. Accordingly, substance or essence is not spoken of them relatively: again, they *are* one. With respect to being—which is, of course, common—each is. Each is the fullness of God; for each person to be, is to be God. Therefore, Augustine argues, Father, Son, and Spirit are one God. The three—taken together—do not "constitute" the one God. Rather, each is fully God, even as each is "in all."

To deepen this dimension of the argument, Augustine introduces in book 7 of *On the Trinity* the language of "subsistence." Such language is to later readers redolent of Thomas. That said, Augustine does not offer an account of "subsistent relations" as does Thomas.[26] Rather, if we are to derive rules about God's oneness and be faithful to the New Testament, we have to take absolutely seriously that it is "one thing for God to be, another for him to subsist, as it is one thing for him to be, another for him to be Father or be Lord."[27] Augustine's point has to do with how language works. Being-language refers to what is common to the three. Subsistence language indicates a relational way of existing that is not common to the three. So Augustine: "He [God] subsists by way of relationship."[28] When the three persons are described, they are described in relation to one another. But the three do not add up to make one God—"while in the supreme triad one is as much as three are together."[29] When we talk about one of the three, Augustine insists that we are talking about one who is God, for that is what each is. Nonetheless, each is (or subsists) by way of relationship. Relationship-talk cannot be confused with being-talk. For example, one begets and another is begotten. That is relational talk. Being cannot beget and be begotten. That would compromise any sense of simplicity in God. We cannot separate Father, Son, and/or Spirit from one another, for the three are one. The one God subsists in an internally differentiated way.

---

24. Augustine, *Trinity*, 6.2.9.
25. Ibid., 6.2.12.
26. What that means will be developed in chapter 4.
27. Augustine, *Trinity*, 7.3.9.
28. Ibid.
29. Ibid., 7.2.12.

Augustine thinks that such talk is close to the New Testament witness. The rule that John 10:30 supplies is that the three are "'one' in terms of being, because he is the same God; 'are' in terms of their relationship, because one is Father, the other Son."[30] Oneness or absolute unity of being indicates "sameness of nature and being without any variance or disagreement."[31] Relational language does not refer as we have seen to being. Such talk refers in the case of John 10:30 one person to another. What each is—God—is so by way of being and *not* by way of relationship. The relationships of the persons do not constitute the one essence of God. Equality of substance is not a function of their relatedness. But the three do bear one and the same life. "The same unity and equality of substance" is said of the three.[32] God is not said to result from the three. God is not the end product of the three. "God is not made bigger than each of them singly."[33] For Augustine, God is complete, and it is this completeness that is shown in the creation, maintenance, and perfection of covenant fellowship with creatures.

There are better and worse ways of talking about God's being. The better way, the way that is most responsible to the New Testament, is to speak of being as common to the three and proper to each one singly. There is also a way that must be resisted. Being cannot thus be "predicated by way of relationship." Being is not a function of the relatedness of the three. If such were the case, "then being is not being."[34] Talk about God's being that is consistent with New Testament talk appreciates that being is common to the three "so that each of them can be called being."[35] Being, for Augustine, is not another way of describing relationship; indeed, the two must be differentiated as with being and subsistence. The substance or being of each is their "is-ness."[36] So Augustine: "The substance of the Father is just the Father, not insofar as he is Father, but insofar as he just is."[37] What makes the Father "God" is his being, not his name, Father. The name Father refers him to another in relation to whom he is Father, namely, the Son.

To sum up so far, we have seen something of how Augustine speaks

---

30. Ibid., 7.4.12.
31. Ibid., 6.1.4.
32. Ibid., 6.1.7.
33. Ibid., 6.2.9.
34. Ibid., 7.1.2.
35. Ibid., 7.3.9.
36. I have made up this word.
37. Augustine, *Trinity*, 7.3.11.

of God's being in a way that takes up New Testament talk. John 10:30 infers that the three not be simply identified with being but rather be rightly distinguished from it. "We do talk of three persons of the same being, or three persons one being; but we do not talk about three persons out of the same being."[38] Were we to talk about "three persons out of the same being," we would hopelessly compromise the simplicity of the divine being and endorse the false notion that being precedes the three. The one divine being is simultaneously three. That is Augustine's basic rule. The three are "'one' in terms of being" and "'are' in terms of their relationship."[39] That is the key point Augustine derives from John 10:30. That, says Augustine, is where Scripture, but especially John's gospel, leads us. God is one in a being sense *and* in a relational sense.

THE FATHER AS THE SOURCE OF BEING

Before we explore Augustine's thinking on the Father as the eternal source of the Spirit, let us step back for a moment to reflect on how Augustine's thinking so far informs this book's thesis. I concur with Ayres that "the full force of Augustine's Trinitarianism" is unlikely to be "economic."[40] Indeed, as one immersed in the metaphysical themes of the Fourth Gospel—what Calvin calls "heavenly teaching"—Augustine's Trinitarianism has its motor on the immanent level. New Testament talk generates rules for describing God's being, the principle of intelligibility for such talk. One of the primary rules is that God does not come to be God in relationship to anything outside God. God has life in himself. What is God? Self-originating being. We see that life on display in the New Testament. The actions of the Son and Spirit disclose a life that is eternal and complete in itself. As we will see, the Spirit is the gift of God, which is precisely what the Spirit is in God, in this life that arises solely in relation to itself.

The reason Augustine spends so much intellectual energy describing the different ways in which substance and relationship language works with respect to God is to ward off heresy. Augustine is determined to

---

38. Ibid. Paul D. Molnar, following T. F. Torrance, makes the same point. "One cannot see the monarchy or oneness of God only in the Father and the supposed source of the divine being of the Son and Spirit." See "Some Implications of Classical Trinitarianism," in *Modern Theology* (forthcoming).

39. Augustine, *Trinity*, 7.4.12.

40. Ayres, *Augustine*, 30.

honour the Trinity as one whose existence is a making known of its essence. Thus what Augustine says about the simplicity of God's being is not a matter of presupposing knowledge of God's essence or being in advance of God's self-revelation. Rather, the New Testament speaks of God as unchangeable, even as God the Son does a "new thing" by coming down for us and our salvation. But that new thing God does is entirely consistent with who God (the Son) has always been, the one whom the Father eternally sires: "The being called the Father, and the being called the Son, is eternal and unchangeable to them."[41]

Furthermore, Augustine has no interest, as do some modern theologians, in arguing that what happens on the level of existence ought to effect what a person is essentially. God's life in history does not make God the one God is. Rather, God's life is "wholly achieved."[42] Augustine thinks that the New Testament encourages this rule. It resists attributing changeability to God. The Son's sending and the Spirit's being breathed eternally manifest the former's generation and the latter's procession.

The being common to the Father is common to Son and Spirit. When we talk about the Spirit, we talk about God—full stop—for that is what the Spirit is: God. The substance of the Spirit is God; the Spirit is (again) God. That much is clear. But what does Scripture infer regarding the Spirit's origin in God? Augustine thinks that the Spirit proceeds from the being of the Father within the one being of God. Does this leave the Son with no role in the Spirit's origin? The Son does have a role, but it is different from the Father's. In Augustine's discussion, prepositions matter.[43] The Spirit's deity is *from* the Father and *of* the Son. The Holy Spirit proceeds from the Father. Likewise, the Spirit is of the Son. "Of" allows for relationships other than those of origin. Let me illustrate. I am my mother's son; I am the son "of" Joan Holmes. I also have a brother named David. But I do not originate from David (my brother) as I do from Joan (my mother). I am of the same blood as my brother but am not from him.

To understand why Augustine is so insistent upon maintaining that the Spirit proceeds (or comes forth) from the being of the Father

---

41. Augustine, *Trinity*, 5.1.6.
42. John Webster, "Soteriology and the Doctrine of God," in *God of Salvation: Soteriology in Theological Perspective*, ed. Ivor J. Davidson and Murray A. Rae (Surrey, UK: Ashgate, 2011), 26.
43. This same is true of Basil's famous discussion in *The Holy Spirit*.

within the one being of God, we must take a moment once again to recall what his opponents—the Arians, the Latin Homoians—were arguing. What is said of God, they averred, is either said accidentally *or* substantially. If begottenness is said of God the Son accidentally, then the Son is not consubstantial with the Father; if begottenness is said of God the Son substantially, then God is a compound being, one who is both unbegotten and begotten. These are the two ways of speaking available to us, and of course God cannot be both, the Arians argued. The Son cannot be thought of as God in the same sense as the Father. Real unity between them is simply a figment of one's imagination. The Son must have come into being *after* the Father. Rather than the Son being coeternal with the Father, the Son and the Spirit are, the Arians argued, the Father's creation. The Son's begottenness and the Spirit's proceeding indicate "some disparity of power or substance."[44] The generation of the Son and the procession of the Spirit indicate an inferior status with respect to the Father.

Augustine argues that his Arian opponents do not read Scripture responsibly. Everything said of God need not be said "according to substance."[45] Moving beyond the substance/accident dichotomy, Augustine introduces, as noted in the previous section, a third category, namely, relation.[46] This category helps to undo some of the Arians' misunderstanding. "Relation" simply means that each of the three "is not so called in relation to Himself, but the terms are used reciprocally and in relation to the other; nor yet according to accident."[47] Relational language works neither on the essential level nor on the accidental level. Begottenness (siring or fathering), for example, is said not according to the Father but to the Son "since in relation to the Father He is said to be Son, and the Father is not Son, but Father."[48] Although the immediate context of these comments concerns the Father/Son relationship, there is a clear pneumatological connection. The Father sends the Spirit, and the Son breathes the Spirit. Sending and breathing are not said according to substance but rather said relatively, that is, relationally.

---

44. Augustine, *Trinity*, 4.5.27.
45. Ibid., 5.1.6.
46. "Relation," as is "substance," is an Aristotelian category. Accordingly, relations "must be understood as items *inhering* in particular substances." See http://plato.stanford.edu/entries/relations-medieval/#2.1 (accessed 6 October 2014).
47. Augustine, *Trinity*, 5.1.6.
48. Ibid., 5.1.7.

New Testament talk of the Spirit being given and sent refers us to the one who gives his gift (the Father) and the one through whom the gift (the Spirit) is given (the Son). Accordingly, when we say the Spirit is God—as we must—"we denote substance," the "what" of the Spirit. It follows, then, that when we refer to the Spirit as the third of the three, we are not speaking "properly, but metaphorically and through similitudes."[49] Talk of the Spirit's procession is not accidental but relational or relative.

When we affirm something relationally, namely, that the Spirit is given, sent, breathed, and so on, or somewhat differently, that the Father is giver and the Spirit is gift, we are also denying something relatively. If the name *Father* is precisely equivalent to *not begotten*, then the being called *giver* is precisely equivalent to *not given*. There are relative affirmations and relative denials taking place, Augustine argues. The Spirit refers to both Father and to Son, because the Holy Spirit is the Spirit both of the Father and of the Son. The Spirit, biblically speaking, is of both but not less than both. But remember that "of" does not work in the same way as "from." The Spirit is "of" the Father in a different way than of the Son. Sent by both, the Spirit is not less than those by whom he is sent.

The basic reason the Spirit is of the Father and of the Son "is apparent when He is called gift of God."[50] The language of "gift" is necessary, Augustine argues, on the basis of Scripture, specifically John 15:26 and Romans 8:9. According to the former, the Spirit *"proceeds from the Father, as the Lord says"*; and, according to the latter, "the apostle's words, *Whoever does not have the Spirit of Christ is not one of his.*"[51] The Spirit is the "gift of the giver." The giver is the Father, and the Son is the "giver of the gift." The Spirit is of both, but not in the same way. The upshot is that, "Therefore the Holy Spirit is a certain unutterable communion of the Father and the Son; and on that account, perhaps, He is so called, because the same name [Holy Spirit] is suitable to both the Father and the Son."[52]

The name Holy Spirit is "suitable" to Father and Son simply because both are said to be a spirit, that is, nonmaterial, and both are said to be holy. In this regard, A. Edward Siecienski comments, "Since he [the Spirit] is the Spirit of both, it logically followed for Augustine that

---

49. Ibid., 5.2.8–9.
50. Ibid., 5.3.12.
51. Ibid.
52. Ibid.

the Holy Spirit must proceed from both."[53] The Spirit is common to Father and Son. So Augustine: "In order, therefore, that the communion of both may be signified from a name which is suitable to both, the Holy Spirit is called the gift of both."[54] Therein lies, as Siecienski indicates, Augustine's challenge: "to make sense of the biblical affirmation that the Holy Spirit 'who proceedeth from the Father' is also 'Spirit of the Son;'" in other words, to read John 15:26 and Matthew 10:20—"from" and "of" the Father—in concert with Galatians 4:6 and Romans 8:16—"of" the Son.[55]

IRREVERSIBLE RELATIONS

The subtleties of Augustine's argument are clearly evident. Augustine believes in order to understand something of the irreversibility of the relations between the three. The Spirit has no Father, just as the Holy Spirit does not have a Son. This is a rule derivative of the way the New Testament speaks. Their relations are eternal. Accordingly, the Holy Spirit—unlike the Son—does not come forth "as born, but as given."[56] In relation to the Father's being, "the Spirit came forth, not as born, but as given," as one proceeding from the Father.[57] The "beginning" of the Spirit is the Father and not the Son. It is from the Father that the Spirit is forever given as gift. Augustine cannot conceive of things being otherwise because of John 15:26—*ekporeuetai* ("to go, come out") from the Father.

The Spirit proceeds as given. This is the Spirit's relationship of origin. Intrinsic to this origin is an opposition of relationship. The one gives (the Father), and the other is given (the Spirit). This happens, as Augustine is careful to point out, within an essential identity. Such opposition of relationship also includes the Son insofar as "that also which is given [the Spirit] has him [the Son] for a beginning by whom it is given."[58] The Father through the Son gives the Spirit. In this sense, and in this sense only, does Augustine teach the dual procession of the Spirit. Accordingly, the Spirit has one beginning—Father and

---

53. A. Edward Siecienski, *The Filioque: History of a Doctrinal Controversy* (New York: Oxford University Press, 2010), 60.
54. Augustine, *Trinity*, 5.3.12.
55. Siecienski, *Filioque*, 59.
56. Augustine, *Trinity*, 5.3.15.
57. Ibid.
58. Ibid.

Son—and "not two beginnings."[59] But the one beginning of the Spirit is twofold. The Spirit comes forth from the Father as given, and yet the Father gives the Spirit by the one in respect to whom the Father is Father, namely, the Son. Or, as Siecienski avers, "For Augustine, the ability to bring forth the Spirit is not something inherently belonging to the Son, but rather is his by a gift of the Father."[60] The Father alone is in the proper sense the one from whom the Spirit proceeds. From the Son too does the Spirit proceed, but only in a mediate sense.

The New Testament speaks of the three as united not only on the level of what they do or will but also at the level of their being. The Spirit is not less God than the Father by virtue of being from the Father. "The Holy Spirit, by being given, has not only this, that He is given, but absolutely that He is."[61] The Spirit is given as one who is God—the gift of God. In reference to the Spirit's self, the Spirit is God. That the Spirit is given eternally as God is a function of the fact that the Spirit is given from the very being of the Father. Accordingly, the Spirit is revealed to be consubstantial with the Father.

In sum, Augustine keeps following the New Testament into the mystery of the Trinity. It is from this mystery that salvation comes. In this mystery is God encountered as God truly is. Not only are the three equal to God's being; the Father is also the source of the being of the Son and Spirit, and the begetter of the Son and the giver of the Spirit. Our knowledge of God is but a glimpse at the being of God we are given to know and love in God's work of re-creation. But what about the mission of the Spirit? What is the relationship between the Spirit's mission and that from which this mission springs, the Spirit's given-ness in God? Indeed, it is fitting to think about how the Spirit's procession—the way in which the Spirit is—is expressed in the Spirit's mission. In the next section, we will do just that by unpacking the Spirit's mission as an extension in time of the Spirit's origin from the Father through the Son.

---

59. Ibid.
60. Siecienski, *Filioque*, 61.
61. Augustine, *Trinity*, 5.3.16.

THE MISSION OF THE SPIRIT: THE GIFT OF THE GIVER

The Spirit's procession (origin) from the Father is revealed in the Spirit's mission. The Spirit is the gift of the giver: the Father gives the Spirit through the Son. God's saving work has the shape that it does because it is *God's* work. What God does is expressive of what and who God is, which is precisely an understanding the New Testament encourages. Augustine's conclusion is that salvation is expressive of actions (immanent processions) internal to the one being of God. The Spirit as the gift of God has an origin in the life of God, not only from the Father but also by the Son. It is this life that the New Testament shows forth.

The Spirit is not only the "gift" but also the "communion" of the Father and Son. "So the Holy Spirit is something common to Father and Son, whatever it is, or is their very commonness or communion, consubstantial and coeternal."[62] The Spirit is coextensive with Father and Son. Augustine uses evocative language to describe this: "It is the Holy Spirit in the triad, not begotten, but the sweetness of begetter and begotten pervading all creatures according to their capacity with its vast generosity and fruitfulness."[63] The "sweetness of begetter and begotten" pervades "all creatures" precisely because that sweetness pervades the triad. That "sweetness" is the Holy Spirit, the gift and communion.

Augustine also refers to the Spirit as "the supreme charity conjoining Father and Son to each other and subjoining us to them."[64] The Spirit's conjoining work in God is in play among us "subjoining" us to the Father and Son. The person of the Spirit is this commonness, communion, sweetness, and supreme charity that conjoins Father and Son and subjoins us to them. The Spirit does all of this as God, for that is what the Spirit is. The Spirit (as with Father and Son) is called God with reference to the Spirit's self. At the same time, the Spirit is a person only with reference to the other two, for the Spirit is always said with reference to Father and Son.

The exegetical basis of Augustine's account of the Spirit's mission of subjoining is deeply indebted to John's gospel.[65] Take, for example,

---

62. Ibid., 5.1.7.
63. Ibid., 6.2.11.
64. Ibid., 6.2.6.
65. For example, thirteen of the twenty-nine scriptural references in book 6 of *On the Trinity* are to John's gospel.

Augustine's programmatic comments on John 2:1–11: "So who then could name Father and Son, and fail to understand there the charity of Father and Son? When you begin to have the Father and the Son, you will have the Holy Spirit; if you do not have the Father and the Son, you will be without the Holy Spirit."[66] The Spirit is to be found where the Father and Son are to be found: the Spirit is their charity. As their charity, the Spirit is their equal, originating from the Father and given through the Son. The Spirit is not made by the Father or the Son but proceeds from the first and as given through the second. In the Spirit's mission of subjoining, we see this but darkly.

Commenting on John 3:29–46, Christ "does not receive the Spirit by measure," Augustine notes that together with God the Father, the Lord Jesus exists in the Spirit "in the source and font of love."[67] The Spirit is always proper to Christ, who exists in the Spirit. We glimpse this in John's language of Christ as giver of the gift of the Spirit. The Spirit in whom Jesus Christ exists is the Spirit he eternally receives from the Father. This is the Spirit who binds him to the Father and the Father to him.

In an important discussion of John 5:19, Augustine avers,

The works of the Father and Son are inseparable. What have I actually said? Just as Father and Son are themselves inseparable, so too are the works of Father and Son inseparable. In what way are Father and Son inseparable? In the way he said himself, *I and the Father are one* (Jn 10:30); in the way Father and Son are not two gods, but one God, the Word and the one whose Word he is, the one and only God, Father and Son bound together by love, and theirs is the one Spirit of love, so that Father and Son and Holy Spirit constitute the Trinity.[68]

Notice several things. God's works, the missions of Son and Spirit, arise from God's life. Unity of being is manifest in indivisibility of works. The common being of the three is revealed in the unity of their works. That God in God's inner life is dynamically one renders talk of the indivisibility of God's works toward the outside intelligible. The work of the three is one because they are one.

---

66. Augustine, *Homilies on John*, 9, 189.
67. Ibid., 271, 324.
68. Ibid., 359–60.

Furthermore, the love by which Father and Son are one is "the one Spirit of love." The Father begets from the depths of his being his equal, the Son. In being begotten of him, the Son is not less than the Father: "What flows and what it flows out from are of one and the same substance ... like light flowing from light."[69] In being begotten of him, "the Father communicates to the Son all that he is, apart from his being Father."[70] Included in that communication is the Spirit. The Spirit proceeds from the being of the Father as given, and this proceeding does not take place apart from the one by whom the Spirit is given, the Son. It is as the Spirit of their love that the Spirit binds us to them.

Importantly, the Spirit that binds together in love in the life of God gives rise to love among us. The Spirit's mission reflects actions internal to the Trinity itself. The Spirit effects love of Christ and Christ's body, the church: "Let us believe, brothers and sisters, that to the extent that someone loves the Church of Christ, to that extent he has the Holy Spirit."[71] The Spirit's mission of fostering love for the Son is commensurate with the Spirit's procession as the love of the Father for the Son and the Son for the Father. The creature's joy is to share in the love that is proper to the Holy Trinity. The Spirit binds us to the Son and thus to his body, his bride, the church. This is, again, the Spirit who is God, God in a substantial or being sense, and God in a relational sense, the third of three. God the Holy Spirit is not only the mutual love of Father and Son but the very love that binds them together, "their mutual gift (*donum*) of his [the Spirit's] love poured out upon humanity."[72]

APPROPRIATING AUGUSTINE

Having briefly seen how Augustine derives principles for speaking about the being of the Trinity from New Testament talk of the three, it is worth taking a moment to summarize how Augustine's Trinitarianism informs this book's thesis. If an account of the Spirit's divinity anchors an account of the Spirit's activity, if indeed that activity cannot be truly received or understood without an account of first principles, what does Augustine teach us about such principles? First, such principles

---

69. Augustine, *Trinity*, 4.5.27.

70. Yves Congar, *I Believe in the Holy Spirit* (New York: Seabury, 1983), 3:85.

71. Augustine, *Homilies on John*, 32, 521.

72. Siecienski, *Filioque*, 60.

describe the mystery into which the New Testament leads. Augustine does not think we know what we are saying when we talk about the Spirit's procession as simultaneous with the begetting of the Son from the Father. But say this we must if we are to truly speak of the God we are given to love, serve, know, and see but darkly. Of course, we also do not know how these acts internal to God are true. Nonetheless, we know them to be true, because God in majestic humility has acted as God *is* for us and for our salvation. Augustine's Trinitarianism is such that God's acts toward the outside reveal acts toward the inside. The Spirit's mission as the gift given is anchored in and expressive of the Spirit's life from the Father and Son, the very being of the one God common to the three.

Second, Augustine is happy to encourage talk about the life of the triune God as proceeding "from the eternal intra-divine acts of the divine three."[73] God's life is from himself. We are given to know that God just is. The Father generates the Son from his very being in the Spirit. This is the Spirit who proceeds from the Father and is given by the Son and who unites the Father to the Son and the Son to the Father in an eternal harmony as the Father's very gift. Accordingly, when we describe who the Spirit is, we are describing the relations whereby the Spirit comes to be; when we describe what the Spirit is, as has been our task, we describe the one being of the Spirit that is common to Father and Son. In the New Testament, we are given glimpses of how the Spirit arises via Father and Son even though we do not really know what we are saying when the Spirit comes to (eternally) be by the Father in a primary sense and the Son in a secondary sense. What we must nonetheless say is that the Spirit is not ontologically subordinate, then, precisely because the Spirit (as with the Son) possesses as one who is given what is the Father's (substance).

Third, that Christ gives the Spirit without measure shows us the extent to which the work that the Spirit's mission accomplishes expresses the Spirit's origin in God. The Spirit is of the Father and of the Son, inasmuch as the Father through the Son gives the Spirit.[74] The Spirit's mission is to reveal the Father of the Son. This is fitting and right, given that the Spirit is given from the Father through the Son, thereby uniting Father and Son in the Godhead and uniting us to

---

73. Ayres, *Augustine*, 3.
74. See Augustine, *Trinity*, 4.5.29.

them. More specifically, Augustine appreciates that the gift (the Spirit) is the love (the "sweetness") of the begetter for the begotten, love that is eternally their gift. It is the revelation of this gift that is the Spirit's mission. In Ayres's words, "Scripture's naming of the Spirit as the highest Love joining Father and Son (and by implication as Light and Wisdom) enables us to understand the Spirit's mission as the immediate transforming presence of God."[75] In short, the Spirit's procession determines the Spirit's mission and in turn should govern any account of the work that such a mission accomplishes.

Fourth, Augustine's exegesis and the rules derivative of it point to the character of the Father's monarchy, the sense in which the Father is "first." The Father generates the Son and gives rise to the Spirit from the Father's very substance. The direction, if you will, is from the Father all the way down. That is not to say that the Son or Spirit is inferior or subordinate in being. It is, rather, to ascribe clear priority to the Father in the life of the Trinity, something that the actions of Son and Spirit toward the outside attest. The Son and not the Father is sent, the Spirit and not the Father is also sent. The Father sends, and this is fitting given that in the actions internal to the life of the Trinity itself, the Father is the source of Son and Spirit. But the Father is not independent of them, Augustine reminds us, for the being of the Father is common to them, and indeed the Father is only Father in relation to the Son.

The Spirit is from the Father, as is the Son, albeit "from" in a different way. The Spirit's origin also points to the Father's monarchy. Even the Son's causality in relationship to the Spirit is entirely of the Father insofar as the Father shares with the Son the spirating of the Spirit. To be sure, we are speaking at the level of relations, and of course we do not know how this is true but only that it is true. The New Testament encourages us to be filled with the Spirit, who is an "irreducible person," "the essence of Father and Son," and "the agent identical to the act of communion between Father and Son."[76] The divine essence, in the person of the Spirit, exists as this act of communion, toward the inside and therefore toward the outside.

I think we see this illustrated in the virgin birth. Jesus is conceived in the power of the Holy Spirit. His earthly birth points to his heavenly

---

75. Ayres, *Augustine*, 229.
76. Ibid., 253, 258.

birth; his mission reiterates his procession. He is born in the Spirit in time, conceived in the Spirit, who is the Father's love for him, and throughout his life is filled with the Spirit, who enables him to be who he is even in death, the Son of God. Thus the Son's mission of obedience reflects the Son's generation from the Father, who in generating him gives him his Spirit, the same Spirit whom the Son pours out upon all flesh and who is "proper" to the Son as one eternally born of the Father. This is the Father who eternally generates the Son in the Spirit. Accordingly, the Spirit is the love of the begetter for the begotten, and the begotten for the begetter.

Last, Augustine points us, rightly so, to the extent to which the God of the Bible is a living God. God is a dynamic reality who exists and therefore acts in a certain way: action as revelatory of being. God's actions in the economy, if we would take Augustine seriously, are not arbitrary. The giving of eternal life — the life God is, from eternity — is the life Jesus supplies by the work of the Spirit in gathering us to him. Jesus is "the bread of life" (John 6:35). The life Jesus gives "without measure" is the Spirit (John 3:34) by whom we share in the Father's relationship to the Son and the Son's relationship to the Father. The triune life is love. "God is love" (1 John 4:8). If Augustine's treatise is received as edifying, it is because he confesses this love to be revelatory of what is and always shall be: the Father's love for the Son, the Son's love for the Father poured out among us by the same Spirit in whom they love one another and us from and to all eternity.

CONCLUSION

It is here that we wrap up our treatment of Augustine in response to the question, "What is the Spirit?" The Spirit *is* God. That is what the Spirit is: God. The being of the Spirit is the one being common to Father and Son. The Spirit possesses that being in a unique way. Herein we glimpse the Spirit's procession in God in relationship to the Father (primarily) and Son (secondarily). From here we turn to Thomas Aquinas. Thomas, also in conversation with John's gospel, extends Augustine's insights, especially regarding the Spirit's identity, that is, "Who is the Spirit?" That question will preoccupy us over the next two chapters. Augustine helped us to see what the Spirit is.

Thomas will help us to go deeper with respect to who the Spirit is. We will recognize Augustine in much of what Thomas says. However, Thomas, as we will see, advances our understanding of the identity of the Spirit in God, the same Spirit who is God together with Father and Son from all eternity.

PART 2

ENGAGING THOMAS

The Hypostatic Subsistence of the Holy Spirit

CHAPTER 4

"RIVERS OF LIVING WATER"

INTRODUCTION

John 7:37–39 is an apt place to begin engaging our second major interlocutor, Saint Thomas Aquinas. The passage runs, "On the last day of the festival, the great day, while Jesus was standing there, he cried out, 'Let anyone who is thirsty come to me, and let the one who believes in me drink. As the scripture has said, "Out of the believer's heart shall flow rivers of living water."' Now he said this about the Spirit, which believers in him were to receive; for as yet there was no Spirit, because Jesus was not yet glorified."[1] The best way to discover Thomas's thinking about the Trinity is to attend to his *Commentary on the Gospel of John*. In it, Thomas uses nonscriptural vocabulary like that of "relations of origin" to describe the interactions between Father, Son, and Holy Spirit on display in the New Testament narratives. Such vocabulary is important as it helps us appreciate something of how giving and receiving works in God's life. In John 7:37–39, we get a glimpse of that giving as expressed in the Spirit's flowing forth from Christ, filling believers with living water. It is this giving that reflects an eternal reality. And it is this reality that Thomas is keen to map via the interactions of the three on display in the narrative of the Fourth Gospel.

Thomas's commentary introduces the reader to highly technical teachings but does so in the midst of commentary, indeed as commentary. Speculative concerns are not teachings that relate at arm's length to the plain sense of Scripture. Rather, they are evoked by the plain

---

1. The text of the Fourth Gospel that Thomas uses is Jerome's Latin Vulgate.

sense of Scripture. For example, the language of "relations of origin" reflects, in Thomas's treatment, the interactions of the three manifest in Scripture. Teaching on the Trinity is speculative teaching in the sense used here inasmuch as it is teaching encouraged by Scripture and serviceable to rightly describing the God Scripture talks about.

To be sure, speculative theology is a term that for many carries negative connotations. Over the course of our study of Thomas, we will see that suspicion is unnecessary. Speculative teaching does not mean abstracting ourselves from the demands of yielding to the Word of God and developing a theological intelligence appropriate to it. Instead, speculative teaching in Thomas's hands takes up terms such as "processions" and "missions" in order to present and synthesize the truth of Scripture. Speculative teaching maps how the works of the three indicate their (common) nature. Our challenge is to attend to Thomas's understanding of extrabiblical language like "processions" and "missions" or that of "relations of origin" so as to see how they make manifest biblical truth. Thus our discussion in the pages that ensue will be "speculative," but only insofar as what is speculative discloses for Thomas the truth of what is at hand in the Fourth Gospel. As with treatment of Augustine in chapter 2, this chapter follows, albeit in a more extensive fashion, Thomas following John. Thomas's comments on a few passages from the Fourth Gospel are the principle of organization.

Thomas exegetes John's gospel as the Word of the Lord. That is the posture of Thomas's commentary. As with Augustine, Thomas hears Jesus' words as words spoken to all included in the reach of the apostles. Jesus speaks in order to convert. That is why Jesus cries out standing, not sitting—"while Jesus was standing there, he cried out" (John 7:37). "The reason for this," Thomas comments," "is to convert them."[2] Jesus' cry, as with his discourse in John 14–16, is addressed to the thirsty, those in need of conversion. For and to the thirsty will flow someone special, and that someone is the Holy Spirit. So Thomas: "The fountain which is taken in is the Holy Spirit."[3] This fountain is the source of a river, and both the fountain and the river that flows forth from it are the Spirit. Thomas's commentary helps us to discover how this works in God, especially with respect to who the Spirit is in God.

---

2. Saint Thomas Aquinas, *Commentary on the Gospel of John* (Washington, D.C.: Catholic University of America Press, 2010), 1085, 2:89.
   3. Ibid., 2:91.

The Spirit is a river of living water "because he proceeds from the Father and the Son."[4] One of Thomas's favourite texts to cite with respect to the Spirit's dual procession is Revelation 22:1, wherein the "'river of the water of life'" is said to come "'from the throne of God and of the Lamb.'" Although Thomas does not engage in a discussion of the relations of origin at this juncture in his commentary on John 7:37–39, it is nonetheless important to signal at the outset a major theme that occupies Thomas and that will in turn occupy us—the Father and Son as the one principle of the Holy Spirit.[5] Thomas's emphasis on the Spirit's proceeding from Father and Son is of course not to compromise the distinct hypostatic reality of the Spirit. Rather, it is to signal up front that Thomas's exegesis of John 14:15, 15:26, and 16:14–15 provide us with significant resources for articulating not only how giving works in God but also how that giving in God is expressed in a new way among us in the Spirit's mission to bind us to the Father through the Son. As we will see, the Spirit is a distinct *who*—a unique identity—in one *what*—the being of God. To the unfolding of this scriptural mystery we now turn.

JOHN 14:16–17: "NOTHING ELSE THAN LOVE"

"And I will ask the Father, and he will give you another Advocate, to be with you forever. This is the Spirit of truth, whom the world cannot receive, because it neither sees him nor knows him. You know him, because he abides with you, and he will be in you."

Several truths arise from Thomas's reading of this passage. First, the relations between the three are real; second, the three are really distinct persons. Equally true, the three are of one nature. That Jesus asks the Father to "give you another Advocate, to be with you forever" (John 14:16) attests these truths. Thomas comments, "The fact that he [Jesus] says, **another**, indicates a distinction of persons in God, in opposition to Sabellius."[6] Sabellius is a third-century figure whose writings are no longer extant but who through the reports of

---

4. Ibid.
5. Thomas writes, "Thus the mission of a divine person is a fitting thing, as meaning in one way the procession of origin from the sender, and as meaning a new way of existing in another." See *ST* I, q. 43, a. 1. For a helpful and brief introduction to the *Summa*, see Nicholas M. Healy, *Thomas Aquinas: Theologian of the Christian Life* (Aldershot: Ashgate, 2003), 4–5.
6. Aquinas, *Commentary on John*, 1912, 3:71.

his opponents championed a doctrine of God as "a radically singular being and of Son and Spirit as merely modes of divine operation."[7] Accordingly, distinctions between the persons are not real; Son and Spirit are but modes by which the one God works. Thomas vigorously disputes this view by introducing the counternotion of "the appropriation of persons."[8] To discredit the view that "another Advocate" indicates that this other Advocate whom the Father will give is of a different nature than the Son, Thomas avers that

> the Son and the Holy Spirit are not consolers and advocates in the same way ... Christ is called an advocate because as a human being he intercedes for us to the Father; the Holy Spirit is an advocate because he makes us ask. Again, the Holy Spirit is called a consoler because he is formally love. But the Son is a consoler because he is the Word. The Son is a consoler in two ways: because of his teaching and because the Son gives the Holy Spirit and incites love in our hearts. Thus the word, *another*, does not indicate a different nature in the Son and in the Holy Spirit. Rather, it indicates the different way each is an advocate and a consoler.[9]

Thomas appreciates that Son and Spirit are not of a different nature even though they act as advocate and consoler in different ways. They advocate differently because they are two and not one. The Spirit is "formally love" and the Son is "the Word." The action of the Son in asking the Father to send "another Advocate" shows forth the eternal Trinity, the mystery of the Trinity in itself. In that Trinity there is real distinction between the persons—against Sabellius—but not a distinction in regards to their nature—over and against Arius. Son and Spirit are one. But they are not one in such a way that different acts and attributes cannot be predicated of each of them. That is what John 14:16–17 teaches regarding God's life. Son and Spirit are truly distinct—not different—from one another and at the same time identical in their one essence or nature.

The Son and Spirit act as advocates; they do the same thing "but in a distinct mode, namely in the mode of their personal properties

---

7. Khaled Anatolios, *Retrieving Nicaea* (Grand Rapids: Baker Academic, 2011), 16.
8. Aquinas, *Commentary on John*, 1912, 3:71.
9. Ibid.

(Word and Love)."[10] What is unique to each expresses their origins. Accordingly, what distinguishes the three is not their essence but their respective properties. Again, the Son is "Word" and the Spirit "Love." Thomas's exegesis demonstrates that "the way of Trinitarian theology ... starts from the action of the persons so as to show, by reasoning, a truth concerning the eternal Trinity in itself (the 'immanent Trinity')."[11] What the interactions of the three manifest are truths concerning their life. It is theology's task to present these truths as intrinsic to the sense of the text itself.

Thomas thinks that John 14:16–17 helps us appreciate what is unique not only to the Spirit's person but also to the Spirit's origin. The Spirit is "from the Truth."[12] The Spirit's mission of abiding "implies origin."[13] The Spirit who is given by the Father is of the Son. Citing John 14:6 — "I am the way, and the truth, and the life" — Thomas concludes that the Spirit "leads to knowledge of the truth, because he proceeds from the Truth."[14] The Spirit's mission is grounded in the Spirit's procession "from conceived Truth, which is the Son."[15] The Spirit leads to the truth because the Spirit is from the Truth. The Spirit speaks Jesus Christ because the Spirit proceeds from Christ. Moreover, the Spirit is "from the Truth and speaks the truth" because "the Holy Spirit is nothing else than Love."[16] The Spirit is Love. "Love," Thomas writes, "proceeds from the Truth, so Love leads to knowledge of the truth: 'He [the Holy Spirit] will glorify me because he will receive from me and declare it to you' (16:14)."[17] The Spirit glorifies the Son and reveals the Son because the Spirit is Love, "the love of God."[18] This is the Spirit's personal property in God and the basis for the Spirit's distinct action toward the outside.

"Love" is the property of the Holy Spirit. But how can this be,

---

10. Gilles Emery, "Biblical Exegesis and the Speculative Doctrine of the Trinity in St. Thomas Aquinas's *Commentary on St. John*," in *Reading John with St. Thomas Aquinas*, ed. Michael Dauphinais and Matthew Levering (Washington, D.C.: Catholic University of America Press, 2005), 44.

11. Ibid., 42.

12. Aquinas, *Commentary on John*, 1916, 3:72.

13. Bruce D. Marshall, "What Does the Spirit Do?" in *Reading John*, 65.

14. Aquinas, *Commentary on John*, 1916, 3:72.

15. Ibid., 3:73.

16. Ibid., 3:72. See also *ST* I, q. 37, a. 1.

17. Ibid., 3:73. Cf. John 15:26: "When the Advocate comes, whom I will send to you from the Father, the Spirit of truth who comes from the Father."

18. Ibid.

if "God is love?" Is Thomas suggesting that the Spirit is love while Father and Son are not? What Thomas argues to the contrary is that "Love" describes something of how the Spirit comes to be in God. The nature common to the three is, of course, love. Again, "God is love." At the same time, however, the Spirit is "personally Love" because the Spirit proceeds as the Love of the Father for the Son and the Son for the Father. "Love" is most appropriately said of the Spirit, and this has something to do with how giving works in God. To John 15:26–27 we now turn and to further unfolding of this giving and of the Spirit as "nothing else than Love."

JOHN 15:26–27: "PROCEEDS AS LOVE"

The Holy Spirit is "the Love of God."[19] In fact, the Holy Spirit's name is "Love," in like manner to "Word" as the Son's name. What is so significant about such a name? For Thomas, a name includes a relation. The name Love expresses particular relations of origin. Thomas explains it this way. The Son sends the Spirit, and the Spirit sent by the Son comes from the Father. That Jesus sends the Spirit is metaphysically significant, Thomas avers. It "indicate[s] his [the Spirit's] procession from another [the Son]."[20] The Son's sending of the Spirit suggests to Thomas that the Spirit is also *from* the Son. Accordingly, the Son's sending of the Spirit reflects how the Son is said to exist in an originating relation to the Spirit: "from whom he [the Spirit] has it that he [the Spirit] is."[21] The Spirit's being is from another. That other is the Son "just as it is from another [the Father] that the Son has whatever he does."[22]

The order of the persons one from another — Spirit from Son and not vice versa — reflects "the order of their nature."[23] The economy rests upon this order and demonstrates this order. It is an eternal order. The Spirit is not after the Father and the Son in any temporal sense but rather together with them is God from eternity. The Spirit is proper to the same essence that Father and Son each possess without confusion or change. Each of the three is God, and each is truly distinguished from the other by the order of their nature.

---

19. Ibid., 3:126.
20. Ibid.
21. Ibid.
22. Ibid.
23. Aquinas, *ST* I, q. 36, a. 2,

The Father and Son as the one principle of the Holy Spirit is taught by John 14:26, argues Thomas.[24] Citing Revelation 22:1, as he does in his discussion of John 7:37–39, Thomas comments that the Spirit being sent by two (the Father and the Son) is thus sent "by [two of] the same and equal power."[25] Although in John 14:26 it is the Father who sends the Spirit, in 15:26 it is the Son. The texts do not contradict one another but rather point to what the Son himself says in John 5:19: "The Son can do nothing on his own." Even the Son's sending of the Spirit from the Father is a sending that the Father undertakes in the Son's name — John 14:26. Moreover, the fruit of that sending, that invisible mission of the Spirit from the Son and the Father, is that "the Holy Spirit makes those to whom he is sent like the one whose Spirit he is."[26] The Spirit makes us like Christ to whom the Spirit belongs and from whom the Spirit proceeds. The shape of the Spirit's working indicates the shape of the Spirit's own procession in God. The Spirit as the "Love of God" conforms us to Christ; this is what the Spirit does.[27] That the Spirit does this expresses the Spirit's origin *from* the Son, and thus the Father in whom the Son does all.

THE ORIGIN OF THE OTHER-DIRECTED SPIRIT

The Spirit conforms to Christ. That the Spirit conforms us to another shows the Spirit's other-directedness. But why? Why does the Spirit testify on Christ's behalf? We have to follow the suggestions that the text supplies. These take us into the realm of the triune life. The Spirit's testimony to the Son infers an opposite relation of origin.[28] Recall that for Thomas the name "Holy Spirit" includes a relation: the Spirit, argues Thomas, is the name of a relation. Specifically, the Spirit is immediately related to the Father, and mediately to the Son. The Spirit is from each, but from each in a different way. Thomas puts it this way: the Spirit proceeds "from the Father immediately, as from Him, and mediately, as from the Son; and thus He is said to proceed from the

---

24. Thomas argues in ibid. that "this term *principle* has not determinate supposition; but it rather stands indeterminately for two persons [Father and Son] together."

25. Aquinas, *Commentary on John*, 2061, 3:126.

26. Ibid., 3:127.

27. Ibid., 3:126.

28. See Aquinas, *ST* I, q. 36, a. 2.

Father through the Son."[29] What renders the three distinct is "a formal distinction ... which has to involve some kind of opposition."[30] The question, of course, is "What kind of opposition?" It is not opposition of an essential nature but rather of a relational one.

Son and Spirit are truly distinct from one another—the Spirit testifies, and the Son is testified. But again, on what basis are they distinct? "They have to be distinguished by some properties that are opposed," argues Thomas.[31] Their actions attest that they cannot be the same. This is why Thomas employs such language. Rather than being sterile, it strives to preserve the mystery of three who are one. Again, such opposition of origin is not "repugnant to their equality. What remains is that the Holy Spirit is distinguished from the Son only by a relative opposition."[32] Relative opposition indicates that the Spirit is different from the Son and vice versa, but only insofar as "one of them is referred to the other."[33] Sent by the Son, the Spirit refers to the Son. But the Spirit does not send the Son. Rather, the Son sends the Spirit, thereby pointing us to how their work expresses an eternal order. Only "relations of origin" oppose Son and Spirit to one another, and that only "insofar as one person [the Spirit] is from another."[34] That—and that only—distinguishes (without separating) Son and Spirit from one another.

Thomas also thinks that John 14:16–17 encourages us to explore how Son and Spirit also have different origins with respect to the Father. Although Son and Spirit receive the same nature from the Father, they receive that very same nature differently. Here we reach the heart of the matter. "The Spirit of truth who comes from the Father" receives "the very same nature ... by proceeding [from the Father]" as does the Son "by being born from the Father."[35] Each proceeds from the being of the Father, albeit differently, one as Word (the Son), one as Love (the Spirit). Here we see once again what relative opposition means in God, the opposition that John 15:26 implies. The Son proceeds via "the property of filiation," which is precisely what it means to speak of the Son as "not from Himself, but from the Father."[36] The Son is born

---

29. Ibid., a. 3, ad 1.
30. Aquinas, *Commentary on John*, 2063, 3:127.
31. Ibid.
32. Ibid.
33. Ibid., 3:128.
34. Ibid.
35. Ibid.
36. Aquinas, *ST* I, q. 36, a. 2, ad 6.

of (filiated by) the Father. The same cannot be said of the Spirit: "The Holy Ghost is from the Father and the Son."[37] The Spirit receives the Father's nature by proceeding, the Son by being begotten.[38] The Son is only from the Father, not from Father and Spirit, whereas the Spirit is from both. The Spirit is from the Father in an "immediate" sense and the Son in a "mediate" sense.

HOW THOMAS DIFFERS FROM "THE GREEKS"

The Son is not begotten of the Father and the Spirit. The Son is eternally begotten of the Father in the Spirit. The Spirit, however, proceeds from the Father in accord with John 15:26. So Thomas: "Because the Son receives from the Father that the Holy Ghost proceeds from Him, it can be said that the Holy Ghost proceeds from the Father through the Son. The meaning is the same."[39] The conclusion that Thomas reaches is a simple one: Son and Spirit are "distinguished only by the order of origin, that is to say, insofar as the birth [or generation] of the Son is a principle of the procession of the Holy Spirit. And so, if the Holy Spirit were not from the Son, the Spirit would not be distinguished from birth."[40]

It is important to note at this juncture that Thomas recognizes his reading of John 15:26 places him at odds with "the Greeks."[41] "For they [the Greeks] say that the Holy Spirit is of the Son, and that the Son acts through the Holy Spirit, but not conversely. And some even admit that the Holy Spirit is from the Son, but they will not concede that the Holy Spirit proceeds from the Son."[42] The issue, in simple terms, is whether "proceeds" demands "from." The Greeks say no,

---

37. Ibid., ad 7.
38. Aquinas, *Commentary on John*, 2064, 3:128.
39. Aquinas, *ST* I, q. 36, a. 4.
40. Aquinas, *Commentary on John*, 2064, 3:128. Interestingly, Thomas argues that the "ancient councils ... contained implicitly ... the belief that the Holy Ghost proceeds from the Father." See *ST* I, q. 36, a. 2, ad 2. What the *filioque* does is render explicit what is clearly implicit. It does not represent a distortion of the ancient councils but rather the fullness of what they affirmed. See further Jaroslav Pelikan, "The Doctrine of the Filioque in Thomas Aquinas and its Patristic Antecedents. An Analysis of the *Summa Theologica* Part I, q. 36," in *St. Thomas Aquinas: Commemorative Studies* (Toronto: Pontifical Institute for Medieval Studies, 1974), 1:325–36.
41. Aquinas, *Commentary on John*, 2064, 3:128.
42. Ibid.

and the Latins, including, of course, Thomas, say yes.[43] But even there, Thomas recognizes the rather flexible nature of the term "proceed": "And so this word [proceed], because it is so general, has been adapted to indicate the existence of the Holy Spirit as from the Son."[44] For Thomas, the Spirit does not proceed from two sources or principles but rather "one principle": that is, "the Son with the Father."[45] To put it differently, there is a unity of "property" between the Father and Son as regards the Spirit's procession, which is "the two Persons together."[46] The procession of the Spirit helps us to better understand that two can be said to be one property of the Spirit, all the while possessing "one common nature."[47] That is indeed the challenge (for Thomas): to speak of how one can proceed from two united in one essence.

Before we move to our most important passage to consider, John 16:14–15, let us take a moment to review the insights reached thus far. Does John 15:26 supply us with a math problem? Is this indeed a case of funny math? It would not seem so, provided that we realize Thomas is set on providing us with some guidelines or rules for mapping Johannine talk. Let us rehearse them for a moment. God is one. The three possess one common nature or essence that does not exist prior to them. Accordingly, the three do not make up something called "God." Furthermore, a relation, for Thomas, is a person: begetter (which implies one begotten), begotten (which implies one who begets), and proceeding (which implies being from another). While a more fulsome account of what Thomas means by this — "subsistent relations" — will have to wait until the next chapter, we ought to note that the three are only relatively opposed. Opposite relations distinguish the persons from one another, to be sure, but not with respect to their common essence. Talk of their different relations of origin attempts to map the New Testament's testimony about their eternal interactions.

What distinguishes the Spirit from the other two in God is the Spirit's procession. Bruce Marshall writes, "In God the Holy Spirit

---

43. By "Latins," Thomas denotes theologians of the Western church, that is, the Latin-speaking church—e.g., Augustine. By "Greeks," Thomas denotes theologians of the Eastern church, that is, the Greek-speaking church—e.g., the Cappadocians.

44. Aquinas, *Commentary on John*, 2064, 3:128.

45. Ibid., 3:129.

46. Aquinas, *ST* I, q. 36, a. 4, ad 6. Note again that Thomas does not use the term "person" in his *Commentary on John*. It is, as Gilles Emery notes, not "an indispensable element of the doctrine of the Trinity." See Emery, "Biblical Exegesis and Speculative Doctrine," in *Reading John*, 31.

47. Aquinas, *ST* I, q. 36, a. 4, ad 1.

proceeds as the Father's love for the Son, the truth which the Father brings forth."[48] The Holy Spirit is "the truth" of the Father's love for the Son that the Father brings forth from eternity. But there is more. As we have seen, "the Spirit proceeds as the Son's love for the Father, whose truth the Son has been brought forth to be."[49] The Spirit, argues Thomas, proceeds from Father and Son as Gift; indeed, "Gift is the proper name of the Holy Ghost."[50] The Gift that the Spirit is "proceeds from the Father as love."[51] The Spirit's procession as love distinguishes the Spirit from the Word, the Son. The Spirit proceeds "as love" whereas "the Son proceeds as a word, whose nature it is to be the likeness of its principle."[52] The personal name of the Holy Spirit—Love—expresses the Spirit's procession, the Spirit's origin, as is the case with the Son. The Gift that the Father gives is eternal: it does not need to be given— although, of course, it is—to be a Gift. The Spirit does not become a Gift in relationship to the creature to whom the Spirit is given. Rather, the Spirit is "the Gift of God giving."[53] This is *who* the Spirit is: Gift of God and therefore gift among us.

JOHN 16:14–15: "ONE IS PRIOR TO ANOTHER"

John 16:14–15 is another key Trinitarian text. Thomas thinks this text helps us to distinguish the Spirit from the Son. "He [the Spirit] will glorify me [Jesus]." The Spirit does not glorify the Spirit's self but rather the Son. The Spirit is other-directed. Thomas refers to the Spirit's glorification of the Son as "the third fruit" of the Spirit's coming, the first being "the rebuking of the world," the second "the instruction of the disciples."[54] The Spirit glorifies another who, like him, is divine. The difference between Son and Spirit is not a matter of essence. Instead, the Son is distinct from the Spirit as the Spirit's principle. This, says Thomas, is "the reason why the Spirit will glorify Christ."[55] The Spirit glorifies the Son because the Spirit is from the Son, "for everything which is from another manifests that from which

---

48. Marshall, "What Does the Spirit Do?" in *Reading John*, 67.
49. Ibid.
50. Aquinas, *ST* I, q. 38, a. 1.
51. Ibid., ad 1.
52. Ibid.
53. Ibid., ad 3.
54. Aquinas, *Commentary on John*, 2105, 3:143.
55. Ibid., 3:144.

it is."[56] The same logic proper to the Son/Spirit relation is also true of the Father/Son relation: "the Son manifests the Father because he is from the Father. And so because the Spirit is from the Son, it is appropriate that the Spirit glorify the Son. He [the Son] says, *he will glorify me, for he will receive from me*."[57] The Spirit's mission is but a new way of existing in relationship to us. The Spirit receives from the Son from eternity, and we see this receiving on display in the interactions of Son and Spirit toward the outside in the economy of salvation.

Thomas is keen to point out the qualitative distinction between the Spirit's receiving from the Son and creaturely receiving—"the Holy Spirit does not receive in the same way creatures do."[58] Thomas explains, "In creatures, that which receives is one thing, and what is received is something else. This is not so in the divinity."[59] Let me explain via an analogy. Let us assume for a moment that I give my eight-year-old daughter a gift on her birthday, as any loving parent should do! The one who receives the gift (my daughter) is different from the gift (e.g., a doll). In receiving the gift, my daughter does not become the gift itself. Daughter and doll are not (and do not become) the same thing. The reason this example—that is, the difference between recipient of the gift and the gift itself—does not apply to divinity is that "the divine persons are simple, and not composed of several elements."[60] While daughter and doll are composed of quite different elements, Son and Spirit are not. "Indeed, the Holy Spirit receives his entire substance from whomever this Spirit receives, and so does the Son."[61] My daughter, in receiving the doll, receives something that remains external to herself: the daughter/doll divide is never overcome; whereas the Spirit receives entirely from the Son, who is in turn from the Father. But note, the Spirit does not receive what is unique or proper to the Son, namely, the Son's generation from the Father. Why? This is because we see a relation of relative opposition at work. The language of generation and procession only works in God in relation to another. The Spirit takes or receives the Spirit's being from the Son. This, Thomas thinks, is how giving works in God.

---

56. Ibid.
57. Ibid.
58. Ibid.
59. Ibid.
60. Ibid.
61. Ibid.

DIVINE RECEIVING

Another difference between creaturely receiving and divine receiving is to be noted. Thomas comments, "The one [the creature] who receives did not have at one time what he receives, as when matter receives a form, or a subject receives an accident: for at some time the matter was without such a form, and the subject without that accident."[62] Again, let me explain. Let us assume that I am asked to paint my daughter's bedroom walls blue. They are currently purple, but my spouse and I think blue would look better and appeal more to her, so I go ahead and paint. Lo and behold, the walls that were purple now become blue. The walls have received a new accident, which is a new colour. The subject (the wall) must not necessarily be blue, even though it now is, because blue possesses an accidental quality with respect to its subject (the wall) that is pleasing to my daughter. Moreover, the walls of the room (the subjects) are composed of matter (drywall, which is itself composed of ground-up rock, water, glue, etc.). The matter (rock) has assumed a particular form (drywall), the drywall (which constitutes the wall—the subject—of the room) having a particular accident (blue paint). Thomas writes, "This is not so in the divinity, because what the Son receives from the Father the Son has from eternity, and what the Holy Spirit receives from the Father and the Son, the Spirit has from eternity. Accordingly, the Holy Spirit receives from the Son like the Son receives from the Father."[63] The walls (the subject) that receive a new paint job (the accident) receive that which they did not have before, blue paint. Whereas in God the Spirit, in receiving from the Son, does not receive what the Spirit does not already have. What the Spirit has, as do the Father and the Son from eternity, is divinity. Simply stated, the Spirit does not receive divine status from the Son (or the Father). The Spirit is God from eternity, as are Father and Son: God the Holy Trinity.

If the Spirit does not receive his divinity from the Son, then what on earth does the Spirit receive? Thomas answers, "When the expression 'to receive' is used of the divinity, it indicates an order in origin."[64] The Spirit, Thomas argues, is consubstantial with the Son and the Father: like them, the Spirit does not participate in divinity but together with

---

62. Ibid.
63. Ibid.
64. Ibid.

them is the one God. However, the Spirit does receive in relation to Father and Son an order insofar as "in God order exists."[65] Thomas calls this "*the order of nature.*"[66] Following Augustine, Thomas argues that the origins of the persons denote a certain order "without priority ... *Not whereby one is prior to another, but whereby one is from another.*"[67] The upshot of this is that in God it is possible for one to receive and another to give, because the one nature is ordered from eternity in this certain way. On the basis of this order are they numerically distinct. Giving and receiving in God works this way, and that is why the three interact among us as they do. John 16:14 encourages us to talk in these terms. The Spirit does not receive from one who is prior but rather from one who also subsists in the same nature.

"All that the Father has is mine," says Jesus (John 16:15). Included in the "all," Thomas comments, is "the Spirit of truth [who] proceeds from the Father."[68] The Son receives all from the Father except of course what makes the Father indeed the Father. What the Father has "is his own essence, own goodness, own truth and own eternity."[69] This raises an important question: Does the "all" imply that the Son "has the characteristic of fatherhood"?[70] The answer would be yes "if our Lord had said, 'All that God has is mine.' But he [the Lord] says, **all that the Father has is mine**, and this keeps a distinction between the Father and the Son, and leads us to understand that all that the Father has is the Son's, except that by which the Father is distinguished from the Son."[71] Their essence is common, and their common nature is what underwrites the force of the "all."

The Son, "by using the word Father ... has not usurped the attribute of fatherhood."[72] By no means, Thomas argues: the essence common to the three is not—and herein lies the force of the whole argument of this chapter—an essence that each has "in the same order."[73] So Thomas: "We have conceded that whatever the Father has the Son has, *but not that the Son has it in the same order as the Father* [emphasis mine].

---

65. Augustine, *Contra Maxim.*, II, 14, quoted in Aquinas, *ST* I, q. 42, a. 3.
66. Ibid.
67. Ibid.
68. Aquinas, *Commentary on John*, 2110, 3:145.
69. Ibid.
70. Ibid. This is Didymus the Blind's objection. See *De Spir. Sanc.* 38.
71. Ibid.
72. Ibid.
73. Ibid.

For the Son has as receiving from another; while the Father has as giving to another."[74] What each has equally—divinity and all the perfections intrinsic to it—is not had in the same way. Giving in God does not work that way. In other words, the Son has all that the Father has as the Son. The Son does not have the all *"in the same order as the Father."* That is not to say for a moment that one has more of the divine nature than another. By no means: the distinctions, for Thomas, are "in the order of having."[75] Thus, Jesus is not deceiving us when he says, "All that the Father has is mine." The "all" is true; but Jesus has the "all" differently than the Father because he is the Son. Again, there exist real distinctions "in the order of having," distinctions that Thomas describes as "relations."[76] Relations—for example, "fatherhood and sonship"—"signify a distinction of order, for fatherhood signifies a giving to another in God and sonship a receiving from another."[77] But again, such receiving refers to another and not to the essence whereby each is. Relational talk simply describes how these three are related to one another. Thomas thinks that such talk provides us with an acceptable way in which to describe how giving in God works.

FROM THE FATHER AND THE SON?

There is, in all of this, a quite compelling logic evidenced for the Spirit's procession *a Patre* and *a Filio*. To appreciate Thomas's thinking, however, we must begin by referring briefly to the procession/generation of the Son from the Father. The Son receives being from the Father, but this does not result in a diversity of natures. The Son proceeds from the Father's nature as "a conjoined principle ... and exists in the same nature, because in God the act of understanding and His being are the same."[78] Fending off the Sabellian heresy, which would argue for a lack of real distinction between Father and Son, Thomas avers, on the basis of John 16:15, that the Word's procession demands one to say "that He Who proceeds receives divine being from another, not, however, as if He were other from the divine nature."[79] The two

---

74. Ibid.
75. Ibid.
76. Ibid.
77. Ibid.
78. Aquinas, *ST* I, q. 27, a. 2.
79. Ibid.

processions (generation and proceeding) remain internal to God. "The Father generates neither by the divine will nor by the Holy Spirit, but by the divine nature."[80] Matthew Levering explains this mystery quite nicely when he writes, "In generating the Son, the Father gives himself absolutely. Only the order of generation differentiates Father and Son: the Father is begetter, the Son begotten."[81]

But what does Thomas's reading of John 16:15 imply regarding the Spirit's procession? "Note that we say that ... the Holy Spirit receives from the substance of the Father and the Son; and that the Father, by virtue of his nature, gives his substance to the Son, and the Father and the Son give to the Holy Spirit."[82] Consubstantiality amongst Father and Son is shared with the Spirit—but not of course in a way that suggests diversity of essence. God is one. When Jesus says that "he will take what is mine and declare it to you," we see an eternal order expressing itself. The Spirit takes and declares because the Spirit receives. This order is irreversible. Accordingly, the Son could not take from and declare the Spirit. Rather, only the reverse is true. The Spirit's declaration of the Son reflects an irreversible eternal order between Son and Spirit. Similarly, Father and Son are not, for example, "from the substance of the Holy Spirit."[83] The Holy Spirit is, rather, from them, just as the Son is from the Father, and the Father is from no one. One is not the other. The three give themselves to us as they do precisely because this is how giving in God works.

The Spirit in being third in terms of order is no less God than the first or second person. Indeed, "what is communicated to the Holy Spirit is what is common to the Father and the Son. Now in the divinity the principle of communication must be the same as what is communicated."[84] Thomas's point is that in God like begets like in such a way that the Holy Spirit receives from Father and Son all that they are—with the exception of their personal properties, paternity (fatherhood) and filiation (the non-word in divinity for "being born"). The one who generates, the one who is generated, and the one who proceeds indicate personal properties that "remain within the agent" in

---

80. Matthew Levering, "Does the Paschal Mystery Reveal the Trinity?" in *Reading John*, 87.
81. Ibid., 88. One of the implications of this is that the Spirit is not "*begotten, but proceeding.*" Thomas is quoting Pseudo-Athanasius. See *ST* I, q. 27, a. 4, on the contrary.
82. Aquinas, *Commentary on John*, 2115, 3:146.
83. Ibid.
84. Ibid.

such a way that "all that exists in God is one with the divine nature."[85] In sum, "so, if the Father gives his essence to the Holy Spirit, the Son must also do so. For this reason he [Jesus] says, **all that the Father has is mine**. And if the Holy Spirit receives from the Father, he will also receive from the Son. And for this reason he says, **therefore I said that he will receive from me and declare it to you**, for according as he receives from me, so he will show you."[86] The Spirit shows among us what he (eternally) receives, namely, essence from the Father and Son.

Thomas's exegesis is fruitful. It shows us the extent to which "the action of the persons in the economy leads to the discovery and disclosure of a truth concerning the Trinity itself."[87] Two truths concerning the Trinity itself emerge from John 16:14–15. The three disclose, first, their unity (common essence) and, second, their distinction (of order) in their interactions among us. In the case of the Spirit, we learn of one who is from the essence of the Father and the Son. Scripture itself discloses this to us and would encourage us to talk this way. Furthermore, there is a soteriological point in talk of originating relations. The interactions of the three narrated in John's gospel are of saving import. To receive the Spirit's declaration of the Son is eternal life. The life that God is, when revealed among us, saves and makes new. God's self-disclosure is a saving self-disclosure. By grace are we made fit to know, love, serve, praise, and share in God's nature as God truly is.

THE PERSON OF THE SPIRIT

The Spirit is a person. But what does that mean? Well, talk of the Spirit's personhood is rather apophatic, which means that human words refer only obliquely to this one. We know that the term can be useful in describing the three we meet in the New Testament. Thomas thinks that the term may be rendered helpful insofar as it points to there being three actors or parties in the New Testament. Hence Thomas's reticence and care in describing what a person is in God. To describe the personhood of the Spirit well requires that we synthesize the exegetical insights arrived at thus far with some help from Thomas's Trinitarian

---

85. Aquinas, *ST* I, a. 27, a. 5; a. 4, ad 1.
86. *Commentary on John*, 2115, 3:146–47.
87. Gilles Emery, *The Trinitarian Theology of St Thomas Aquinas*, trans. Francesca Aran Murphy (Oxford: Oxford University Press, 2007), 13.

treatise in *ST* I.[88] Although the next chapter will unfold the Trinitarian treatise in the *ST*, appeal to it now is necessary in discussing what Thomas thinks a person is in God. This we will now do. As with the previous sections of the chapter, our thesis remains in full view. We will talk about the Spirit's personhood—the unique *who* of the Spirit—in a way that tracks New Testament (Johannine) talk, with a view to mapping the work of the Spirit as arising from who the Spirit is in God. As we will see, the *person* of the Holy Spirit can, for Thomas, only be haltingly described by keeping three points in play. Indeed, personhood requires a gentle unfolding of them: (1) the Spirit's procession (origin) in God; (2) "the role of *relation* in grasping the meaning of person"; (3) and that "the divine processions are in the identity of the same nature."[89] These points taken together allow Thomas to speak of a person as a subsisting relation. To this task of describing what constitutes the Spirit as a person we now briefly turn.

ORIGIN

First, the procession of the Spirit is one of two processions in God. In a broad sense, *procession signifies origin* insofar as the Son and Spirit are said to proceed from the Father. The Father does not proceed from them. The New Testament teaches that they come forth from him. Son and Spirit have their mode of being with reference to the Father, who is from no one. In addition, procession also denotes something specific and particular to the Holy Spirit. The Spirit is the very procession of Love within the Trinity itself. The Spirit (Love) proceeds by way of Love (the Father's Love for the Son and the Son's Love for the Father) as "the procession of Love."[90] "Love" is the Spirit's personal property.

---

88. Thomas's treatise on Trinitarian theology is structured in such a way as to lead us to true knowledge of the intra-Trinitarian mystery, specifically what distinguishes Spirit from Father and Son, and what is said to constitute the Spirit as Spirit in relation to Father and Son. Thus q. 27 of the treatise on the Trinity handles the matter of processions, q. 28 that of relations, and qq. 29–42 that of persons.

89. Emery, *Trinitarian Theology*, 50; Aquinas, *ST* I, q. 28, a. 1.

90. Aquinas, *ST* I, q. 28, a. 4.

RELATION

Second, the Holy Spirit's procession of Love expresses a set of relations (properties or characteristics). These relations are "real relations"; they indicate real plurality in God.[91] The Spirit is related to Father and Son by procession. If procession expresses an origin (from the Father and Son), then relation "in God" is suggestive of "a real opposition."[92] By opposition Thomas simply means that their relational differences are real. When we hear the term "opposition," we note a degree of hostility, of otherness not productive of unity. Thomas does not talk about opposition in the usual sense. He uses the term only to fend off false teaching. Such teaching would understand relation as an accidental category. By way of an explanation, consider the sky. The sky on any given day may be blue (sunny) or gray (rainy). Blue is said accidentally of the sky as is gray, for the sky is often not blue but gray. Blue or gray are accidental qualities in relation to the sky. The sky is not any less the sky for being either blue or gray. The interactions of the three narrated for us in the New Testament are not accidental to God. Their interactions and the (relative) opposition displayed in them are real. In the garden of Gethsemane Jesus does not cry out to himself but to his Father. That he cries out to one whom he is not (his Father) gives us a glimpse of what Thomas means by relations implying opposition. The three really interact.

The Spirit is really distinct from the others, but distinct in a relative way. The Spirit *is* in relation to them. Relatedness assumes real difference that goes all the way down in God. Relatively distinct, but not essentially distinct, are the three. The "relative" serves only to resist one's thinking that their distinctions betray an essential difference. The three are one God, not three Gods. The Spirit proceeds from Father and Son in God and is related to them in this way. But Father and Son do not proceed from the Spirit. Think John 16:14–15. As with Augustine, Thomas argues "but in so far as relation implies respect to something else, no respect to the essence is signified, but rather to its opposite term."[93]

---

91. Ibid., a. 1, ad 2.
92. Ibid., a. 3.
93. Ibid., a. 2.

COMMON NATURE

Third, the one substance "is not diversified" by these processions because they "are in one and the same nature."[94] Each is not like the other, to be sure; but that does not impair their essential unity or suggest a diverse essence. Processions are internal to God's life. It is a matter of the divine nature communicating itself.

THE PERSON AS A SUBSISTING RELATION

Divine persons are subsistent relations. The previous three points about what a person is in God lead to this. Indeed, such talk is important to believers. It reminds them, so Thomas argues, that there is not any gap between the three and the one. The one God does not lie behind the three. The three are not extrinsic to the one essence of God. Christians are monotheists. Talk of a person as a subsistent relation helps Christians to understand what kind of monotheists they are. Thomas puts it this way:

> But relation in God is not as an accident in a subject, but is the divine essence itself; and so it is subsistence, for the divine essence is subsistence. Therefore, as the Godhead is God, so the divine paternity is God the Father, Who is a divine person. Therefore a divine person signifies a relation as subsisting ... *And this is to signify relation by way of substance, which is a hypostasis subsisting in the divine nature* [emphasis mine]; although it remains that that which subsists in the divine nature is the divine nature itself. Thus it is true to say that the name *person* signifies relation directly, and the essence indirectly.[95]

Thomas's main point is that a subsistent relation is a relation that is not at arm's length from or accidentally related to the essence of God. It is, instead, a "relation by way of substance."[96] The relations of the three are "the divine essence itself."[97] The Holy Spirit is therefore the divine essence itself. When we see the three interacting in the New Testament, their common essence is on display. They interact as God

---

94. Ibid., a. 1, ad 4.
95. Ibid., q. 29, a. 4.
96. Ibid.
97. Ibid.

precisely because they are God. It follows, then, that the three do not require anything or anyone outside themselves to exist in relationship. The three are not extrinsic to the divine essence itself. Divine paternity (God the Father), as with filiation (God the Son), and proceeding (God the Holy Spirit), signify for Thomas "a relation as subsisting."[98] In the simplest terms, this is to describe a relation that possesses or has being. In other words, this is a "relation by way of substance, which is a hypostasis subsisting in the divine nature."[99]

We thus return full circle. Talk of the Spirit's personhood indicates a subsisting relation. The Spirit is a relational reality. This is important to believers. The three encountered in the covenant of grace are God. The Holy Spirit is a person, described in terms of a subsisting relation, which exists *in* God. The Holy Spirit "is endowed with the divine being."[100] What the three persons are—that is, God—are "that whereby He [God] is." What God is and that whereby God is, says Thomas, "are the same."[101] Person indicates, for Thomas, a relation of identity with regard to the one essence. In sum, the language of subsistent relations for Thomas is twofold. It denotes, first, relation to another, which involves opposite relations of origin. Subsistent relation indicates, second, relation as proper to the divine essence—hence, subsistent relations.

CONCLUSION

In sum, this chapter has sought to describe the interactions of the three in a few passages from John's gospel with the help of Thomas. Thomas's exegesis yields a rich account of who the Spirit is and how the Spirit acts in God and among us. Talk of the Spirit's acts naturally yields in Thomas's account talk of the life from which those deeds arise. We found the same to be the case with Augustine. For both thinkers, the triune life is of material import. Where Thomas is also helpful is

---

98. Ibid.
99. Ibid. Note the way Thomas equates "substance" and "hypostasis." Of this, Emery comments, "Since, as we have seen, the person is defined as a 'substance' (an 'individual substance of a rational nature'), it can be called both *substance* and *hypostasis* ... The main hazard for Latin terminology is that *substance* and *hypostasis* have a close etymological connection, indeed a literal correspondence ... [As a result,] Latin Trinitarian theology had to find another word with which to translate *hypostasis*: they chose *subsistentia*" (Emery, *Trinitarian Theology*, 112–14).
100. Ibid., 124.
101. Aquinas, *ST* I, q. 29, a. 4, ad 1.

with respect to the function of extrabiblical language in describing the mystery of God in the New Testament. Precision concepts do not abstract us from the text. Rather, in Thomas's hands they help us not to speak about what is going on there in ways that are false.

In the next chapter, I will unfold some of what Thomas thinks are the fruits of the Spirit's relation to the Son's saving work. Such an inquiry will yield greater understanding of the Spirit's identity. I will also think about how the pneumatological teaching informs an account of the Son's enactment of his kingship among us. The second trial scene in John's gospel—John 18:33–38—is in Thomas's reading most productive. The task ahead is to describe something of the first principles present in this passage. We will see that the Spirit's mission to bear us anew in Christ's rule is the *temporal expression* of the Spirit's eternal procession. To this mystery do we now attend.

CHAPTER 5

THE KINGSHIP OF JESUS AND THE SPIRIT

INTRODUCTION

We begin with John 18:33–38, a passage commonly referred to as the second trial scene. The centre of the scene is Pilate's question: "So you are a king?" Jesus' answer to the question is instructive. We will see the extent to which it informs Trinitarian discourse. Specifically, Thomas thinks that the exchange yields important truths regarding how the Spirit's activity in relation to Jesus manifests the Spirit's procession from the Father and the Son. If the previous chapter sought to follow Thomas's thinking on the "who" of the Spirit in conversation with the Fourth Gospel, this chapter will extend that inquiry in relation to the Trinitarian Treatise in *Summa Theologica* I. The matters at hand are the Spirit's personal properties and the immanent distinctions of the three. Attention will be given to the Spirit's acts as derivative of how the Spirit originates in God.

Jesus is distinct from the Father and the Spirit even as he is one with them. Articulation of the character of this distinction in God's life — as far as we are given to know — is the task ahead. Thomas avers that the Spirit's deliverance of us over to the reign of Jesus shows us something about the Spirit's eternal procession from him and his Father. The Spirit's realization of Jesus' kingdom amongst us reveals new things about the Spirit's procession from the king. This chapter deepens the previous chapter by taking up these new things in relationship to Thomas's treatment of them in *ST* I, qq. 27–43.

JOHN 18:36: "MY KINGDOM IS NOT FROM THIS WORLD"

Jesus' kingdom "does not have its origin in earthly causes and human choice."[1] Its source has to do with the reason for Jesus' birth. Pilate cannot comprehend this source, since Pilate can only comprehend kingship on horizontal terms as but a brute and cynical exercise of power. However, the source of Jesus' kingship is not horizontal; it lies, rather, with Jesus' origin. "Even if I testify on my own behalf, my testimony is valid because I know where I have come from and where I am going" (John 8:14). Sent from the Father into the world, born, as Chrysostom says, "from the Father, by an eternal birth; just as I am God from God, so I am king from king."[2] Jesus' kingship is intelligible only in relation to its spring—Jesus is "a king from God the Father."[3]

Jesus' words also assume a real distinction between him and the Spirit. Whereas the Scriptures are happy to speak of the Son as born, Scripture does not use the language of "begetting" in relationship to the Spirit. On the contrary, the tradition, following the Scriptures, confines the language of begetting or birth to the relation of the Father and the Son. The Spirit is spirated (breathed) by Father and Son—what Thomas calls "common spiration"—but the Spirit is never described as born. Both Son and Spirit proceed from Father inasmuch as he is their common source; but the Spirit is not from the Father in the same way as is the Son. The Son is from the Father, from whom he takes his being. The Son is also the one from whom another proceeds, namely, the Spirit. But in the case of the Spirit, there is no one who is from him, for the Spirit receives his being from the Father through the Son. Neither Son nor Father is said to receive their being from another in the same way that the Spirit does.

The second trial scene, as Thomas reads it, encourages reflection on how the language of "born" is true of only one of the three. Thomas, in his commentary on John 18:37, launches into a brief but extremely dense speculative discussion as an *explanation* of Jesus' answer to Pilate—"My kingdom is not from this world." Indeed, Thomas thinks that Jesus' own words license thinking about an immaterial kingship

---

1. Saint Thomas Aquinas, *Commentary on the Gospel of John* (Washington, D.C.: Catholic University of America Press, 2010), 2351, 3:221.
2. Ibid., 3:233–24.
3. Ibid., 3:223.

within God.[4] Let me explain. King Jesus is the perfect expression and likeness of the one from whom he proceeds; in generating him, the Father communicates his entire being. As a commentary on this mystery, Thomas calls the Son "the very concept of the divine intellect and the Word of God."[5] Now this language of "intellect" might seem a bit strange in the context of commentary on the second trial scene, but for Thomas it serves a crucial explanatory role. An intellectual procession remains within the mind or person: it is internal to them. This is different from other kinds of processions, namely, external ones. Such talk is true not only in the case of the Son's origin: it also, as we will see, has bearing on talk of the Spirit's origin. The Word's procession from the Father is an intellectual procession insofar as the Word is one with the one who speaks the Word. The Word has the same nature and so can be said, moreover, to reign just as does the one from whom he proceeds. The Word is born to reign from eternity. His eternal birth from the Father's essence *qualifies* him to exercise the office of king. His birth from eternity grounds his kingship.

Furthermore, he is born for a purpose in order that we might fulfill our vocation, which is listening to the truth, his voice. He descends even unto death so as to return to the Father with us. Without Jesus' testimony we cannot receive our "being-towards-the-image-of-the-Trinity."[6] Jesus Christ is the image, the voice, the Word whereby we are raised up for life with the Trinity.

How can one belong to the truth, listen to Jesus' voice? How can a community respond in faith to his reign and love as Jesus commands Peter to do (John 21:15–19)? The answer to these questions takes us to the Spirit, who has a different origin in God than the Son. To listen to Jesus is to love him. To love him is to receive the Spirit whereby the Father loves him and he loves the Father. Here we see the extent to which pneumatological language is, according to Thomas, implicit in the second trial scene. Who belongs to the truth? Those who are in the

---

4. This immaterial or spiritual kingship is realized materially in the temporal missions of the Son and Spirit.

5. Aquinas, *Commentary on John*, 2365, 3:224. Cf. *ST* I, q. 34, a. 1, ad 2: "For the interior word proceeds in such a manner from the one who expressed it, as to remain with him." Accordingly, the one "Who proceeds in God by way of an emanation of the intellect is called the Son ... inasmuch as in God the Word proceeding does not differ really from the divine intellect." Aquinas, *ST* I, q. 34, a. 2; q. 34, a. 2, ad 2.

6. Gilles Emery, *The Trinitarian Theology of St Thomas Aquinas* (Oxford: Oxford University Press, 2007), 217.

Spirit. Consider Thomas's comment on John 17:22, wherein Jesus prays "that they may be one, as we are one." Thomas writes, "Now there is a twofold unity in God. There is a unity of nature: 'I and the Father are one' (10:30); and a unity of love in the Father and Son, which is a unity of spirit."[7] Thomas continues, the Father and Son are "one by a love which is *not a participated love and a gift from another* [emphasis mine]; rather, this love proceeds from them, for the Father and Son love themselves by the Holy Spirit."[8] Thomas's thoughts on John 10:30 and 17:22 help us to interpret John 18:37 as a Trinitarian statement.

In sum, to belong to the Son (the truth) is to belong to a kingdom not from this world. To belong to the Son is to belong to the Father, for they are one. In addition to this, the Spirit is not external to them or they to the Spirit. Father and Son do not participate in the Spirit. To say they are "one by a love which is not a participated love" deepens our sense, Thomas argues, of the Spirit's proceeding.[9]

"NOT A PARTICIPATED LOVE"

Who is the Holy Spirit, then? The Spirit is the "love proceeding" from Father and Son.[10] The love in which they love one another is not external to them. It is not a force or presence in which they participate. The Father and Son do not love each other by way of someone or something outside of them. Rather, Thomas's point is that the love whereby they love one another has a name and is a personal subsistence: the Holy Spirit. The Holy Spirit—the name itself assumes relation— "proceeds by way of the love whereby God is loved, [accordingly] that person is most properly named *The Holy Spirit*."[11] Furthermore, to say that the Spirit is "the divine person [who] proceeds by way of the love whereby God is loved" involves the language of "will." But what does Thomas mean when he says that the Holy Spirit proceeds "by way of the will as Love"?[12] Likewise, how is such a procession different from the Word's procession described in terms of "intellect"?

To appreciate the significance of "will" language, let us back up

---

7. Aquinas, *Commentary on John*, 2214, 3:180.
8. Ibid., 3:180–81.
9. Ibid., 3:180.
10. Aquinas, *ST* I, q. 37, a. 1, ad 4.
11. Ibid., q. 36, a. 1.
12. Ibid., a. 2.

for a moment. Recall that Thomas thinks that the Spirit proceeds from the Father and the Son: this is a comment on "the order of their nature."[13] The Spirit has a common origin with respect to Father and Son. What is from the Father—the Spirit—is also from the Son. But the Spirit is from them by way of "will." Explaining this, Gilles Emery writes, "Love consists, rather, in a lively momentum, a movement, an impulse towards the beloved being, arising in the will when one loves something: the one whom I love is present in my will, inclining me towards him … divine Love is a subsistent relation whose nature is that of God himself."[14] The Father loves the Son in the Spirit; the Son loves the Father in the Spirit. Since God is pure act, the language of "will" is hardly stagnant. The Love by which Father and Son are one "is not a participated love; rather, this love proceeds from them" as a vital momentum on the part of the Father toward his beloved Word.[15] The beloved Word reciprocates the Father's Love in that same vital momentum. This movement bears a name, and that name is the Holy Spirit. Hear Emery once again: "Procession by way of intellect (the generation of the Word) and procession by way of the will (the procession of Love) have a comparable structure … In the same way that the word remains *in* the knowing subject, the imprint of love emerges *within* the lover's own affectivity."[16] But this is not to isolate the beloved's "grip … in the heart of the one who loves," for Love is the very presence of that "grip."[17] Again, that Love is a subsistent relation, and that relation has a name, the Holy Spirit.

While the language of "will" is not the language of Scripture, Thomas thinks that it illuminates Scripture. The Spirit, as noted above, is the fruit of the mutuality of Father and Son. The Spirit's activity expresses their very mutuality. Indeed, without the Spirit there would be no mutuality. The Love that proceeds from them by will highlights the dynamism of God's life. Such Love, in other words, moves toward giving in God and toward the outside.

The word that Jesus gives to his disciples is his Father's word, and it is given, comments Thomas, "by the inspiration of the Paraclete."[18]

---

13. Ibid.
14. Emery, *Trinitarian Theology*, 226.
15. Aquinas, *Commentary on John*, 2214, 3:180–81.
16. Emery, *Trinitarian Theology*, 228.
17. Ibid., 229.
18. John 17:14; Aquinas, *Commentary on John*, 2222, 3:183.

If such is the case, then, the Spirit's procession as Love is seen in a new way in time. The Spirit as the Gift of "love proceeding" inspires receptivity to the word of Jesus.[19] That the Spirit inspires such love among us for Christ, the one born to be king, is because of the Spirit's procession. The love of God that the Spirit pours out, the love that the Spirit actually is, is a love "eternally inclining toward being given."[20] "Will" language makes sense in Thomas's thought as an expression of this inclination. "Love proceeding" as Gift, "the Love through which the Father and Son love one another and love us," is the Holy Spirit.[21]

Here we get a glimpse not only of how the Spirit preserves otherness in God but also how that otherness provides a rationale for why there is something—the creation—and not nothing. When Emery describes the Holy Spirit as the "source and structuring principle of creation," he is referring to the productivity of this otherness in God.[22] If creation is the "temporal effect" of the eternal procession of the Spirit, this is only because the Spirit as Love and Gift of Father and Son communicates and celebrates that Love toward the outside.[23] Here we see the Spirit exercising a distinct agency in God that is expressed as Love and Gift toward the outside.

"LOVE PROCEEDING"

Jesus' rule communicates eternal life. The Spirit, the very Gift of that life, unites us to the life of the Father and Son. That the Spirit is the Love whereby Father and Son love one another, and in turn us, demonstrates again a deep and basic Trinitarian truth. The Spirit's acts are in utter conformity with and revelatory of the personal property of the Spirit: "love proceeding."[24] The Spirit who joins human beings to the Trinity proceeds from the heart of the Trinity. Accordingly, it is not a stretch to think that "St Thomas draws the whole economy together under the sign of the Holy Spirit."[25] "Being Love in person, the Holy Spirit nests human beings into friendship with God,

---

19. Aquinas, *ST* I, q. 37, a. 1, ad 4.
20. Emery, *Trinitarian Theology*, 237.
21. Aquinas, *ST* I, q. 37, a. 1, ad 4; Emery, *Trinitarian Theology*, 416.
22. Emery, *Trinitarian Theology*, 247.
23. Aquinas, *ST* I, q. 43, a. 2, ad 3; Emery, *Trinitarian Theology*, 257.
24. Aquinas, *ST* I, q. 37, a. 1, ad 4.
25. Emery, *Trinitarian Theology*, 258.

making them 'contemplators of God,' and giving them through this contemplation a 'dwelling in God.'"[26] The Spirit's action in the world whereby the Spirit leads us to the Father through the Son expresses the truth about the Spirit's origin and hypostatic existence in the life of the Trinity itself as the "love proceeding" from Father and Son.[27] Again: the Spirit would not lead to Father and Son were he not *of* them, *from* them! Similarly, the Spirit would not unite us to them were the Spirit not responsible for uniting them to one another. Were the Spirit not Love, their Love, the Spirit's work of fostering love for the Father and Son would have no ground. The economic action of the Spirit that draws us to Christ and in him to the Father is revelatory of the Trinity itself, displaying or exhibiting "the fundamental structure of his [the Spirit's] eternal procession ... *a Patre and a Filio.*"[28]

Consider John 8:23: "You [the Jews] are from below, I am from above; you are of this world, I am not of this world." Commenting on this, Thomas writes, "We should note with respect to the first [the Jews' deprivation] that everything in its development follows the condition of its origin. Thus, a thing whose origin is from below naturally tends below if left to itself. And nothing tends above unless its origin is from above."[29] Jesus is "from above," meaning that the key to understanding his mission is the one who sent him. Jesus' mission is unintelligible apart from the sender. Jesus is the sent one. Accordingly, Jesus' sending is reiterative of his procession. Because he is eternally born of the Father, he is sent from the Father. The language of "I am" as in "I am from above" harkens back to Exodus 3:14: "'I AM WHO I AM' (Ex 3:14), for existence itself (*ipsum esse*) is proper to God," Thomas writes. He continues:

> For in any other nature but the divine nature, existence (*esse*) and what exists are not the same: because any created nature participates its existence (*esse*) from that which is being by its essence (*ens per essentiam*), so that his existence (*suum esse*) is his essence (*qua essentia*). Thus, this designates only God. And so he [Jesus] says, **For if you do not believe that I am**, that is, that I am truly God, who has existence by his essence, **you will die in your sin**.[30]

---

26. Ibid., 264.
27. Aquinas, *ST* I, q. 37, a. 1, ad 4.
28. Emery, *Trinitarian Theology*, 272.
29. Aquinas, *Commentary on John*, 1178, 3:118.
30. Ibid.

Jesus teaches that "he is existence itself (*ipsum esse*)."[31] There is no God lurking behind Jesus by whom he is made divine—Jesus is not divine by participation. Jesus is proper to God. As the only begotten Son of the Father come among us to seek and to save, Jesus receives from eternity a nature identical to the one who begets him from eternity: this is a procession by intellect in God. Father and Son share a common nature: what is said of one is said of the other "excepting what touches on the incommunicable personal property (paternity, filiation, procession)."[32] The incommunicable personal properties signify, once again, opposite relations of origins. One is not like the other. We make sense of this by invoking language of properties to articulate how one is not like the other precisely because each one has a different origin in God than the other.

A COMMON SOURCE?

What light does the discussion of Jesus' origin, indeed his hypostatic subsistence, shed on our attempt to deepen understanding of the Spirit's origin, the unique "who" of the Spirit? To answer the question well, we need to note Thomas's translation of John 8:25: "Then they asked him, 'Who are you?' Jesus replied 'the source (beginning) who is also speaking to you."[33] The text, as Thomas receives it, encourages a discussion of how "source" language applies not only to Jesus but to the other two. "The Father is also called the source or beginning. In one sense the word 'source' is common to the Father and the Son, insofar as they are the one source of the Holy Spirit through a common spiration."[34] One might ask, then, if the Father, Son, and Spirit subsist in one essence, indeed possess a common essence, how can it be that something—"common spiration"—is common only to two and not to three? Here we see how "source" language does not work at the level of being. Were it to work on that level, Thomas's language would suggest a divided essence.

Thomas, however, is not speaking according to essence but to relations. Father and Son form one single principle of the Holy Spirit: the

---

31. Ibid.
32. Emery, *Trinitarian Theology*, 276.
33. The NRSV translates it thus: "They said to him, 'Who are you?' Jesus said to them, 'Why do I speak to you at all?'"
34. Aquinas, *Commentary on John*, 1183, 3:119.

Spirit in that sense is common to them. The relationship of the Spirit to Father and Son contains relative opposition in that something said of Father and Son — "source" — is not said of the Spirit. The Father and Son spirate the Spirit; the Spirit does not spirate but is, rather, related to them as one spirated. Giving in God, Thomas argues, works this way. Does this imply that the Spirit has nothing to give to Father and Son? By no means: recall Thomas's comments about the Love that is the Spirit not being a "participated Love." Father and Son come to one another only in the Spirit. Each (Father and Son) is in the Spirit, and they together (Father and Son) are in the Spirit.

The Greek Fathers are not hostile to such a take — so Thomas argues. The Spirit has the Son as a source too: from the Father through the Son.[35] But the Greek Fathers and the Byzantine scholars of Thomas's own day nonetheless had different emphases than Thomas. They do not understand the Son as also a causal "principle" of the Spirit. Emery writes of this, "Thomas did not know why those whom he calls the 'Greeks' sometimes agreed to say that the Spirit *flows out* from the Son (*profluit*), but not the Holy Spirit proceeds from the Son (*procedit, ekporeutai*); it was that, for them, *ekporeusis* can only have the Father as principle."[36] It is important to note that Thomas understands source language to be appropriate to the Father and Son with respect to the Spirit: the Spirit comes forth from them, is related to them by an origination relation. Such talk is derivative of the biblical witness. In the New Testament, the Spirit is poured out by God (the Father) and breathed by the Son. Thomas thinks that such activity points to how relations to these two are constitutive of the Spirit's hypostatic subsistence.

Generation and procession (the two originating relations in God) attest that the Spirit's procession is principally from the Father, who communicates his essence by generation to the Son and by spiration to the Spirit through the Son. Accordingly, "the Son receives his breathing of the Holy Spirit from the Father ... To say that the Holy Spirit proceeds from the Father *through the Son* implies that the Holy Spirit also proceeds *from the Son*."[37] The Spirit, argues Thomas, is originated via the Father and Son in such a way that the Father in begetting the Son (paternity) communicates everything to the Son (filiation), including

---

35. This formulation in Thomas's mind also implies "from."
36. Emery, *Trinitarian Theology*, 280.
37. Ibid., 291.

the Son's being the principle of the Holy Spirit. What is common to Father and Son is an originating relation with respect to the Spirit. Because the Father and Son are really distinct—but not different—owing to opposite relations of origin (paternity and filiation), Thomas thinks that there must be two distinct sources within a unity of essence from which the Spirit is "love proceeding."[38] The upshot is that the persons are really distinct from each other but not from their common essence. Once again, it is a matter of appreciating how language works in God. Relation distinguishes the persons, yes; but the essence is not thereby distinguished. The relations of the three distinguish them from one another but not their essence. So Thomas: "The divine essence, however, is not only really the same as one person, but it is really the same as the three persons ... *The essence is the three persons*, so likewise it is true to say, *God is the three persons*."[39] In keeping with this, what distinguishes the Spirit from Father and Son is not a greater degree of essence: Father and Son would then be higher than or superior to the Spirit. What renders the Spirit a distinct personal subsistence in God is the Spirit's immanent procession from the Father and the Son as "love proceeding"; the Spirit is God in an essential sense, the essence simultaneously common to Father and Son.[40]

The point that Thomas appreciates in all of this is that the Spirit *is* by procession. One cannot follow the biblical testimony and talk otherwise. Procession is an action common to the Father and Son, but the Spirit's origin as "love proceeding" is not true of either the Father or the Son. Hence the reason for Thomas's employment of the language of "opposition." "To proceed" is said only of the Spirit. This is one "principle of difference" with respect to the Spirit's personal subsistence. It is proceeding, and this only.[41]

There is also a second way in which Thomas elucidates this "principle of difference," and that is in regard to "*relation* by way of form."[42] By this, Thomas simply means distinguishing relations. Different origins imply distinguishing relations. "Whence, since the persons agree in essence, it remains that the persons are distinguished from each other

---

38. Aquinas, *ST* I, q. 37, a. 1, ad 4. Emery makes the following perceptive comment: "It is the divergent ways in which the Byzantines and the Latins interpret their patristic heritage which is the issue" (Emery, *Trinitarian Theology*, 295).

39. Aquinas, *ST* I, q. 39, a. 6.

40. Ibid., q. 37, a. 1, ad 4.

41. Ibid., q. 40, a. 2.

42. Ibid., q. 40, a. 2.

by the relations."[43] This is an extremely important point to recognize. Origins alone for Thomas do not make the person(s)! Proceeding, to be sure, signifies an origin unique to the person of the Spirit; but the name *Holy Spirit* "signifies the relation which is distinctive and constitutive of the hypostasis."[44] Put simply, you cannot talk about origins without talking about relations. One cannot talk about the Spirit in isolation from Father and Son.

This is in a sense the apex of Thomas's account of how the Spirit uniquely originates in God: the Spirit is a person on the basis of the relations that constitute the Spirit as Spirit and thus distinguish the Spirit from Father and Son. So Thomas: "For since the divine Persons are the relations themselves as subsistent, there could not be several Fathers [in God] ... For God understands and wills all things by one simple act. Therefore there can be but one person proceeding after the manner of word, which person is the Son; and but one person proceeding after the manner of love, which person is the Holy Ghost."[45] There is only one Father because God himself is a "simple act." God (the Father) knows himself as Father in the one he generates (the Son), the one to whom he gives existence "in the divine nature."[46] The Spirit proceeds from the Father through the Son as the Love by which the Lover (the Father) begets the Beloved (the Son).[47] Thomas teaches that there is not only real distinction among the three but a real unity. One *is* really the Word of the Father; another *is* really the love of the Father for that Word and the love of that Word for the Father.

Our love for the Father and the Son is, as Thomas notes in commenting on John 14:15–17, "the same love."[48] The Christian does not love the Father differently than the Son and vice versa, for "the love by which we love God is from the Holy Spirit."[49] Love for God is from God, and that love is the Holy Spirit. We love God in the Spirit for God is that love. The Spirit's work of fostering love for Father and Son flows from *who* the Spirit is as love proceeding.

In sum, to talk of the Spirit as "love proceeding" is to talk of the Spirit as one who receives essence in relation to the Father and the Son.

---

43. Ibid., q. 40, a. 2.
44. Ibid.
45. Ibid., q. 41, a. 6
46. Ibid., a. 5.
47. Ibid., a. 5, ad 1.
48. Aquinas, *Commentary on John*, 1909, 3:69.
49. Ibid.

The Father and Son communicate essence to the Spirit. The Spirit is their love going forth, the very love in which they love. This is the order that the Scriptures talk about with respect to the three, an order that is true of God although we know not how. The Spirit brings to us the life of the Son, teaching us what he taught, advocating for us, effecting in us love of the Father and Son, their love. Indeed, such love *is* the Holy Spirit, the "divine essence after a distinct relation."[50] Thomas thinks it important to talk about what sets the Spirit apart from Father and Son in God's life precisely because such talk helps us to make sense of why the Spirit acts as the Spirit does. If this section has sought to unfold the Spirit's origin and relations to the Father and Son in terms of love, the next section will unfold the mission of Love as derived from the being of the Spirit. To the mission of the Spirit do we now look as an extension in time of the Spirit's proceeding in God—the unique "who" of the Spirit—after the manner of Love. We will see that the Spirit's mission is to express his origin as Love. Such Love finds its fulfillment in our being drawn in the love of the Trinity.

THE MISSION OF THE HOLY SPIRIT

What is the mission of the Holy Spirit? And why is talk of the Spirit's mission illuminated by talk of the Spirit's origin? This penultimate section takes up these two questions. "Mission" for Thomas simply explains the temporal procession of the Spirit. Mission is a matter of describing the Spirit's acts in time. The Spirit, as the Son, is sent. Consider, for example, John 14:26 and 15:26: "whom the Father will send in my name ... whom I will send to you from the Father." The Spirit is *breathed* by the Son and *sent* by the Father in the Son's name. This mission of the Spirit points to "a new way of existing in another," a new way of proceeding, following biblical texts like John 14:26 and 15:26.[51] The Spirit is not forever sent. Rather, the Spirit is sent, as is the case with the Son, in "the fullness of time" (Gal 4:4). Why is the Spirit sent by the Father in the name of the Son? Why is the Father, for example, not sent? The Father as one who sends and the Spirit as one sent is, Thomas argues, the "temporal effect" of the eternal procession

---

50. Emery, *Trinitarian Theology*, 353.
51. Aquinas, *ST* I, q. 42 a. 5, ad 1.

of the Spirit. It is in the Spirit's sending that we see the Spirit "rendering himself present [in time] *in an innovative way.*"[52]

Thomas is adamant that the visible mission of the Spirit does not signify any kind of ontological change on the part of the Spirit. Rather, the Spirit is given to us in order to accomplish love among us. Thomas, as with Augustine and Barth, always wants the reader to see that the Spirit remains God in all that the Spirit does. Accordingly, "that a divine person may newly exist in anyone, or be possessed temporally by anyone, does not come from change in the divine person, but from change in the creature."[53] Put simply, the Spirit does not become another in coming to abide in us. This is why the New Testament language of sending is so important to Thomas. The Spirit cannot be said to always exist in us—the Spirit does not indwell us by virtue of our being born—precisely because the Spirit is sent to us. The Spirit is a gift rather than a property natural to us.

What is the gift of the Spirit? The Spirit is "the gift of sanctification."[54] The Spirit is the gift of love that sanctifies.[55] The Spirit does not sanctify in God because God is holy. But when sent among us, the Spirit does sanctify. Sanctification is what takes place when the Spirit exists in us "in a new way."[56] That new way is charity, the blossoming of love. The Spirit's sending bears fruit. By the Spirit "the known and beloved reality [Father and Son] ... [is] present in the one who knows and loves [that is, ourselves]."[57]

Here we reach the heart of the matter. Why is the Spirit sent? "The Holy Spirit is sent so that the enamored saints can reach up to God in a way that participates in the personal character of the Holy Spirit—love."[58] The Spirit's mission—the Spirit's being sent by the Father through the Son—expresses the "who" of the Spirit. In the Spirit's acts and the fruit they bear do we see the work of *God* the Spirit. Precisely because the Spirit has "His origin from another," is the Spirit able to dwell "in a new way within someone" as the Love breathed forth by the Word.[59] The Spirit is, eternally, this Love come to exist among us in a new way.

---

52. Ibid., q. 43 a. 1, ad 3; Emery, *Trinitarian Theology*, 367.
53. Aquinas, *ST* I, q. 42 a. 2, ad 3.
54. Ibid., a. 7.
55. Ibid., a. 5, ad 2.
56. Ibid., a. 6.
57. Emery, *Trinitarian Theology*, 383.
58. Ibid., 387.
59. Aquinas, *ST* I, q. 43, a. 5.

The Spirit transforms us into those who, like Jesus, "testify to the truth" (John 18:37). Christ's rule, his testimony, is ever to be the object of our knowledge and the Spirit he breathes the object of our love. Jesus Christ continues to undo our sad love affair with idols so as to uphold us in the astonishing claim that we are reconciled to him in order to listen to his voice. Christ through his Word and Spirit is at work; although he and his Spirit's mission of authoring and gifting sanctification is invisible, their mission is nonetheless present and effective. The Spirit as love and gift is at work in a new way conforming us to Christ's rule, bringing his "sanctification to achievement within us."[60] The Spirit is sanctifying, communicating his gifts to us through the proclamation of the Word and the sacrament that seals us in the promises of the same. The mission of the Son and Spirit continues, invisibly to be sure, but continues nonetheless. Not held hostage by our sin and death, Son and Spirit communicate themselves. This, as Gilles Emery notes of Thomas, is where "the treatise on the Triune God concludes: a mystery which communicates itself."[61]

Thomas thinks that the most faithful way to expound this self-communicating mystery is to talk about first principles—the Spirit's origin and relation to Father and Son—and from there to proceed to the Spirit's mission. The latter (mission) he derives from the Spirit's origin. He understands those principles, moreover, to be material. Without first principles, one does not know whether the Spirit's mission really comes from God, is really the mission of *God* the Spirit. But with them in hand, we see that the Spirit's mission is the Spirit existing among us in a new way: sent from the Father in the name of the Son.

BACK TO THE BASICS: PILATE'S QUESTION

The question Pilate directs to Jesus, one that engendered great fear, is as contemporary as ever: "Where are you from?" (John 19:9). It is only in light of Trinitarian teaching that we can answer this question. It is hard to conceive that the man before Pilate is, has always been, the great "I am." Were Pilate born "from above," he would see that

---

60. Emery, *Trinitarian Theology*, 387.
61. Ibid., 412.

the man before him has an origin that is "from above." Trinitarian doctrine explains this origin. It makes the "intimate alliance" between the immanent mystery and the workings of the economy plain.[62] It helps us to see that what is above us and what has come among us are one.

The action of Jesus is not explicable without the reference to his origin; his generation from the Father is the very rationale for what he says to Pilate. Christ's actions remain oblique to Pilate, however, because he has not experienced the new birth of the Spirit. Were Pilate born of the Spirit, he would see and know that Christ is of another and the Spirit of him and his Father. Jesus' testimony discloses something immanent, his origin. But Pilate does not receive this testimony. The speculative reference of Jesus' words does not convict Pilate. The Word who stands before Pilate, the Spirit he breathes and whom the Father sends in his name, are not so subtly grieved. Even though Pilate tries "to release him," he remains in the end a cynical political operator beholden to the crowds' assessment of Jesus: "Everyone who claims to be a king sets himself against the emperor" (John 19:12). One of the origins Jesus claims to have would not have gotten himself into such a tangle, Pilate reasons. An origin "from above" would surely be more transparent, less vulgar, more sublime, and certainly not Jewish.

Trinitarian doctrine teaches that the mission of the Spirit is derivative of the Spirit's procession. Augustine and Thomas learn from the Fourth Gospel the extent to which the missions of Son and Spirit make sense only in light of first principles. Why does the Spirit act among us as the Spirit does? The Spirit is Love proceeding. As Emery notes of Aquinas, "the *doctrine* of the economic Trinity ... is, rather, the final fruit of the exploration."[63] The first principles of the Spirit drawn from the Spirit's acts toward the outside enable us to return to those acts and receive them as they are: *God's* acts.

Jesus' presence, as Hans Frei taught, is a function of his identity.[64] Jesus identifies himself before Pilate as one born to be king. This is but the new way in which Jesus dwells among us as one originated by another. Jesus' mission in time to be king, to be among us for whom he

---

62. Emery, *Trinitarian Theology*, 413.
63. Ibid., 415.
64. Hans W. Frei, *The Identity of Jesus Christ: The Hermeneutical Bases of Dogmatic Theology* (Eugene, OR: Wipf and Stock, 1997).

was born, is elucidated by teaching on the Trinity. Indeed, such teaching supplies us with an account of "who" he is. Accordingly, one does not obtain an account of the Trinity in itself, apart from the witness of Scripture. Scripture, rather, encourages appreciation of the three as really being mysteriously three and really being mysteriously one. But why? Because all God does for us and for our salvation comes from God. "Trinitarian reflection begins from the action of the persons in the world in order to come round to that action anew."[65]

In sum, Pilate is unable and unwilling to reconsider the one before him. Despite the fear in Pilate becoming more and more pronounced, the soldiers' mock declaration—"'Hail, King of the Jews!'"—is unrecognized (John 19:1). Were Pilate listening with the grain of the Spirit to Jesus' testimony, he would have become a party to the genuine truth. He would have come to see that the King before him was born from another. This King—despite the efforts of Pilate's and the leaders' of Jesus' own people to abandon him to the cross—is forever born of his Father, and so is raised from the dead. On the third day, the Spirit, in raising Christ from the dead, evidences the depth of the love of Father for Son and Son for Father, a love that our "no" to them cannot destroy.[66] The Spirit as Love and Gift of Father and Son ensures that their love perdures even in the face of death. The Spirit keeps on giving the Gift of Love to the Father and Son and to us.

CONCLUSION

Thomas has much to teach us about the procession and mission of the Holy Spirit. He argues, following the Fourth Gospel, that the Spirit is God; that is what the Spirit is. The Spirit is united in essence with God the Father and God the Son. The Spirit shares absolute and undivided unity together with Father and Son in the one essence of God. One essence is proper to the three, intrinsic to them, and is that by which each is. This is what Thomas's language of subsistence honours. Talk of the Spirit's subsistence is Thomas's way of being faithful to the way the New Testament talks. The New Testament does not conflate the three. Instead, it really distinguishes them. The three are

---

65. Emery, *Trinitarian Theology*, 416.
66. Aquinas, *ST* I, q. 37, a. 1, ad 4. Paul understands both the Spirit and the Father to have raised Jesus. The seeming "inconsistency" is irrelevant. See Romans 8:1–17.

really three. Thomas in this chapter took us to the place where we were able to see what distinguishes Spirit from Father and Son in God, what makes the Spirit a unique "who." Accordingly, we learned that the Spirit is distinguished from Father and Son only by a relative opposition of relation. "Love proceeding" is said only of the Spirit. Proceeding is the Spirit's relation of origin. Such talk, Thomas thinks, is intrinsic to New Testament texts like John 15:26.

A pneumatology responsible to the biblical witness will take seriously that the three are really united in essence; they are one "what," but really distinguished from one another. The Spirit is not after Father and Son, nor are they ever said to be without the Spirit. Not in a participated sense is the Spirit the love of Father for Son and Son for Father. Father and Son are Father and Son only in the Love of the Spirit. The Spirit is the "love proceeding" as the Gift whereby the Father and Son love one another and the world.[67] We participate by grace in the life that has always been.

What is the spiritual aim of an account of the Spirit? Contemplative knowledge of the blessed Trinity is the aim.[68] It assumes discourse that describes the being and identity of the God encountered in Scripture. Such discourse is, of course, scientific in nature, meaning that it is discourse bound to and by the object of which it seeks in faith to speak. But scientific discourse is not an end in itself. Rather, it serves a spiritual aim. In Emery's words, Trinitarian theology "constitutes a spiritual exercise in the authentic meaning of the term: a contemplative and speculative exercise on the part of the theologian who seeks to grasp 'something of the truth' in order to disclose the faith 'for the consolation of believers.'"[69] This book represents this exercise. Thomas teaches us about a set of terms that help us to speak with a degree of truth about the Spirit's being and identity and activity in God and among us. To the extent that scientific discourse equips the saints to speak about this with appropriate confidence and clarity, it is edifying.

It is now time to take up our last major classical interlocutor, Karl Barth. Barth shares with Augustine and Thomas a concern for God's prevenience. Barth understands why talk about God remaining God in

---

67. Ibid.
68. I will discuss contemplation in chapter 10.
69. Emery, *Trinitarian Theology*, 418.

all that God does is so important. As we follow some of Barth's engagements with the Fourth Gospel, we will note many changes of idiom in comparison with Augustine and Thomas. What does not change, however, is the locating of the Spirit's redemptive work in the Spirit's divinity. Barth's talk of what the divine Spirit does is the focus of the next two chapters.

Spirit Christology

There has been a push amongst some more contemporary theologians for a "Spirit Christology." One of the most significant and able exponents of it from the Roman Catholic theological world is Thomas G. Weinandy. What Weinandy seeks to do is to supplement Thomas's account of subsistent relations "whereby the persons exist as who they are only in relation to one another" by offering "an active role to the Holy Spirit."[1] Indeed, this is something that Thomas, building as he does on Augustine, "did not do."[2] This is problematic for Weinandy, given that "it [the role of the Spirit] bears upon the identity of the Son within the Trinity as well as his activity within the economy of salvation."[3]

I mention Weinandy at the outset of the excursus because, in assigning a more heightened role to the Spirit in the triune life and in the economy, he is responding to what is a (perceived) weakness in the tradition. To what extent Weinandy reads the tradition in the form of Augustine and Thomas responsibly is well beyond the purview of this excursus to determine. That said, there is an intuition at work in Weinandy's thought that gives us a clue to what Spirit Christology is all about. I will engage this intuition. The intuition is that the unique personal identity of the Spirit in God's inward and outward movements has been shortchanged. The tradition is to blame for this.

Weinandy's concerns resemble those of a theological colleague here in New Zealand, Myk Habets. Habets too argues that the tradition has erred. In Habets's view, the tradition has fallen prey to a diminished view of the Spirit, abetted in large part by a zealous overapplication

---

1. Thomas G. Weinandy, "Trinitarian Christology: The Eternal Son," in *The Oxford Handbook on the Trinity*, ed. Gilles Emery and Matthew Levering (Oxford: Oxford University Press, 2011), 389. See also Thomas G. Weinandy, *The Father's Spirit of Sonship: Reconceiving the Trinity* (Edinburgh: T&T Clark, 1995), 8.
2. Weinandy, "Trinitarian Christology," in *Oxford Handbook*, 389.
3. Ibid.

of what he calls a "Logos Christology."[4] While Weinandy's concerns are with Augustine and Thomas, Habets is more vexed by what he perceives to be a wide-ranging problem in "classical Christology," namely, its championing of a Christology "from above and [its being] concerned with the descent of the eternal Son."[5] Habets's alternative is to champion a "Christology that moves from the functional testimony to ontological implications"—in other words, from below to above.[6] By moving in this direction, speculation is avoided, Habets argues, and "the gulf between Jesus' humanity and divinity (the two nature Achilles heel of classical Christology)" is bridged "by means of the Holy Spirit."[7]

While it would be irresponsible to argue that a senior Roman Catholic theologian and a younger Reformed Baptist theologian both understand the train to have gone off the tracks at the same time and for the same reasons, each nonetheless is responding to a (perceived) lacuna in the tradition. The solution, in Habets's case, is to practice "theological reflection with the Spirit and … [reexamine] the *loci* of theology from that vantage point."[8] If Habets's recent monograph is any indication, this is the dominant motivation of some Spirit Christologists: to rescue what "was relegated to the heterodox fringe of the tradition" with respect to "the fourth century Logos Christology [which] dominated the minds of great theologians."[9] The complement "relegated to the heterodox fringe" is a Spirit Christology, the "'normative link of pneumatology with Christology." This is precisely what was torn apart by "a radical dissociation between reflection on the divinity of the Word of God and the divinity of the Spirit."[10]

Whether such a genealogy can be sustained—indeed, whether the tradition, together with the fathers, "generally upheld the now long-standing Logos Christology that stresses incarnation over inspiration, ontology over function, and a methodology from above as opposed to one from below"—is of course highly contestable.[11] My sense is that

---

4. Myk Habets, *Anointed Son: Toward a Trinitarian Spirit Christology* (Eugene, OR: Pickwick, 2010), 36.
5. Ibid.
6. Ibid., 17.
7. Ibid., 52.
8. Ibid., 8.
9. Ibid., 54.
10. Ibid., 70.
11. Ibid., 80.

Habets's discussion is so broad and sweeping and clearly in service of pointing out the problem—the suppression of a Spirit Christology in favour of a Logos Christology—that the developmental nuances of catholic Trinitarianism are largely lost. To argue, as Habets does, that "classic Christology has been all too ready to appreciate the divine nature of Jesus, without also appreciating his humanity" is a comment that I find untenable.[12] Which of the Latin or Greek Fathers would be guilty of arguing this, I wonder? Is his brush too broad?[13]

Were there a greater appreciation of the role of the Spirit in Jesus' life, the Gospels would, Habets argues, have been read so as to bolster this "pneumatological perspective ... [that] Jesus is who he is because of the Spirit."[14] Habets argues that it is the role of the Holy Spirit that has been and largely continues to be neglected "in all of the manifold expressions of his [the Spirit's] relationship to Jesus and the Father."[15] The upshot again is that the Spirit's work in Christ's conception, at the cross, and in the resurrection is not mined for its dogmatic promise. "The Christ of the Spirit is functionally transformed into the Spirit of Christ," the result being an either/or rather than a both/and: "The Christ of the Spirit" and "the Spirit of Christ."[16] Only if the Spirit's work in the incarnate Christ is accorded dogmatic significance can the dominating Logos Christology be truly complemented by a Spirit Christology, "a Christology from below to above ... [which] is more than sufficient to account for the identity of Jesus."[17]

The language of "from below" is key. It is here that we can see what a Spirit Christology—in Habets's work—seeks to accomplish. It accounts for Jesus' identity as a function "of the presence and operation of the Spirit of God in him."[18] The move is from Jesus' humanity to what is above, "to ontological conclusions" to be drawn therewith, especially in regard to the Spirit's being first in the economy.[19] The

---

12. Ibid., 159. Thomas F. Torrance addresses this with characteristic subtlety in *The Trinitarian Faith* (Edinburgh: T&T Clark, 1988), 146ff.

13. A less iconoclastic account can be found in R. Michael Allen's *The Christ's Faith: A Dogmatic Account* (London: T&T Clark, 2009). Allen, also a Reformed theologian, argues in his monograph that Spirit Christology at its best honours a simple dogmatic insight regarding "the need to extend the classical affirmation of the Spirit's significance in the life of Jesus dogmatically, with biblical and creedal roots for such insistence" (141).

14. Habets, *Anointed Son*, 117, 160.

15. Ibid., 161.

16. Ibid., 162.

17. Ibid., 191.

18. Ibid., 193.

19. Ibid., 206, 227.

Spirit's being first in the economy, however, does not shortchange the preeminence of the Son. Here Habets, following Weinandy, sees the active role of the Spirit in the Son in the economy to rest in the Trinity itself. "What makes this *perichoresis* intelligible is the active role of the Holy Spirit within the Trinity. The Father begets the Son in the spiration of the Spirit so the Spirit makes the Father to be the Father of the Son and the Son to be the Son of the Father. The Spirit thus proceeds from both Father to Son and Son to Father and so becomes distinct in his mutual relation to them as the Love by which they come to be who they are for one another."[20]

Starting with the Spirit and the subsequent development of "a third article theology relevant for the 21st century" does not mean that one starts with the Spirit in God, that is, in the Trinity itself.[21] Habets is not arguing—fortunately—for the reversible character of the relations of the persons in the Trinity. One starts as it were with the Father, but not the Father alone but the Father who "begets the Son in the spiration of the Spirit."[22] Or, in Weinandy's words, "The Father begets the Son in the love of the Spirit who conforms him to be the loving Son of the Father."[23] Starting with the Spirit means, according to what has been said, giving the Spirit a heightened prominence in the interior and exterior life of the Holy Trinity. This heightened role comes to the fore in the activity of the Spirit rendering the triune "*perichoresis* intelligible."[24]

Weinandy's concern to develop an account of subsistent relations that understands them as "relations fully in act" is, I think, a commendable project. To extend Augustine and Aquinas, as Weinandy does, by arguing that "not only does the Holy Spirit proceed from the Father as the one in whom the Father begets the Son in love, but the Holy Spirit also proceeds from the Son as the one in whom the Son loves the Father who has begotten him"[25] seems exegetically sustainable and dogmatically profitable, and also in keeping with the thrust of Thomas's thought.

What is less commendable about Spirit Christology is the notion

20. Ibid., 225.
21. Ibid., 231.
22. Ibid., 225.
23. Weinandy, "Trinitarian Christology," in *Oxford Handbook*, 395.
24. Habets, *Anointed Son*, 225.
25. Ibid., 389.

that one must "start" with the Spirit, as Habets would have it. As Bruce D. Marshall writes,

> Considerable theological problems of its own [are raised]. Perhaps the most far-reaching of these is the disharmony it [starting with the Spirit] would create between the scriptural pattern of divine redemptive action in the world, where the Father sends the Son and the Father and the Son both send the Holy Spirit, and the pattern of eternal divine processions, about which—if the Son in any sense originated from the Holy Spirit—the redemptive mission, following a contrary pattern, would fail to teach us.[26]

Marshall's intuitions are on the mark. While the highlighting of "the active role of the Holy Spirit within the Trinity" is laudable, where Habets's proposals go awry is to argue that "in the economy, the Spirit is prior to the Son."[27] Even in the ministry of Jesus, for example as demonstrated by John 3:34, which anticipates the Johannine Pentecost in John 20:19–23, the Spirit cannot be said to be "prior to the Son." This is not to eclipse the truth that the Spirit conceives and bears the humanity of the Son in the womb of Mary. But it is to say with Marshall that the "scriptural pattern of divine redemption action" would be disrupted with the embrace of the notion that one can start with the Spirit, that one can get to Christology with pneumatology.[28] Given that Jesus' whole mission is that of giving "us his own Spirit, which conforms us to himself," I do not know how one can champion starting with the Spirit, given that the Spirit comes from the Son and is poured out upon us through the Son—"the Spirit is given to us through him"—in order to make us over in his image.[29]

What a Spirit Christology seems to do, if one is to take Habets as one of its representative voices on the Protestant side, is to confuse immanent processions and temporal missions. The missions of the persons follow upon or are derivative of the processions. The temporal

---

26. Bruce D. Marshall, "The Deep Things of God: Trinitarian Pneumatology," in *The Oxford Handbook on the Trinity*, ed. Gilles Emery and Matthew Levering (Oxford: Oxford University Press, 2011), 407.

27. Habets, *Anointed Son*, 227.

28. So Kathryn Tanner: "One with the Word, the humanity of Christ receives what is the Word's very own—the Word's own Spirit." See *Christ the Key* (New York: Cambridge University Press, 2010), 71.

29. Ibid., 173.

action of the persons in the economy teaches us about the "the pattern of eternal divine processions."[30] Given that the Spirit's action in the economy is not to lead us to the Spirit's self but rather to Christ and thereby to his Father, I do not know how one can start with the Spirit, given that the Spirit "works directly to unite us with Jesus Christ and his Father," and does so "by teaching us to know who Jesus is."[31] The Spirit does not teach us about the Spirit but "first of all leads us to Jesus Christ," thereby indwelling us, this being "the chief way he instructs us concerning who he [the Spirit] is."[32] As Kathryn Tanner notes, "The Son is the shape of the Spirit's working"; if this is truly the case, I do not understand how one can argue that one is to start with the Spirit, as the Spirit would ever only have us start with the Son.[33]

To put my concerns somewhat differently, what I think has happened in Habets's case is a confusion of the order of knowing and teaching in relation to the order of being. As regards "the non-temporal origination of the persons," the Spirit originates as gift and love.[34] "This type of origination or this relation will give us what is basic to the identity of the Holy Spirit."[35] In terms of the Trinity in itself, the Spirit proceeds from the Father and Son as gift, which is the key to the Spirit's identity. In the economy, the Spirit works, for example, to give rise in Mary's womb to the humanity of the Son, empowers the Son and rests on him throughout his ministry, and is said to raise him from the dead. Such temporal action rests on an irreversible sequence in the immanent life of the Holy Trinity. Accordingly, to start with the Spirit in terms of the order of teaching or the order of knowing would seem to reverse how the persons of Son and Spirit—by virtue of their processions—are related to one another in God's life. The Son is begotten, and by virtue of being generated by the Father, he shares with the Father in the act of spiration, whereby from him too does the Spirit proceed. The actions of the persons in the economy are anchored in their origins: the Son is sent as one begotten by the Father, and the Spirit is "breathed" by the Son who is one with the Father so as to take what is the Son's and

---

30. Marshall, "Deep Things," in *Oxford Handbook*, 407.
31. Ibid., 400.
32. Ibid., 411.
33. Tanner, *Christ the Key*, 206.
34. Marshall, "Deep Things," in *Oxford Handbook*, 411. "Among the three only he is spoken of as 'gift' to *us* because to him alone does it personally belong to *be* gift" (p. 405).
35. Ibid., 403.

declare it to us. The asymmetry between Son and Spirit, just so that the Son does not proceed from the Spirit but the Spirit comes forth from the Son, is what is attested in their temporal missions. The way in which we know is derivative of the order of the three in God.

The issue at stake in Spirit Christology is one of the Spirit's identity, indeed, what grounds the Spirit's unique hypostatic identity within God. The Spirit exists by way of originating relations. The Spirit comes forth from Father and Son but not as one who is after them. As Marshall writes, "The Spirit proceeds from the Father and Son eternally as love in person, the fruit and seal of the Father's infinite donation of himself to the Son, infinitely returned by the Son."[36] If such is the case, then starting with the Spirit to complement a historically dominant Logos Christology—debates about such a genealogy notwithstanding—seems somewhat misguided, as again the economy, resting as it does on eternity, teaches us of a personal identity that is so indissolubly related in an originating way to Father and Son that it cannot be conceived otherwise.[37] The Spirit subsists as one of three in God and as God; the Spirit is gift and love with which the Father loves the Son and the Son the Father.

The Spirit's acts teach "us concerning who he [the Spirit] is."[38] In Weinandy's words, "The Holy Spirit is love fully in act."[39] Knowledge of this mystery is something that we by faith receive as a fruit of the Spirit's mission. Teaching on the Spirit should help us glimpse the order internal to God's being. Indeed, it should derive from it. The work of the Spirit in conforming us to the Son and freeing us for him "cannot enter into his [the Spirit's] identity itself."[40]

In sum, work (and presence) is a function of identity and being. Knowledge too is derivative of an essential identity to which being is ascribed. In other words, knowledge of someone is derived from the being of that person, their nature; in the case of the Spirit, the Spirit's unique subsistence. My worry regarding Spirit Christology—at least insofar as Habets's monograph is representative—is that we are being asked to start with one whose identity is other-directed. I am convinced that the best way to honour the Spirit is to try to keep talking in New

---

36. Ibid., 412.
37. John 17:26.
38. Marshall, "Deep Things," in *Oxford Handbook*, 411.
39. Weinandy, "Trinitarian Christology," in *Oxford Handbook*, 390.
40. Marshall, "Deep Things," in *Oxford Handbook*, 402.

Testament terms. One starts with the Spirit by starting with the Son, by whom the Spirit is given, and in turn the Father, who sends the Son in the Spirit. The Father sends the Son in the Spirit in order "that the love with which you have loved me may be in them, and I in them" (John 17:26).

PART 3

ENGAGING BARTH

THE OTHER-DIRECTED SPIRIT

CHAPTER 6

THE REDEMPTIVE SPIRIT

INTRODUCTION

Karl Barth is the last major classical interlocutor to feature in our account of the Holy Spirit. As Augustine and Thomas, Barth will not leave us room "for a facile self-dispensation from the burden of metaphysical thought."[1] This is because of one theological conviction above all else, the majestic reality of *God*. It is theology's task to describe this God, especially the extent to which God remains *God* in all that he does for the life of the world.

Barth does not unfold the "who" of the Spirit in God's life in a manner similar to Augustine's or Thomas's. That is not to suggest that Barth is indifferent to such talk. Rather, Barth's pressing concern is the freedom of God—God's remaining God in the creation, maintenance, and perfection of covenant fellowship with creatures. Accordingly, Barth thinks language like that of "relations of origin" can be helpful to the extent that it deepens appreciation of this central insight. This is why it is fitting to include Barth in our account alongside Augustine and Thomas. With them he shares a common interest that God's acts among us arise from the life of God—Father, Son, and Holy Spirit. Our account in this chapter and the next will examine not only how Barth secures this point but also whether his way of doing so is satisfactory.

Barth has a profound sense of God's ontological self-sufficiency

---

1. D. M. MacKinnon, "The Relation of the Doctrines of the Incarnation and Trinity," in *Creation, Christ, and Culture: Studies in Honour of T. F. Torrance,* ed. Richard W. A. McKinney (Edinburgh: T&T Clark, 1976), 103.

and of God's freedom in relationship to all he does. God's freedom is on display in the accomplishment of humanity's reconciliation and redemption in Jesus Christ, the covenant of grace. God's freedom is the proper ground, indeed, the premise, Barth argues, of God's being for us. At every step, Barth is keen to point out that the latter rests on the former. If God's being is contingent on God's acts, then God's acts are necessary to God's being. Acts thus become the means by which God becomes God rather than "an act of Trinitarian self-repetition."[2]

As with Augustine and Thomas, Barth has a strategy for helping us see how the Spirit's acts are anchored in the Spirit's antecedent divinity. Barth's strategy is different from Augustine's and Thomas's, and yet it has deep affinities with theirs. We see this at work in part in Barth's engagement with John's gospel. Although Barth does not supply us with a full-blown commentary on John's gospel as does Augustine (in the form of his homilies) or Thomas (in the form of his lectures), Barth's *Erklärung* of John's gospel from the mid-1920s is nonetheless highly suggestive of how the Spirit not only (1) remains God the Spirit but also (2) how the Spirit originates in God. To be sure, his *Erklärung* does not cover the whole of the gospel but rather 1:1–8:59. Nonetheless, Barth's *Erklärung*, especially of John 2:23–3:21, infers interesting things regarding the Spirit as one of the three irreducible modes of the one divine being.

What also needs to be said is that we treat Barth (as we did Augustine and Thomas) in a manner that accords with his own procedural commitments. Barth's ordering of the material on the Spirit in §12 of *CD* I/1—the Spirit's work in advance of reflection on the eternality of the Spirit—serves a distinct purpose. As we will unfold, this is based on Barth's reckoning to describe the same subject, God the Spirit, *twice*. Barth describes the redemptive features of the Spirit's work (§12.1) before and in dependence on what is primary—the Spirit's "Godness" (§12.2). The Spirit's divinity is the premise and ground of the Spirit's impartation of freedom to the creature. To use language akin to Thomas's, it is the Spirit's procession that is manifest in the Spirit's mission. We ask of Barth, as we did Thomas and Augustine, what he thinks the Fourth Gospel teaches of how the Spirit originates

---

2. George Hunsinger, "Karl Barth's Doctrine of the Trinity, and Some Protestant Doctrines after Barth," in *The Oxford Handbook on the Trinity*, ed. Gilles Emery and Matthew Levering (Oxford: Oxford University Press, 2011), 312.

in God and how that is revealed in the Spirit's work to the outside, in which the Spirit remains God's Spirit and not our Spirit.

In the next chapter, we will also take up Barth on how the Spirit's work relates to the Spirit in God's inner life. Our concern, however, is not with his exegetical work but with his more synthetic and later work, namely, *CD* IV, §§62, 67, and 72, especially as it relates to how the Spirit does things. Although we do not find in *CD* IV a freestanding account of the immanent Spirit (which is what Barth gives us in §12.2), an economic treatment of the Spirit is in Barth's hands never just that. As we will see, his treatment of the gathering, upbuilding, and sending work of the Spirit in relation to the Christian community trades on and amplifies what he says in §12.2. However, Barth does not say anything fundamentally new in *CD* IV. He does say the same thing, but he says it differently (that is, in relationship to Christ's prophecy) and with more of an ecclesial focus. This is worth our attention. As with §12.1, §§62, 67, and 72 presuppose the Spirit's antecedence as the ground of the description of the Spirit's encompassing, liberating, transforming, and rendering transparent of all things in relationship to the purposes of the Risen One and his Father.

Before we turn to Barth on the Fourth Gospel, we need to be clear about how Barth uses the term "revelation." For Barth, God's revelation is *self*-revelation. Revelation as self-revelation is "reiterative" in character, which means that God acts among us as God is.[3] In Christ and the Spirit, we are given to know and love God as God truly is. God self-discloses, argues Barth, not because God is in need of so doing or constrained by something outside of God. Rather, God gives of the divine self in an utterly saving way because God is free to do so. God is a God who shares with sinners the life God has in himself and from himself. Barth uses the term "revelation" in the service of describing this truth.

BARTH AND THE FOURTH GOSPEL

Barth lectured on John's gospel in the winter semester of 1925/1926 at the University of Münster, and he repeated the lectures in Bonn in the summer semester of 1933, just months after Hitler was elected

---

3. See Eberhard Jüngel, *God's Being Is in Becoming: The Trinitarian Being of God in the Theology of Karl Barth*, trans. John Webster (Grand Rapids: Eerdmans, 2001), 73, 83.

chancellor of Germany.[4] As with Augustine's homilies and Thomas's lectures on the same gospel, Barth is "offering an *Erklärung*, an exposition or theologically interested reading."[5] As we read Barth's lecture on John 2:23–3:21, we see his "theologically interested reading" at work. Indeed, his reading crackles with language that you would expect to encounter at this period of his career: for example, *Ereignis* [event], *Existenz* [existence], and *Krisis* [crisis], terms that Barth puts in the service of reading John.[6] A case in point: Jesus places Nicodemus before "*die große Frage der Erkenntnis seiner eigenen Existenz* [the great question of the knowledge of his own existence]."[7] Throughout his comments on this passage, Barth goes to great lengths to draw attention to Jesus as the active agent, "the revealer of his Lordship," the one who is the only "reality," the only one in whom we can be made trustable to himself.[8] This is not to say that Barth champions a kind of christomonism. In accord with the logic of the passage, it is the Spirit who "makes alive, who gives the life of the child of God to the one who does not yet have this life."[9] Barth is emphatic that it is the Spirit who makes us God's children, that the new birth of the Spirit is God's work, and that it is water baptism that attests such as having happened.

While Barth does not explore in any extended sense the metaphysical underpinnings of the Spirit's acting thus in creating children, he takes it for granted that the Spirit's work has its reality in the Spirit's divinity. Barth thinks that the passage honours God's immanence, in particular, the immanence of the Spirit. Accordingly, the Spirit who bears anew is "not the invisible, noble spirit part of the human, but rather the absolute God who turns to and communicates to the human,

---

4. See Karl Barth, *Erklärung des Johannes-Evangeliums (Kapitel 1–8): Vorlesung Münster Wintersemester 1925/1926, wiederholt in Bonn, Sommersemester 1933*, ed. Walther Fürst (Zürich: Theologischer Verlag, 1999). All translations of Barth's text are my own. Note also Barth's and Eduard Thurneysen's sermon titled "Jesus and Nicodemus," in *Come, Holy Spirit: Sermons*, trans. George W. Richards et al. (London: Mowbrays, 1978), 101ff. This sermon was preached between 1920 and 1924. For a most helpful engagement with Barth's concerns during the 1920s, see John Webster, *Barth's Earlier Theology* (London: T&T Clark, 2005).

5. John Webster, *The Domain of the Word: Scripture and Theological Reason* (London: Bloomsbury/T&T Clark, 2012), 77.

6. See Barth, *Erklärung des Johannes*, 209.

7. Ibid., 211.

8. Ibid.

9. Ibid., 213. Note that Barth uses the language of "Sakrament" to describe Christian baptism. For a recent exploration of the exegetical bases of the later Barth's aversion to the language of sacrament, see the fine PhD thesis of Jonathan Peter Slater, "Karl Barth's Doctrine of Baptism: An Assessment of Its Plausibility as Exegesis" (PhD diss., University of St. Michael's College, 2013).

the Spirit who is the God of the human, God in the act of his being [*Gottseins*] in coming to the human."[10] The Spirit is and remains God, Barth argues, in bearing us anew for life. God the Spirit remains Lord, remains God in the act of his being.

That we are made by the Spirit into those who correspond to the reign of God "is to be understood as a wonder that is made comprehensible only in its incomprehensibility [*Unbegreiflichkeit*]."[11] Accordingly, Barth is not championing a kind of contentless apophaticism but rather a kind of unknowing generated by the particularities of God's self-introduction. His point is simply that Nicodemus must be taught, as we must, that God acts toward us as God is. We know God by God. However, in making himself known, God does so "without having become comprehensible."[12] Accordingly, Nicodemus stands under "*der Krisis*," as do we all, insofar as Nicodemus asks, "How can these things be?" (John 3:9).

These things are not "a human-earthly possibility and reality." "The new creation," Barth argues, "is *God's* work and act."[13] So Barth: "Revelation is in this exclusive sense, revelation. Revelation exclusively supposes itself, has made itself exclusively available because it is *God's* revelation, because its content is τὰ ἐπουράνια, the new birth of the human through the Spirit, indeed revelation, that to which we bring nothing precisely because it has found us."[14] God loves Nicodemus just as God loves the world—as it *is*. God's revelation is not a response to our merit, or in the case of John 2:23–3:21, Nicodemus's having merited it. "He [Nicodemus] finds himself face to face with something new and incomprehensible, something that he cannot fathom ... Jesus gives him a jolt and throws him out of this mood."[15] The world, as Nicodemus, is in the dark. But God loves the world—despite its being in the dark "*as it* is ... God loves it as it *is*, and his love has no other ground than in him*self*."[16] God loves the world, deeply estranged as it is from him, from the very depths of God's being. The world (Nicodemus included), Barth argues, is the "object [*Gegenstand*] of real divine love, namely that

---

10. Barth, *Erklärung des Johannes*, 214.
11. Ibid.
12. Ibid.
13. Ibid.
14. Ibid., 217.
15. Barth and Thurneysen, "Jesus and Nicodemus," in *Come, Holy Spirit*, 102–3, 106–7.
16. Barth, *Erklärung des Johannes*, 220.

of the world loved by God … [a love] that is comprehensible precisely in its incomprehensibility [*Unbegreiflichkeit*]."[17]

Barth is happy to use the language of decision [*Entscheidung*] to express what Jesus' discourse creates in relation to Nicodemus—the possibility of a decision of belief or unbelief. Jesus generates this decision by virtue of the *Krisis* he (Jesus) is. Accordingly, Jesus' judgment of our ongoing affair with false gods, as expressed in John 3:19—"people loved darkness rather than light because their deeds were evil"—is nothing but good news. Jesus says no to our infatuation with the darkness, thereby overcoming it. The light of Jesus is the light of "a new creation made by the Spirit who begets children of God."[18] Just so, "the one born of the Spirit is revealed to have been born in God … He is the *peccator iustus* [sinner justified]. And that means having life eternal."[19]

If Barth's comments on John 2:23–3:21 are more than a mild indication of the overarching concerns of his commentary, it is safe to say that the language of *Krisis* is front and centre. Such language has a basic theological function. It reminds us that the Spirit makes Christians.[20] The language of *Krisis* indicates agency: God the Holy Spirit is the active agent of new birth. Following the Fourth Gospel, Barth thinks that revelation—Jesus Christ—is in us as that which *God* the Spirit accomplishes. The Spirit forms Christ in us.

Barth's reading does not, as does Thomas's, reflect on where the Spirit's regenerating work comes from. Barth is concerned with describing the acts of the Spirit in bearing anew. That said, in honouring the *Krisis* that God is, Barth reminds us of the Spirit's divine being. God remains God in coming to us; God's being is the very ground of his loving encounter with the world. So Barth: "Jesus came to drag men out of all their dreaming of religious ideas, their feelings, and conversations and to put them beside the supreme reality—God … But even for this we must be born anew … We can come to God only through God himself."[21] God the Spirit is the agent who brings about the new birth.

Barth's *Erklärung* of John 4:1–42 has affinities with his reading of

---

17. Ibid., 221.
18. Ibid., 224.
19. Ibid., 224.
20. Barth, *CD* IV/2, 330. Barth writes, "He [the Holy Spirit] makes them Christians … And as He does all this, showing Himself in all this to be the Spirit of Jesus Christ, He is the Holy Spirit."
21. Barth and Thurneysen, "Jesus and Nicodemus," in *Come, Holy Spirit*, 109, 110.

John 2:23–3:21. What one encounters in revelation, Barth argues, is not "a divine effect." Rather, in revelation, as John 3:35 attests, "there exists a necessary, inner-divine relation between Father and Spirit as is the case with Father and Son in such a way that the encounter of God for and with humanity is not simply a divine effect [*Wirkung*] ... but rather the pure act [*actus purus*] in which God is for his own sake, in which God loves himself from eternity and in eternity. That is the mystery of *birth* by the Spirit, the mystery that issues in *worship* in Spirit and in truth. *God and the movement of his own life in himself is the mystery* [emphasis mine]."[22] The last sentence is especially important to consider. It is the movement of God's life that is at issue. The mystery of the new birth indicates the mystery of *God* and the movement of the life of God. The God who is "pure act" is the agent of the new birth. In the new birth, the inner relations of the three are manifest. The Trinity is the active agent.

[handwritten margin note: Not extrinsic to God. Only working of divine processions in time.]

The indivisible work of the Trinity has its focal point in the activity of the Spirit. It is the Spirit (and not Father or Son) who is said by Jesus to bear this life. But why, we ask? This is where talk of God's life is in order. Such talk supplies us with the rationale for why the Spirit acts as the Spirit does in bearing anew. For Barth, the doctrine of the Trinity explains, however much it may strain language, the origins of God's acts. The doctrine unfolds why God's life moves as it does.

"THE MOVEMENT OF HIS OWN LIFE"

God has life from himself. On no one or no thing is God dependent in order to be God. That much is clear from the acts of the three. But how does one truthfully talk about God's "own life" and of how the Spirit originates in God? The architecture of Barth's account in *CD* I/1 helps answer these questions. *God the Holy Spirit* (§12) is divided into two parts, (1) *God as Redeemer* (pp. 448–66) and (2) *The Eternal Spirit* (pp. 466–89).[23] In the first part of the section, Barth attends to the work of the Spirit. In the second, he attends to the Spirit as "of the essence of God Himself."[24] The second part does not draw attention away from

---

22. Barth, *Erklärung des Johannes*, 249.
23. It is my view that the sections of *CD* preceding II/2 are not the "old Barth." There is strong continuity across the corpus. Accordingly, *CD* II/2 does not represent a revolutionary change in Barth's thinking.
24. Barth, *CD* I/1, 466.

the first but describes the first in a new and different way. The second part helps us appreciate the basic truth that the Spirit, by whom we come to see and hear—"Grace," Barth argues—"is antecedently in God Himself."[25] The second part helps us to see, moreover, how it is that the Spirit is really different from the other two divine persons.

As is the case with Augustine's *On the Trinity* and Thomas's *Summa Theologica*, what Barth offers in his great synthetic work, *Church Dogmatics*, is a classical account of the themes of church teaching in a way that is derivative of his engagement with Scripture. Here in §12.2 (*The Eternal Spirit*) we see the extent to which Barth's exegetical labours of the period inform his talk of the Spirit's work. However, the work of the Spirit is the work of the Spirit of God, who is, Barth argues, a distinct agent "no less and no other than God Himself, distinct from Him whom Jesus calls His Father, distinct also from Jesus Himself, yet no less than the Father, and no less than Jesus, God Himself, altogether God."[26] An account of the operations of the Spirit must be accompanied by an account of the eternal Spirit. The latter is not an addendum. Without reflection on the Spirit's eternality, Barth argues, we do not know whether it is *God* at work to free us for Jesus Christ.

A doctrine or dogma of the eternal Spirit is "more or less plainly hinted at in the New Testament even though it obviously was not and is not to be found there. The dogma itself, then, is not in Scripture; it is exegesis of Scripture."[27] The dogma of the eternal Spirit as "of the essence of God himself" is "exegesis of Scripture."[28] What Scripture teaches, Barth argues, is that "the Spirit is in revelation [what] He is antecedently in Himself. And what He [the Spirit] is antecedently in Himself He is in revelation."[29] Notice that Barth does not collapse the work of the Spirit into the person of the Spirit. The Spirit is a distinct agent. The source of that agency is God's life. The Spirit in revelation is "God." This is who the Spirit shows the Spirit's self to be. The agency of the Spirit in revelation corresponds to the Spirit's life in God. The question remains, however, of how the Spirit comes to be in God.

Barth turns to the Niceno-Constantinopolitan Creed of 381 to

---

25. Ibid.
26. Ibid., 467. It is worth noting that Barth says this in the first part of §12 (*God as Redeemer*, §12.1) after having described the work of the Spirit as consisting "in freedom, freedom to have a Lord, this Lord, God, as Lord" (ibid.).
27. Ibid.
28. Ibid., 466, 467.
29. Ibid., 466.

expound this mystery.[30] The Creed provides conceptual tools for unfolding how the Spirit's acts rest upon the Spirit's origin in God—"who proceeds from the Father and the Son."[31] Barth thinks that what makes the Spirit Lord is "the fact that He [the Spirit] is the common factor in the mode of being of God the Father and that of God the Son. He is what is common to them, not in so far as they are one God, but in so far as they are the Father and the Son."[32] The Spirit "is a third mode of being of the divine Subject or Lord."[33] Accordingly, what distinguishes the Spirit from the first and second modes, Barth argues, is that the Spirit is "the common factor" of Father and Son.[34] The Spirit arises in relation to Father and Son; they do not arise in relation to the Spirit. The Spirit originates in relation to Father and Son as the "togetherness or communion," or better, "the fellowship, the act of communion, of the Father and the Son."[35]

Barth, as Augustine, speaks of the Spirit as "their [Father and Son] own principle. But this principle is the breathing of the Spirit or the Holy Spirit Himself."[36] The Spirit is, put simply, equivalent to an originating relation. The person of the Spirit, if you want to use the language of person, is nothing but the being breathed by Father and Son.[37] How does the Spirit originate? By the breathing of the Father and Son. "There is nothing here but relatings, no somewhats doing the relating. The language strains."[38] And yet, the Creed serves as "the exegesis of Scripture." To talk about the Holy Spirit "antecedently in Himself" is to talk about this originating relation, this being breathed.[39]

Why does Barth follow the tradition in speaking this way? Because it points to a basic biblical truth. The Spirit as this originating relation in God grounds, for Barth, our knowing "Him [the Spirit] thus in revelation. But He is not this because He is it in His revelation; because He is it antecedently in Himself, He is it also in His revelation."[40] That

---

30. Ibid., 468ff.
31. Ibid., 469.
32. Ibid.
33. Ibid.
34. Ibid.
35. Ibid., 469, 470.
36. Ibid., 470.
37. I owe this way of thinking to Denys Turner, *Thomas Aquinas: A Portrait* (New Haven, CT: Yale University Press, 2013), 126. It nicely captures Barth.
38. Ibid., 126.
39. Barth, *CD* I/1, 470.
40. Ibid., 471.

there cannot be a *"vice versa!"* is crucial to Barth's argument.[41] The agency the three exercise in their work toward the outside does not make them divine. If that were true, Barth argues, then God would be who God is on the basis of what God has done. That cannot be, however, as it suggests that God's work impacts God's being, which is something Barth will not have. The work of Spirit is the outworking of an origin, a particular originating relation with respect to Father and Son. The Spirit "really sets free and really makes us the children of God" because the Spirit is antecedently God.[42]

Recall that for Barth God is "pure act."[43] Hence the Spirit in being this relatedness to Father and Son is a profoundly dynamic reality. Barth notes, "In this work of His on us He [the Spirit] simply does in time what He does eternally in God."[44] The Spirit's work simply reiterates or repeats in time "the specific element in the divine mode of being of the Holy Spirit."[45] The specific element is again the Spirit's being "the act of communion" of Father and Son.[46] The Spirit is this act of communion. Therein lies the Spirit's inner dynamism, the Spirit's "reality in His relation to the other divine modes of being."[47]

At this point we begin to see a rule at work that governs Barth's thinking about the relationship of the economic to the immanent. Barth writes, "Material dogmatic statements about the immanent Trinity can and must be taken from definitions of the modes of being of God in revelation."[48] Barth's account of *The Eternal Spirit* (§12.2) succeeds that of his account of *God as Redeemer* (§12.1) as proof of this rule. The Spirit's procession in God from the being of the Father

---

41. Ibid.
42. Ibid.
43. Barth, *Erklärung des Johannes*, 249.
44. Barth, *CD* I/1, 471. Cf. IV/3.2, 760, wherein Barth writes, "Just as the Holy Spirit, as Himself an eternal divine 'person' or mode of being, as the Spirit of the Father and the Son (*qui ex Patre Filioque procedit*), is the bond of peace between the two, so in the historical work of reconciliation he is the One who constitutes and guarantees the unity of the *totus Christus*."
45. Barth, *CD* I/1, 469.
46. Ibid., 470.
47. Ibid., 474.
48. Ibid., 485. Note: Bruce L. McCormack argues that Barth "was not consistent with his own rule [i.e., nothing can be said about the immanent Trinity that does not find its basis in the economy]; and yet, it is equally clear that he was not aware of the inconsistency—and that is a point of no small importance." Accordingly, McCormack's constructive proposals are to be understood as "*possible conclusions* [emphasis mine] to be drawn from a more consistent application of the rule which Barth himself did not envision but which he clearly was seeking." See "The Lord and Giver of Life: A 'Barthian' Defense of the *Filioque*," in *Rethinking Trinitarian Theology: Disputed Issues and Contemporary Questions in Trinitarian Theology*, ed. Guilio Maspero and Robert J. Wozniak (London: T&T Clark, 2012), 231.

and Son is derivative of New Testament talk. For Barth, one proceeds from the work of the three to their immanent life as far as *the order of knowing* is concerned. But that is not to suggest for a moment that the immanent reality of God is a function of God's saving work in Israel and Jesus. God does not arise out of what God has done; God's doing does not achieve God's being. In the case of "the temporal reality" of the Spirit, Barth understands that it has "eternal content."[49] That "eternal content" is "the immanent *Filioque*," the Spirit as the "bond of peace between the two [Father and Son]."[50] God's acts arise from God's life. The Spirit's agency is derivative of the Spirit's origin.

Barth thinks that the "immanent *Filioque*" is not only a teaching that Scripture encourages but also is implicit in the Creed of 381.[51] "The Eastern view," especially since the hardening championed by Photius in the ninth century, does not accord so well with the fullness of Scripture's testimony.[52] Barth's argument, drawing as it does on well-known New Testament texts like Galatians 4:6 and Romans 8:9, is quite simple. There must be a "*relatio originis*"—a causal relation—between the Son and Spirit.[53] Were there not such a relation, it would be improper for "the Spirit [to] be called the Spirit of the Son."[54] New Testament patterns of speech demonstrate an originating relation. So Barth: "If the rule holds good that God in His eternity is none other than the One who discloses Himself to us in His revelation, then in the one case as in the other the Holy Spirit is the Spirit of the love of the Father and the Son, and so *procedens ex Patre Filioque*."[55] The "immanent *Filioque*" expresses itself in the acts of the three toward the outside. The economy demonstrates the "full consubstantial fellowship between Father and Son as the essence of the Spirit."[56]

To sum up this section, Barth covers some doctrinal terrain similar to Augustine and Thomas. In order to say with confidence that the Spirit remains God the Spirit in all that the Spirit does, we must talk,

[margin handwritten note: Spirit of Christ, therefore Spirit from Christ.]

---

49. Barth, *CD* I/1, 481.
50. Ibid.; IV/3.2, 760.
51. Ibid.
52. For an account of this hardening, see Yves Congar, *I Believe in the Holy Spirit* (New York: Seabury, 1983), 3: 57–58. Congar writes, "Photius enshrined pneumatology in a form of expression [a scheme consisting of two branches] which put out of the question an agreement with the West or even with those Latin Fathers whom the Orthodox Christians accept as their own" (p. 59).
53. Barth, *CD* I/1, 482.
54. Ibid.
55. Ibid., 483.
56. Ibid., 481, 482.

however strained it may seem, about the "immanent *Filioque*." The "immanent *Filioque*" follows teaching on the "economic *Filioque*." The former is a way of saying the latter but in a different way.[57] For example, Barth states that the "presupposition" of his discussion in *CD* IV/1 §62.1 (*The Work of the Holy Spirit*) is *CD* I/1 §12.[58] The work of the Spirit in §12.1 (*God the Redeemer*) has a presupposition: it is §12.2 (*The Eternal Spirit*). Thus it is to be expected that Barth restates in §62.1 what he wrote in §12.2: "He [the Spirit] eternally proceeds from the Father and the Son, as He united the Father and the Son in eternal love, as He must be worshipped and glorified together with the Father and the Son, because He is of one substance with them."[59] The work of the Spirit in revelation (Jesus Christ) shows the Spirit to be antecedently in himself God, and "in God independently, just like the Father and the Son."[60] The Spirit is not only in God, but is God, God the Holy Spirit. The Spirit's work among us corresponds to the Spirit's life in God. The Spirit unites Father and Son in love. Such love, Barth thinks, is the Spirit. "The Holy Spirit is the love which is the essence of the relation between these two modes of being of God."[61]

THOMAS AND BARTH: WHAT IS THE DIFFERENCE?

Barth's treatment of *The Eternal Spirit* (§12.2) succeeds his treatment of the operations of the Spirit (§12.1), whereas Thomas ends his treatment on the Trinity in *ST* I with the divine missions (q. 43). Thomas has to talk about the person of the Spirit (q. 36) and the name of the Spirit as "Love" and "Gift" (qq. 37–38) before he can talk about the mission of the Spirit (and indeed of the Son). Is there anything at stake, theologically speaking, in the different sequencing of topics? And if so, how does that further inform not only our understanding of Barth but also the shape of a responsible pneumatology?

Barth's treatment of *The Eternal Spirit* functions to remind us that "the reality of God which encounters us in His revelation is His reality

---

57. Ibid., 481.
58. Barth, *CD* IV/1, 644.
59. Ibid., 646.
60. Barth, *CD* I/1, 474.
61. Ibid., 480.

Not dismissing analogy for univocality.

in all the depths of eternity."[62] Thomas would concur. Remember, the Spirit's mission, for Thomas, is but a temporal extension of the Spirit's procession, "*the being spirated by the Father through the Son.*"[63] That said, Thomas contemplates the person of the Spirit in advance of the work, not as a kind of exercise in "natural theology," but rather to help us to see the mission (the work) as the person existing "but in a new way."[64] For Thomas as for Barth, the mission (act) follows from the person (being). Indeed, and without oversimplifying, I think it is fair to say that Thomas would not disapprove of Barth's rule that "material dogmatic statements ... must be taken from definitions of the modes of being of God in revelation."[65]

That said, I do think Thomas would argue that Barth's rule is incomplete. Let me explain. Metaphysics or "speculation" does not— over and against Bruce McCormack — "supplement it [the Christocentric approach] with metaphysical speculation (as touching upon the divine essence)."[66] It seems that McCormack misunderstands the function of metaphysical speculation for Thomas. As Gilles Emery notes, "Teaching on the economic Trinity is just as speculative as reflection on the imma- nent Trinity. The doctrine of the economic Trinity is seen as the fruit of a meditation which, with the helping hand of the study of the Trinity in itself behind it, elucidates the Trinitarian economy by the eternal being of God."[67] Here we have the basic difference between Barth and Thomas. Barth's account in *The Eternal Spirit* describes the work of the Spirit from a particular angle. The work of the Spirit is *God's* work. For Thomas, however, you can only come to a truthful understanding of the work by first taking account of the immanent procession of the Spirit. What is at stake, if anything, in this?

Discussion of both economic and immanent Trinity is metaphysical.

Two of the church's greatest teachers have different accounts of the way in which theology proceeds. Emery helps us to appreciate this. He

---

62. Ibid., 479.

63. Turner, *Thomas Aquinas*, 126.

64. Bruce L. McCormack, "Processions and Missions," in *Thomas Aquinas and Karl Barth: An Unofficial Catholic-Protestant Dialogue*, ed. Bruce L. McCormack and Thomas Joseph White (Grand Rapids: Eerdmans, 2013), 120; Aquinas, *ST* I, q. 43, a. 7. In *CD* I/1, 465, Barth (unfor- tunately) equates contemplation of God with manipulation. The quote runs: "It is precisely ἐν πνεύματι that we shall be ready either way to turn from ourselves to God and to pray to Him, not to contemplate God and manipulate Him."

65. Barth, *CD* I/1, 485.

66. McCormack, "Processions and Missions," in *Thomas Aquinas and Karl Barth*, 111.

67. Gilles Emery, *The Trinitarian Theology of St Thomas Aquinas* (Oxford: Oxford University Press, 2007), 415.

argues of Thomas that theology works in three stages. The first stage is "the acknowledgement of the revelation of the Trinity through its action in the world, listening to and following the witness of Scripture."[68] Barth would concur: this is what §12.1 undertakes— *God as Redeemer*. In the second stage, "beginning from their economic revelation, this theologian [Thomas] puts forward a speculative reflection on the persons, in their distinction and their unity. This is the doctrine of the 'immanent Trinity,' or in Thomas' own language, the doctrine of the Trinity 'in itself.'"[69] Barth would also concur with Thomas's intention, although Barth would not use the language of speculation. This is what I understand Barth to be doing in §12.2 (*The Eternal Spirit*). Barth's intentions are speculative—as defined above—and so compatible with Thomas's.

Where Barth and Thomas evidence a degree of difference is in regard to a third stage. Of this third stage, Emery writes,

> A third and final phase uses the two initial movements as a guide into a speculative reflection on the action of the persons within this world. This is where a genuine *doctrine* of the "economic Trinity," the Trinity as "principle and end of creatures," is conveyed. In the same way that it sets off from Scripture in order to lead us back to Scripture afresh, Trinitarian reflection begins from the action of the persons in the world in order to come round to that action anew.[70]

If Thomas is correct, then, speculative reflection does not understand itself to be touching on the divine essence *per se*. Similarly, it neither explains what is going on in the missions nor supplements them. Rather, speculative reflection understood in the sense above *conveys* what is going on in God's activity toward the outside.

"Speculative reflection" is not a matter of essentialism, of speculating on the essence of God in a manner detached from the acts of the three. Likewise, it is not natural theology. Rather, speculative reflection is the third step in the order of *teaching*. Thomas's teaching on the Trinity reverses the order of knowing. We know God because of the acts of the three. Thomas, however, teaches how the Spirit originates in God before he unfolds the Spirit's mission toward the outside. In Thomas, the order of teaching (procession to mission) does not map onto our knowing

---

68. Ibid.
69. Ibid., 415–16.
70. Ibid., 416.

(from mission to procession). However, in Thomas, our knowing must be derivative of the order of being in God's life. We are given to know by faith these three as they really are. However, for Barth in *CD* I/1, his teaching on the Spirit does map onto the way in which we come to know the Spirit. Hence Barth moves from the mission (the work) to the procession (the divinity of the Spirit). That is the order of knowing that coincides, in Barth's account, with the order of teaching.

Despite the differences between the order of teaching and Thomas's positing of a third stage of speculative reflection, the affinities between Barth and Thomas are far greater. Both concur that one can only attend to the work of the Spirit well if one has a robust sense of *what* and *who* is working therein. Although the differences of expression are undeniable, the intention is the same. Accordingly, Barth's treatment assumes a basic asymmetry between the immanent and economic inasmuch as the Spirit's divinity in the pure act that is God is revealed in the Spirit's agency in the economy—"The wind blows where it chooses" (John 3:8). As with Thomas, Barth thinks that the Spirit can only make us present to Jesus Christ with ears to hear and eyes to see because of the Spirit's consubstantiality with him and his Father. The work of the Spirit trades on and implies "the deity of His essence."[71] God is present as God in his work. The Spirit sanctifies because the Spirit is himself holy, gives life because the Spirit in himself is life and love. God "is in Himself the Spirit, love."[72]

For Barth, teaching on the divinity of the Spirit accompanies an account of the redemptive Spirit. The former occasions statements that tell us, however broken the language becomes, of how the third of the three is in God. For example, the Spirit is "the active mutual orientation and interpenetration of love, because these two, the Father and the Son, [who] are of one essence, and indeed of divine essence, because God's fatherhood and sonship as such must be related to one another in this active mutual orientation and interpenetration."[73] The Spirit is love in God, "the active mutual orientation and interpenetration of love."[74]

It is in §12.2 that Barth takes up, pneumatologically speaking, "the burden of metaphysical thought."[75] This is not again to suggest that

---

71. Barth, *CD* I/1, 457, 460.
72. Ibid., 483.
73. Ibid., 487.
74. Ibid.
75. MacKinnon, "Incarnation and Trinity," in *Creation, Christ, and Culture*, 103.

Barth is uninterested in metaphysical thought in later volumes of the *CD*. Nonetheless, the orientation of Barth's account through *CD* IV is, as we will see, rather more economic than immanent. Speculative discourse is not something into which Barth leads us, which is precisely where, if indeed one follows Thomas via Emery, a genuine doctrine of the economic is conveyed.[76] Rather, Barth's concern is to let such discourse secure his overriding concern to honour the divinity of the Spirit in all that the Spirit does.

For a reader of Barth such as McCormack, the question of an "immanent *Filioque*" is perhaps moot. This because of what happens in *CD* II/2. Without getting overwhelmed by a debate internal to Barth scholarship, it is worth signaling the importance of *CD* II/2, wherein Barth rearticulates the doctrine of election in a manner determined by the "in Christ" of Ephesians 1:4. Accordingly, *CD* II/2 (and thereafter on McCormack's reading) generates the point of convergence with Thomas, namely, "the shared affirmation of a single eternal act in which both the processions and the missions take place."[77] Accordingly, God's act of self-constitution (the processions) cannot be differentiated from the covenant of grace (the missions). Barth in *CD* I/1 does want to distinguish but not separate the two. I do not think Barth ever departs from this. Indeed, I see Barth in *CD* I/1 asking the same question McCormack ascribes to the "later" Barth: "What must God be if the missions are what they are?"[78] Barth, having described the activity of the Spirit in *God as Redeemer* in §12.1, tells us that this is the work of *The Eternal Spirit* (§12.2). The one who acts thus — redeems — is God; §12.2 explains the ground of the redemptive work of the Spirit in terms of the divine being of the Spirit.

The debate internal to Barth's studies yields an important point that will allow us to make the transition to further consideration of how the Spirit does things. The issue in all of this is the manner in which God relates to time. John Webster argues that it is "out of the ceaseless repose of his own life" that God engages time. God's life is "the first object of systematic inquiry."[79] The "repose of his [God's] own life" denotes "the primacy of theology proper."[80] One's ordering of the topics of

76. Emery, *Trinitarian Theology*, 416.
77. McCormack, "Processions and Missions," in *Thomas Aquinas and Karl Barth*, 111.
78. Ibid., 113.
79. Webster, *Domain of the Word*, 146.
80. Ibid.

theology—the order of teaching—is to reflect this primacy: "The being of God *in se*, followed by the treatment of the works of God, with the theology of the divine missions as the hinge between the two."[81] Although we see that Barth in *CD* I/1 does not order the material in this way insofar as the outward movement is treated in advance of the inward (the order of teaching), Barth is adamant that the work of the redemptive Spirit proceeds from God's life. The redemptive work of the Spirit is that of God the Spirit.

By turning toward a more in-depth engagement with Barth's account of the work of the Spirit in the next chapter, the outward movement of the Spirit, we ask whether further insight is achieved regarding the movement of the eternal Spirit in God. Barth is too skilled a reader of Scripture to leave the consequences unexplored. And so we move toward an exploration of what light the work of the Spirit, especially in relation to Christ's own self-impartation (his prophecy), yields with regard to the inner life of God. This is the broad objective of the next chapter.

CONCLUSION: GROUNDING GOD'S OUTWARD MOVEMENT

We have attended to how Augustine, Thomas, and Barth read some of the key Trinitarian texts in the Fourth Gospel. They agree that the mission of the Spirit is a revelatory mission. It arises in God, disclosing how the Spirit originates in God. Barth, in both his lecture cycles on the Fourth Gospel and the first part volume of his *Church Dogmatics*, emphasizes that God the Spirit is the subject and agent of his redemptive work. We learn from Barth that the work of the Spirit encourages us to talk about the source of that work. In so doing, we learn that its ground—the Spirit's Godhead—expresses itself in the Spirit's work, for example, new birth.

The Son's generation from the Father is expressed in an outward sense by his sending. So too is the Spirit's bearing us from above expressive of the love that the Spirit is *in* God. This love is expressed

---

81. Ibid. In the chapter "Perfection and Participation," Webster describes the works of God in terms of "God's *will*." Thus "what ties together the realities of God in himself and God's economic presence is God's *will*, directed to creatures as sovereign decision and determination in their favor." See *The Analogy of Being: Invention of the Antichrist or the Wisdom of God*, ed. Thomas Joseph White (Grand Rapids: Eerdmans, 2010), 391.

in the Spirit's voice. "He [the Spirit] speaks both of Him [Christ] and for Him."[82] This does not suggest an inert Christ or a depersonalized Spirit. Rather, as will be shown in the next chapter, Christ creates correspondence to his life in the Spirit. The New Testament describes this as an event, says Barth, "the outpouring of the Holy Spirit as proceeding from Him [Christ]."[83] But where does this outpouring come from? It comes from God's life. Barth, as Augustine and Thomas, helps us to see that the Spirit proceeds among us as does the Spirit in God. There is real correspondence.

John 20:22 refers to "breath" — "He [Jesus] breathed on them" — as the breath of his Spirit.[84] Jesus breathes on his disciples his Spirit, "the fulfillment [Barth notes] of this repeated promise."[85] The Spirit promised is the Spirit given among us, as is the case in God. The Johannine Pentecost teaches us that the testimony of the other "advocate" is not restricted to the mode of promise (John 14:16). "He [the Spirit] is sent by Jesus Christ and comes to man. According to Jn. 20:22, He blows as His breath in the freedom described in Jn. 3:8."[86] The Spirit is indeed given, breathed by Christ to be received by all and so to return all to Christ and thus to the Father. The promise is fulfilled. The Spirit as "the authorisation to speak about Christ" is authorisation to speak of the resurrected Christ.[87] The Spirit is indeed the Spirit of Christ *resurrected*. Barth unfolds this point with particular acumen. In the next chapter, we will treat his account of that point with a view to what it teaches us about the life of the Spirit in God, in relation to Father and Son. Barth never divorces his account of how the Spirit does things from the one — the resurrected and exalted one — who breathes the Spirit he eternally receives from the Father. That is because there exists a real correspondence between the Son's breathing of the Spirit and the source of that breathing in God's life. It is with Barth's continual help that we further contemplate this mystery.

---

82. Barth, *CD* IV/2, 326.
83. Ibid., 325.
84. Barth, *CD* I/1, 450.
85. Ibid., 452.
86. Barth, *CD* IV/1, 648.
87. Barth, *CD* I/1, 455.

CHAPTER 7

THE SPIRIT OF CHRIST

INTRODUCTION

In this chapter, we will look at the Spirit's acts in relation to the Christian community, the body of Christ. Such a vantage point supplies us with a wealth of knowledge surrounding the nature of the Spirit. Once more, our interlocutor is Barth. While in the previous chapter we looked at the immanent dimension of teaching on the Spirit, in this chapter, we will look at the works so as to extend the last chapter. This way of building my argument agrees with Barth's own commitments. With Augustine and Thomas, we moved from their exegetical work to their more synthetic work. With Barth, however, we have to move somewhat differently. If the previous chapter sought to point out the main concern of pneumatology—honouring the divinity of the Spirit in the Spirit's redemptive work and the source of that divinity—this chapter will describe similar ground. It will do so in relationship to Barth's account of the Spirit's work in the Christian community. Although Barth does not say anything new in these paragraphs, he does say it differently. As a result, we see further how Barth contributes to the book's thesis. Pneumatological teaching describes not only what the Spirit does but also its source in God's life. Thus "we are not now in a different sphere; we are simply looking at it [the Spirit] from a different angle."[1] The angle that we look at in this chapter is that of how the Spirit does things in relationship to Jesus Christ and his community.

For Barth, as we have seen and will continue to see but in a new way, one can only talk about or know in a responsible manner the

---

1. Barth, *CD* IV/1, 644.

Spirit by describing the Spirit's being.[2] Being, in Barth's mind, as in Augustine's and Thomas's, grounds knowledge. Knowledge of the Spirit's activity is derivative of the Spirit's being. The consubstantiality of the Spirit with Father and Son is the ground of the Spirit's activity. As we discuss the activity of the Spirit, we must be mindful of what it implies regarding the Spirit's divinity and how the Spirit originates in God.

Some might find Barth a strange choice as one of our main interlocutors in a text on pneumatology.[3] Barth is often criticized for diminishing the hypostatic uniqueness of the Spirit by talking about the Spirit almost exclusively as "the power in which Jesus Christ attests Himself."[4] Such talk is said to depersonalize the Spirit and to leave the Spirit with nothing to do that the Son cannot do better. Eugene Rogers puts it this way: "It's as if the ditty from *Annie Get Your Gun* were an acknowledged premise like this: Anything Spirit can do, Son can do better, Son can do anything better than She [the Spirit]."[5] To be sure, Barth has a different pneumatology than does Rogers. The question remains, however, whether Rogers's criticism that Barth does not appreciate the extent to which the Spirit is said to rest on the Son—over and against language of the Spirit being the power of the Son or the essence of the Father and Son relation—renders Barth's pneumatology deficient.[6]

THE SPIRIT AND THE GATHERING OF THE CHRISTIAN COMMUNITY

Barth's account of the work of the Spirit in *CD* IV is bound up with the church, or his preferred term, "the Christian community." The Christian community is the community created by the Spirit. The reason Barth connects talk of the Spirit with talk of the community is that "the Holy Ghost leads him [a person] into the community

---

2. Ibid., 657.

3. Even one as sympathetic to Barth as Bruce McCormack avers that Barth's pneumatology has weaknesses, namely, "the reduction of the Spirit to the 'act of communion' between Father and Son." See "The Lord and Giver of Life," in *Rethinking Trinitarian Theology*, ed. Guilio Maspero and Robert J. Wozniak (London: T&T Clark, 2012), 237.

4. See, e.g., Barth, *CD* IV/1, 648.

5. Eugene F. Rogers Jr., *After the Spirit: A Constructive Pneumatology from Resources Outside the Modern West* (Grand Rapids: Eerdmans, 2005), 9.

6. See, e.g., ibid., 32.

and not into a private relationship with Christ."[7] In leading to Jesus, the Spirit leads to the Christian community. The work of the Spirit as the very "power in which Jesus Christ attests Himself" has duration and shape.[8] That shape has to do with the church. So Barth: "To be awakened to faith and to be added to the community are one and the same thing."[9]

The Spirit's work in relation to Jesus and his body reflects, Barth argues, who the Spirit is in eternity, that is, the Spirit *of* Jesus Christ. Barth's Christocentric account of the Spirit's work in relation to the community thus corresponds to how things are in eternity. That the Spirit works in the economy as the Spirit does is no accident. The Spirit gives rise to the event of "His [Christ's] real presence as the living and speaking Lord" on the basis of the Spirit's antecedent existence. "The reflection of what the Holy Spirit was in eternity and will be in eternity does not cease to fall on it [the Christian community]."[10] The Christian community is a spiritual community, meaning that it is created in the Spirit of Christ. The Spirit's work has the Christ-centred shape that it does because it is a repetition of who the Spirit is in God. In Eugene Rogers's words, "What the Trinity does in the economy has its character from what the Trinity does in its own life."[11]

Barth's account of the work of the Spirit in *CD* IV does not take the Spirit's divinity for granted. In unfolding the "spiritual" and yet "concrete" criterion of apostolicity as the work of the Holy Spirit, he asks: "But in that case, who and what is the Holy Spirit? Is He the sovereign God, who as Spirit moves where He will, awakening the hearts of men to the unity of faith and their lips to attest it?—or is He something quite different?"[12] As articulated in §12.1, the Spirit's work anticipates the question of being (§12.2), "Is He the sovereign God?" Does the Holy Spirit show the Spirit's self to be God? The answer is yes, of course. The Spirit cannot be other than "God in the power which quickens man to this profitable and living knowledge of His action."[13] The Spirit acts as God because the Spirit is God.

The focal point of the Spirit's quickening is the church. The church

---

7. Barth, *CD* IV/1, 689.
8. Ibid., 648.
9. Ibid., 688.
10. Ibid., 691.
11. Rogers, *After the Spirit*, 117.
12. Barth, *CD* IV/1, 716.
13. Ibid., 646.

can be what it is in Jesus *by* the power of the Holy Spirit. Jesus Christ is by the Spirit "invisibly present as the living head in the midst of it as His body."[14]

Even at the introductory stage of our discussion, we notice the extent to which the work of the Spirit has an other-directed focus. The acts of the Spirit have their principle of intelligibility in relationship to Jesus and also his Father, and thus to Jesus' body, the church. To argue otherwise is to depart from New Testament patterns of speech. Commenting on Romans 8:15–17, Barth writes, "He [the Spirit] is the Spirit of faith, who bears witness to us that we are the children of God by the fact that we may cry, 'Abba, Father,' and that at bottom we cannot cry anything else."[15] The work of the Spirit is the work of "the Holy Spirit of the living Lord."[16] The "of," for Barth, makes all the difference. Indeed, the immanent "of" is reflected in the economic "of." It is *God* the Spirit who is at work "as the Spirit has promised to be in the midst of every community gathered by Him [the Spirit] and in His name."[17]

In sum, the Spirit gives rise to the Son's body, the church, gathering and enabling it to be a modest reflection of Jesus Christ himself. The Spirit, as Jesus' gift breathed, generates a body for Jesus. This is the Christian community. It is a community that Jesus is not ashamed to call his own, a body that "cannot escape a wonderful similarity with its Lord who became a servant."[18] That the Spirit does so is because the Spirit is of him from eternity. We see that what the Spirit does corresponds to who the Spirit is in God.

THE SPIRIT AND THE UPBUILDING OF THE CHRISTIAN COMMUNITY

Barth's account of the upbuilding of the community in *CD* IV/2 (§67) often describes the Spirit in the following terms: "The powerful and living direction of the Resurrected, of the living Lord Jesus, and therefore the Holy Spirit ... effects the upbuilding of the Christian

---

14. Ibid., 725.
15. Ibid., 733.
16. Ibid., 728.
17. Ibid., 674.
18. Ibid., 739.

community."[19] The Spirit, together with the risen Lord Jesus, is "the principle of sanctification," the living direction of the Risen One.[20] It is the Spirit whom Barth describes as "the quickening power" of the sanctification that is Jesus Christ.[21] The Spirit's agency in upbuilding is exercised exclusively in relationship to Jesus Christ. Barth writes at the outset of his account of §67.2 (*The Growth of the Community*) that "the true Church in the event or occurrence or act of its upbuilding as a community … takes place in the power and operation of the Holy Spirit, and the corresponding action of those who are assembled and quickened by Him."[22] The church's upbuilding, as its gathering, is a spiritual event. Its operative reality is the Spirit. Accordingly, the church's centre lies outside of itself—in Jesus Christ in the power of the Holy Spirit. We see something of the priority of the church's essence—Jesus Christ—in relation to its existence. To the extent that the church is truly the church, it will, for Barth, share in the Spirit in Christ. By the power of the Spirit can those assembled by the (written and proclaimed) Word act as witnesses to the Word.

If we are to grasp something of the relationship between what Barth argues in §12.2 and here (§67.2), I think Barth's sense that the "true Church" takes place in the event of Jesus imparting himself in the Spirit is highly significant. The origin of the church is the event that creates, sustains, and perfects it, namely, the humiliation and exaltation of the Son. The church's origin—Jesus Christ—issues in upbuilding actions: "God and men build the community in consequence."[23] Those actions that contribute to its growth are actions the community undertakes, to be sure; but the power by which those actions are undertaken is Jesus—"Jesus is the power of life immanent within it [the Christian community]."[24] The church's acts do not make it what it is, Christ's body. Indeed, the community's acts of obedience issue from its being. The relationship between being and action is irreversible. So Barth: "It is in this sense that the Holy Spirit as the self-attestation of Jesus is the quickening power by which Christianity is awakened and glorified and built up to a true Church in the world. As the self-attestation of Jesus

---

19. Barth, *CD* IV/2, 614.
20. Ibid.
21. Ibid., 617.
22. Ibid., 641.
23. Ibid., 644.
24. Ibid., 651.

the Holy Spirit achieves the communion of saints (*communio sanctorum*) and causes it to grow (intensively and extensively)."[25] The church can truly act as the church—can be itself—only in the Spirit.

The irreversible relationship between the Spirit and the church is worth thinking about. Such irreversibility is derivative of a more basic truth, namely, the irreversibility in God of essence and existence, and of being and act. That is to say, the Spirit remains Lord or God in the Spirit's raising of sinners from the dead. The Spirit "quickens from above, from a distance, from God; from the God who dwells in light unapproachable."[26] Barth, however, does not take us any deeper than that. Nowhere does Barth in §67 or §62, while engaging in rich descriptions of the Spirit's work in relationship to Christ and the community, reflect on how the Spirit is God. Barth is happy to say that the Spirit is "from God" and to leave it at that. The discussion of the Spirit's procession from Father and Son undertaken in §12.2 is no doubt assumed but not extended.

Is Barth's account, then, bereft of further pneumatological insight? I think not. Only once does Barth in §67 tell us why he does not take the work of the Spirit and relate it—overtly, anyhow—to the Spirit's consubstantial unity with Father and Son. So Barth: "He [Jesus] is the One who exists in His *history* ... The being of the Head of the community is the event of the life of this man ... In heaven, hidden in God, *He whose being is this once for all act, this particular history* [emphasis mine]."[27] "He whose being is this once for all act" recalls, whether we are speaking of Son or Spirit, what Barth teaches in *CD* I, namely, that the Son and Spirit act as they are. Being, in other words, is predicated of their history, but not occasioned by their history. They do not have their being because of their history. However, their being is this history.

In making this move, Barth does not collapse God's being into God's act. God's being is the antecedent reality by which these acts occur. Barth's point is simply to remind us that the gathering, upbuilding, and perfecting of the Christian community by the Spirit is the work of *God* the Spirit. God is free to be himself, argues Barth, in creating, maintaining, and perfecting covenant fellowship with the

---

25. Ibid., 652.
26. Ibid., 653.
27. Ibid., 695, 696. The German runs, "*Im Himmel, in Gott verborgen, ist Er, dessen Sein dieser einmalige Akt, diese besondere Geschichte ist, das Haupt seiner Gemeinde.*"

creature. This God can and does so because God is the one who loves in freedom.

That Barth will not untether the Spirit from Christ reflects how things are in God. Barth writes that "the only content of the Holy Spirit is Jesus," pointing to something of a causal relation by which the Spirit originates in relationship to Jesus.[28] To be sure, Barth does not overtly "back up" to discuss the immanent procession of the Spirit. We do not hear of how this activity corresponds to God's life, to the originating relations by which the three are. And yet there are hints. Barth writes, "There is a real identity, not present in *abstracto*, but given by God and enacted in the mighty work of the Holy Spirit, between the Holy One, the kingdom of God as perfectly established in Him, and the communion of the saints on earth, which as such is also a communion of sinners ... It [the community] lives because and as its Lord lives."[29] The church lives in the Lord who is the Spirit. The Spirit's work of enacting a real identity between Jesus Christ and his community mirrors the unity of Christ and the Spirit from eternity.

The register of Barth's account is, as has been said, economic. Barth's point is that Jesus and his Spirit exist as they eternally are in this history of which the Christian community is the firstfruits. The being of Jesus and the being of the Spirit are present and given in the once-for-all act of reconciliation, "this particular history" where humanity is reconciled to the Father through the Son in the Spirit.[30] There cannot be any isolation of being from act; that, again, is not to say that Barth collapses being into act. It is to say, rather, that the Jesus who saves, who indeed rules, upholds, and orders his community, is "at every moment in the quickening power of the Holy Spirit."[31] It is to also say that Jesus' ruling and his Spirit's quickening attests that he with the Spirit is *God*, and that their common being is indicated in their indivisible acts, in this event of ruling and quickening. Accordingly, it is not being and then act, but being in act.

---

28. Ibid., 654.
29. Ibid., 656, 657.
30. Ibid., 696.
31. Ibid., 710.

THE SPIRIT AND THE SENDING OF THE CHRISTIAN COMMUNITY

In §72 (*The Holy Spirit and the Sending of the Christian Community*), Barth keeps reminding the reader that the Holy Spirit in sending the community is God. Although §72, oriented as it is to "the concept of the prophecy of Jesus Christ," contains few references to the actual work of the Spirit, the basic point regarding the Spirit's divinity remains present.[32]

As Barth expounds the prophecy of Christ, by which he means "this new thing [that is, the new reality] has already happened and is constantly shown to have already happened," we can understand something of the deep continuity between *CD* I/1 (§12.2) and *CD* IV/3.2 (§72). "The person who bears this name [Jesus Christ] ... is Himself God in His gracious address to the world."[33] Jesus addresses himself to us and claims us as God. Just as Barth wants to acknowledge the Son's divinity in all his works, the same is true of the Spirit. What Barth says of Jesus can be said of the Spirit insofar as the one who bears the name Holy Spirit "is Himself God."[34] The Spirit is God himself in the power that makes alive in relationship to Jesus Christ. The "immanent *Filioque*" functions in this paragraph to remind us that it is *God* who is at work here.[35]

Although the focus of Barth's account in §72 is Christ and "the new reality of world history" in him, and the task entrusted to the community as that of "attest[ing] this new thing to the world," the pneumatological dimension of Christ's prophecy is not shortchanged. Indeed, the "pneumatologico–ecclesiological" elucidates the "christologico–ecclesiological."[36] Barth puts it this way: the "order of grace" is also "the order of the act of the Holy Spirit," which is the "order of the being of Jesus Christ and His community."[37] The Christ who confronts us, Barth argues, is inseparable from his community. This is not to conflate Christ and his community, but it is to say that Christ wills to reflect himself in the community, however marginal and seemingly inconsequential its

---

32. Barth, *CD* IV/3.2, 681.
33. Ibid., 713, 710.
34. Ibid., 710.
35. Barth, *CD* I/1, 481.
36. Barth, *CD* IV/3.2, 758.
37. Ibid., 759.

existence may be.[38] Barth thinks that the very being of Jesus Christ has power, and that power is "the Holy Ghost who calls, gathers, enlightens and sanctifies all Christians on earth, keeping them in the true and only faith in Jesus Christ."[39]

Following Barth, the Spirit exercises the Spirit's agency only in relation to Jesus Christ. The Spirit undertakes the acts of an agent—the Spirit "calls, gathers, enlightens, sanctifies"—as God, "the power of the being of Jesus Christ in its relationship to the community."[40] "The Holy Spirit as his [Jesus's] Spirit" acts, which is to say, "Jesus Christ in the power of the Holy Spirit."[41] Jesus acts in the Spirit because he is a spiritual person. Jesus can never be isolated from the Spirit, in whom he exists. That Christ and the Spirit act as they do, that the Spirit is indeed the power and reality of Jesus' being, indicates "one and the same reality. But neither renders the other superfluous."[42] The Spirit's unique hypostatic or personal reality is not obviated by the Spirit's other-directedness, that is the Spirit's Christ-directedness. What we see, rather, is a person who *is* in relationship to the Father and through the Son.

Jesus Christ cannot "be reduced" to the Spirit. The one is not the other. The reason "neither is dispensable," that one is inseparable "from the other," the reason "neither can be true except as elucidated by the other," is that "the Holy Spirit is the power of God proper to the being of Jesus Christ in the exercise and operation of which he causes his community to become what it is."[43] Why is the Spirit proper to Jesus' being? What John Webster calls the "backward reference" supplies us with an answer.[44] So Barth: "Just as the Holy Spirit, as Himself an eternal divine 'person' or mode of being, as the Spirit of the Father and the Son (*qui ex Patre Filioque procedit*), is the bond of peace between the two, so in the historical work of reconciliation He is the One who constitutes and guarantees the unity of the *totus Christus* ... He is the One who constitutes and guarantees the unity in which He is at one and the same time the heavenly Head with God and the earthly body

---

38. See ibid., 745.
39. Ibid., 758.
40. Ibid.
41. Ibid., 752.
42. Ibid., 759.
43. Ibid., 759.
44. John Webster, *The Domain of the Word* (London: Bloomsbury/T&T Clark, 2012), 143.

with His community."[45] Barth grounds the uniting work of the Spirit as described in §12 in the perfection of God. Specifically, just as the Spirit binds Father to Son and Son to Father in God's life, so too does the Spirit bind the community to Christ, uniting the ascended Jesus with his earthly body, the Christian community. In short, the rationale for the Spirit's uniting of Christ with his community lies in God. The Spirit does among us what the Spirit does in God. The Spirit exists as the Spirit in God and just so as the Spirit among us.

The Spirit as "the bond of peace" between Father and Son is, Barth continues, the very "capacity and authority" of "the historical work of reconciliation."[46] The reconciliation that God in Christ achieves has the authority it does because it *is* spiritual. It is also as spacious as it is because it is spiritual. Barth's argument that the "christologico-ecclesiological" rests on the "pneumatologico-ecclesiological" thus comes to full fruition.[47] Christ is not only born among us of the Spirit, but his work of reconciliation has the effect it does only because of the Spirit. "The basis and secret of the people of God" is "two exalted names," Jesus Christ and the Holy Spirit.[48] Each is God; "neither can be separated from the other, but each is necessary to elucidate the other."[49] That "Jesus Christ acts and works and creates in and in relation to the Christian community by the Holy Spirit and therefore again in the mystery of God" indicates, Barth argues, the hypostatically eternal character of the Spirit.[50] The agency of the Spirit takes place in the name of Christ. The Spirit elucidates the name of Christ among us and in God. Barth thinks that it is in the Spirit that Father and Son come to one another in God's life, and in that same Spirit does the Father's Son come among us. The Spirit is the agent who as "an eternal divine 'person'"[51] will take what is Christ's and declare it to us (John 16:14).

Barth's moves make sense, exegetically speaking. The Spirit does seem to derive something of his life from the Son. Even as the Son is conceived by the Spirit and receives the empowering Spirit throughout

---

45. Barth, *CD* IV/3.2, 760.
46. John Webster, "Perfection and Participation," in *The Analogy of Being*, ed. Thomas Joseph White (Grand Rapids: Eerdmans, 2010), 385; Barth, *CD* IV/3.2, 760.
47. Barth, *CD* IV/3.2, 758.
48. Ibid., 752.
49. Ibid.
50. Ibid.
51. Ibid., 760.

his ministry, the Spirit has being in the glorifying of the Son, and thus the Father who glorifies himself in the Son. Here we see something of the Spirit's acts in God being extended into time. The Spirit lives by glorifying the Son, creating and upholding not only the Son's humanity but also his community, and perfecting them for all eternity to the glory of the Father. The Spirit's glorifying of the Son, his being breathed by the Son, his being given by him—"they all point back."[52]

The prophecy—prophetic speech—of Jesus Christ is intelligible only in the Spirit. Jesus speaks then and now in and by the Spirit. It is in and by the Spirit that Jesus Christ is present, that he transcends all of our yesterdays and todays, indeed, that women and men are able to call on him and receive him "in the life of His [Christ's] community of this or that century, land or place."[53] Again, it is by virtue of the Spirit's gracious act, the agency of the gracious Spirit, that there exists a "people of His [Christ's] witnesses in world-occurrence."[54] And this is so because the Spirit "is Himself God, *Dominus* [Lord], *vivificans* [life-giver], *cum Patre et Filio simul adorandus et glorificandus* [who with the Father and the Son is worshiped and glorified]."[55] The acts of the Holy Spirit explain not only who the Spirit is in God but how the Spirit originates. The mystery is that in God the who of the Spirit and the how of the Spirit are one. The Spirit is not someone who relates to the Father and Son but is the being, the relation, that comes forth from them.

BARTH'S RULE

The rule that emerges from our engagement with Barth in *CD* IV is that the acts of the Spirit explain who the Spirit is and provide a glimpse of how the Spirit originates. What and who is the Spirit? The Spirit is God, the one who glorifies the Son (John 16:14). Why does the Spirit do this? Because the Spirit *is* the love and life proceeding from the Father for the Son and the Son for the Father, from and to all eternity. The Lord of that love and life bears fruit in the form of the community of Jesus Christ, women and men who confess Christ, for "to confess Him is its [the community's] business."[56]

---

52. Webster, *Analogy of Being*, 383.
53. Barth, *CD* IV/3.2, 761.
54. Ibid., 762.
55. Ibid.
56. Ibid., 787.

Barth's account of the work of the Spirit and the sending of the Christian community can in many respects be heard as an extended commentary on John 16:13: "he [the Advocate] will not speak on his own, but will speak whatever he hears." What the Spirit speaks is Jesus Christ, and Jesus speaks only what he hears from the Father. What the Spirit hears—Jesus Christ, the Father's Word—is, as we have seen, a Word that generates a community. Jesus Christ ascended and seated at the right hand of the Father speaks and indeed comes, Barth argues, not in the flesh but in the Spirit. That Barth will not set the Spirit free from Jesus, just as Jesus will not describe himself apart from the Father, points in my view to the very depths of the perfection of the triune life. Just as Jesus has his existence now and in eternity from the Father who is the one who generates him, so too does the Spirit have the Spirit's "whence and whither," his "specific basis of existence" in the Son.[57]

At the same time, the Son is "in the Father" and therefore in the Spirit, whom the Father shares with the Son from eternity. It is these three who are nothing but these relations. The Spirit is not less than the other two, Barth argues, just because the Spirit is from them and the other two are not from the Spirit. Barth's sense that the Spirit does not exist on the Spirit's own but only in relation to the Son points to a causal truth, a truth about how the three exist. The Spirit's pattern of speaking only what he hears gives us a strained glimpse of how the Spirit originates by virtue of the other two. The Spirit's pattern of speech points to how the Spirit only speaks of the one through whom the Spirit is, the Son.

To sum up this section, I think that Barth's account of the "work of the prophecy of Jesus Christ Himself, or of the Holy Ghost" unfolds a basic truth about the divine life.[58] Jesus works in the Spirit—indeed, by the power of the Spirit, as one who from eternity is *in* the Spirit. The Spirit's consubstantiality with Father and Son is seen in the Spirit's attestation of Jesus, whose word (his prophecy) is not his own "but [is from] the Father who sent" him (John 12:49). The Spirit does not speak his own words but only those that the Spirit hears. What the Spirit hears from the Father is Christ and what the Spirit speaks is Christ. Accordingly, I think that Barth's christologically concentrated account of the Spirit's work helps us to see not only what and who but

---

57. Ibid., 830.
58. Ibid., 847.

also how the Spirit is in God. The Spirit establishes the community in Christ and therefore in his Father because the Spirit is *in* Christ, who is from the Father.

CONCLUSION

Barth's account of the Spirit helps us to understand what John 16:14—"He [the Spirit] will glorify me"—infers regarding God's life. With Barth, whether it be the material from *CD* I or *CD* IV, we see that the Spirit remains God in all that the Spirit does, never becoming our Spirit but rather remaining the Spirit of the Father and Son. The reason for this has to do with *how* the Spirit is in God. To be sure, Barth does not say anything that is fundamentally different from Augustine or Thomas. Barth also encourages Nicene orthodoxy. Having said that, Barth receives the witness of Scripture and the church's teaching tradition in a fresh way. Barth presses a point with which Augustine and Thomas are sympathetic.

Where Barth is most helpful, pneumatologically speaking, is in aiding us to see why we must say the kinds of things Augustine and Thomas have said. Why the talk of who and how the Spirit is in God? Because the New Testament encourages such talk. By such talk are we reminded that it is truly God at work to seek and to save. Specifically, the New Testament teaches that God remains God in all that God does for us and for our salvation. *God* the Spirit glorifies the Son and in him the Father, and in so doing he gives us a share in that glory. Barth's other-directed account of the Spirit in *CD* IV helps us to see the mystery of the Spirit's hypostasis as intelligible primarily in relation to an "of," the Spirit *of* the Son. The "of" arises in God's life, uniting Father and Son and us to them.

Barth affirms with Augustine and Thomas the basic premise of pneumatological teaching, the immanent dimension (the eternal Spirit). This dimension is the premise of a history, yes, but a history in which the Spirit is God. The Spirit acts as God in this history on the basis of the relation to Father and Son that the Spirit is. Put differently, the capacity for the Spirit's work lies on the immanent level. It is only because of the pure act that God is that there is an economy of grace in the first place. Accordingly, the "of" is what qualifies the Spirit to do what he does: the Spirit is the one breathed by the relations of Father

163

and Son from eternity and therefore among us in a sanctifying way. Barth understands that acts denote unique properties or characteristics that point to how the three come to be in relation to one another. The Spirit's glorification of the Son among us reflects what the Spirit does in eternity.

This chapter extended the previous chapter inasmuch as we noticed how Barth describes twice the same ground. The Spirit who fills Jesus and whom Jesus breathes is *his* Spirit, whom Jesus shares with the Father as he receives his being from eternity from the Father. Barth thinks that John's gospel encourages such talk. The rationale for the Spirit's declaration of the Son arises in God's life, and the soteriological payoff of such talk is immense. Through the Spirit are we related to the Father in the Son. By the Spirit is the Son's relationship to the Father repeated in us. This is why Barth's account of the Spirit repeatedly presses the same point regarding the Spirit's remaining God in sanctifying the creature.

Those who hear Jesus receive his Spirit. Jesus knows them, and they know Jesus just "as the Father knows Him and He the Father."[59] Salvation is a matter of knowing the Father as does the Son, who gives us his Spirit. This is again why Barth so emphasizes the point about God being God in all that God does. It allows us to say, following the New Testament, that to know God as God truly is, is life, eternal life. Life in the Spirit is a matter of the Son knowing us and us knowing him "as the Father knows Him and He the Father."[60] By the Spirit does Jesus live in us through faith. Barth's account deeply complements and extends the two that have gone before. As we will see in a moment, Barth's treatment encourages us to talk about a few more key themes whose principle of intelligibility lies in the being and identity of the Spirit. Those themes have to do with the question "What does the Spirit do?" The next section answers this question.

---

59. Barth, *CD* II/2, 780.
60. Ibid.

PART 4

CORRELATES

REGENERATION, CHURCH, AND TRADITION

REGENERATED SIGHT

A LOOK BACK AND A LOOK AHEAD

In this chapter, we make a transition. We move away from a systematic engagement with the metaphysics of the Spirit with respect to the Fourth Gospel and toward other themes that teaching on the Spirit should engage, namely, regeneration (chapter 8) and church and tradition (chapter 9). In order to reflect well on regeneration and faith, I introduce the motif of sight. Sight provides a useful way into a sketch of regeneration. In what follows, I will reflect in a fairly ad hoc way with Augustine principally, and Thomas and Barth secondarily, so as to articulate the kind of sight simultaneous with regeneration. I think this is a fitting move, given the ground covered thus far.

Following the New Testament witness, regeneration involves us in the domain of the Spirit. It is the work of God the Spirit toward the outside. The Spirit does not regenerate in God's life, because God's life is perfect and complete in itself. Rather, it is we who need regeneration and faith. Although the Spirit's activity toward the outside is utterly consistent with the Spirit's relatedness to the Father and Son in God's life, it is not the same. The works of the Spirit in regenerating and giving rise to faith are a consequence of the Spirit's procession in God and the fruit of the Spirit's mission among us.

Why do regeneration and faith only now become independent themes and subjects of our discussion in this book? The reason is that we have to talk first about what qualifies the Spirit to act before we can understand what the Spirit does. The previous six chapters have unfolded what qualifies the Spirit to do what the Spirit does in terms of Augustine's, Thomas's, and Barth's thought in light of the Fourth

Gospel. What we discovered is that who the Spirit is in God—"*the being spirated by the Father through the Son*" — is what grounds an account of the Spirit's mission and the works it accomplishes.[1] Hence regeneration and faith, as well as the sight concomitant with them, extend first principles.[2] Without talk of first principles, it is impossible to answer a question like "Why does the Spirit not regenerate us in the Spirit but only in Christ?" The Spirit regenerates in Christ because the Spirit comes from him; Christ breathes the Spirit, not the other way around, precisely because that is how things are in God. But again, why? Because the three accomplish among us works that are utterly consistent with and manifest who each is in God. For example, because the Father *is* the generating of the Son, it follows that the Father sends the Son. It is now time to unfold these themes, sensitive to what they teach us about the identity of the agent(s) who accomplish(es) them.

JOHN 3:5, THOMAS, AND SPIRITUAL REGENERATION

We begin our account of regeneration with Thomas's reading of John 3:5. It is helpful because it emphasizes the eschatological character of regeneration and its connection with baptism. Thomas also has interesting things to say about how regeneration is related to sight. Thomas begins by discussing the "spiritual regeneration" evident "in the New Law," the new covenant. Spiritual regeneration is inward and "by grace" rather than outward and "by incorruption."[3] This dynamic points to the eschatological character of regeneration. Thomas cites 2 Corinthians 4:16 in explaining the difference between "by grace" and "by incorruption": "Even though our outer nature is wasting away, our inner nature is being renewed day by day." We do *see*, indeed, enter into Jesus' kingdom here and now, Thomas argues, but only imperfectly. Such sight is possible only by grace. And yet we shall one day see without corruption, unshackled from what "is wasting away." Grace works its way from the inner to the outer. The renewal of the inner

---

1. Denys Turner, *Thomas Aquinas: A Portrait* (New Haven, CT: Yale University Press, 2013), 126.
2. Ibid.
3. Saint Thomas Aquinas, *Commentary on the Gospel of John* (Washington, D.C.: Catholic University of America Press, 2010), 433, 1:165.

being anticipates the eschatological renewal of the outer, our bodies. So Thomas: "But there is perfect regeneration in heaven, because we will be renewed both inwardly and outwardly. And therefore we shall see the kingdom of God in a most perfect way."[4] Spiritual vision or sight is the eschatological fruit of "perfect regeneration."

How does the Spirit bring about such sight? The Spirit uses water. Thomas, commenting on John 3:5, gives three reasons for this. First, Thomas argues that the Spirit takes up water because of the condition of human nature. "For man consists of soul and body, and if the Spirit alone were involved in his regeneration, this would indicate that only the spiritual part of man is regenerated. Hence in order that the flesh also be regenerated, it is necessary that, in addition to the Spirit through whom the soul is regenerated, something bodily be involved, through which the body is regenerated; and this is water."[5] Water unfolds the character of the Spirit's regeneration of the "spiritual part of man" but also "the body." Thomas argues that John 3:5, in recording Christ as saying "without being born of water," teaches that our rebirth involves not only the spiritual dimension but also the material.

Second, water is "necessary for the sake of human knowledge."[6] Our natural way of knowing "spiritual things" is "by means of sensible things, since all our knowledge begins in sense knowledge. Therefore, in order that we might understand what is spiritual in our regeneration, it was fitting that there be in it something sensible and material, that is, water, through which we understand that just as water washes and cleanses the exterior in a bodily way, so through baptism a man is washed and cleansed inwardly in a spiritual way."[7] Thomas thinks that our regeneration, spiritual as it is, is attested in a material way via water. The waters of baptism illuminate in an outward sense inward spiritual cleansing.

The third and final reason Thomas gives as to why water is intrinsic to regeneration has to do with the Word. It is also the most interesting. Thomas writes, "Water was necessary so that there might be a correspondence of causes for our regeneration in the incarnate Word."[8] Rebirth and renewal by the Spirit is one cause of regeneration, just as rebirth and renewal in the waters of baptism is another. The two causes

---

4. Ibid.
5. Ibid., 168.
6. Ibid.
7. Ibid.
8. Ibid.

correspond to one another in the Word. Water and Spirit "cause" regeneration *in* the Word. Of course, the water has no agency of its own; it only causes rebirth because of the Spirit's use of it. The Spirit is the agent of regeneration—following John 3:5. However, Thomas does not forget that the Spirit inheres in the Word, and so is the Word also said to regenerate.

This last point in Thomas's discussion of the Spirit's use of water, following John 3:5, illuminates the *mutuality* of Spirit and Son in regeneration. On the one hand, Jesus Christ is the agent of regeneration. On the other hand, by the Spirit do we indwell Christ, and so is regeneration said to be *from* the Holy Spirit. All that said, the distinct agency of the Son and the distinct agency of the Spirit in regenerating manifests what is true of their life together in God. Thomas gives us a glimpse of this when he writes that "we are regenerated as sons of God, in the likeness of his true Son."[9] Note that we are not regenerated as sons and daughters of the Spirit but only of the Son. The Spirit does not birth us in the Spirit's self but only in the Son, which is fitting, given that in God the Spirit is the love proceeding, love by which Father and Son love one another.[10] So Thomas: "Therefore, it is necessary that our spiritual regeneration comes about through that by which we are made like the true Son and this comes about by our having his Spirit."[11] Christ's Spirit, says Thomas, makes us like him. That is the Spirit's mission. Spiritual regeneration is *from* the Spirit of the Son. The Spirit does not makes us like the Spirit but "like the true Son." We are made like the Son by "a spirit of adoption" (Rom 8:15). Why is this? Because the pattern of the Son's and Spirit's working in regeneration corresponds to how things are in God. Why are we regenerated as sons and daughters in the Son rather than the Spirit? Thomas thinks that it has to do with the Spirit's identity in the Trinity. Because the Spirit is breathed from the Father through the beloved Son, the Spirit truly regenerates in the Son. The direction of the Spirit's regenerative work expresses the divine

---

9. Ibid., 167.

10. I think it would be fair to say that Sarah Coakley would be quite critical of this way of phrasing things. This would arguably be an instance of the Spirit becoming "the secondary communicator of an already privileged dyad of Father and Son." See *God, Sexuality, and the Self* (Cambridge: Cambridge University Press, 2013), 101. However, I do not think this is the case, given that "the mystery proper of the Holy Spirit" is of one "who manifests Himself by manifesting the divine Word." See Boris Bobrinskoy, *The Mystery of the Trinity* (Crestwood, NY: St. Vladimir's Seminary Press, 1999), 25.

11. Aquinas, *Commentary on John*, 442, 1:167–68.

life itself. Because the Spirit is from the Son, the Spirit unites us to the Son, and in him to the Father.

In summing up this section, I ask, "What can we take from Thomas?" as we begin to sketch an account of spiritual regeneration and the sight intrinsic to it. In describing regeneration following John 3:5, we should recognize its inward and outward dimensions. The inward man is being renewed day by day in the Spirit. Water baptism indicates the form that renewal takes. The Spirit is at work mortifying the flesh and vivifying in Christ. The outward man is also no less the focus of the Spirit's renewal, although its perfection is an eschatological reality. While one waits patiently for the Son's coming again in glory, and thus one's own rising in glory, one lives, to use Barth's nice turn of phrase, "with Christ in penitence."[12] But of course to be "with Christ in penitence" is to be with Christ "also in confidence."[13] Such penitence and confidence come about by the awakening power of the Spirit to faith.[14] Thomas understands that mortification of the flesh is only one dimension of the Spirit's regeneration of us in Christ, for the Spirit mortifies in order also to raise us to new bodily life, which is precisely what the Spirit's use of water in baptism teaches. Indeed, we do not remain in the waters but are raised, inwardly cleansed. By the Spirit, we can really live as if sin and its concomitant death are no more. In keeping with this, Thomas's reading of John 3:5 complements this book's thesis, because he helps us to see something of how the agency of Son and Spirit in regeneration reflects the divine life itself. The pattern of their working reflects an immanent reality, their origins in God.

AUGUSTINE ON REGENERATE VISION

In this section, we think about sight in conversation with Augustine. From him, we learn a few key features of the content of regenerated sight. Augustine begins one of the most pneumatologically concentrated sections of *On the Trinity* (15.5) with these words: "Now we must discuss the Holy Spirit as far as it is granted us with God's help to *see* [emphasis mine] him."[15] How do we see the Spirit, especially in

---

12. Barth, *CD* IV/1, 775.
13. Ibid.
14. See ibid., 778.
15. Saint Augustine, *The Trinity*, part 1, vol. 5 of *The Works of Saint Augustine* (Hyde Park, NY: New City, 1991), 15.5.27.

a manner that agrees with Augustine's description of the Spirit as "the common charity by which the Father and the Son love each other?"[16] We begin to see this, Augustine argues, by submitting to the divine Word itself. Sight is generated by the word.[17] The divine Word, writes Augustine, "has made us search with greater diligence into things that are not set out in open display, but have to be explored in obscurity and dragged out of obscurity."[18] Augustine searches to see how the Spirit is in God, indeed to drag this truth out of obscurity.

Forceful language

Sight derivative of the Word coincides with love. One does not strive to see so as to master or dominate but in order to love. To see is to love. "Unless therefore the Holy Spirit is imparted to someone to make him a lover of God and neighbour, he cannot transfer from the left hand to the right."[19] One cannot see God or love God out of resources internal to the self or the community. Sight is not a Pelagian endeavour. Rather, God is loved by God's Spirit, just as Father and Son love one another by that same Spirit. We *see* something of the Spirit's procession in God by loving and receiving the Spirit as the gift of God.

The love for God that the Spirit creates among us has a particular shape. That shape reflects the Spirit's immanent identity as love *in* God. This is why it is important to *see* how the Spirit is in God. To recall a now familiar Augustinian emphasis: "the Spirit is distinctively called by the term charity, although both Father and Son are charity in a general sense."[20] In "the inseparable trinity," the Spirit "is the gift of God who is love."[21] Why go down this path in developing an account of regenerate sight? Without an account of the Spirit as "the love which is from God and is God," we would not see where this love comes from.[22] "Scriptural evidence," Augustine argues, "conspires to prove that the Holy Spirit is the gift of God, in that he is given to those who love God through him."[23] The Scriptures prove the Spirit's identity among those who love God through that same Spirit.

The kind of sight that Augustine encourages is intellectual. It sees

---

16. Ibid.
17. Ibid.
18. Ibid.
19. Ibid., 5.31.
20. Ibid.
21. Ibid.
22. Ibid., 5.32. See Romans 5:5, one of Augustine's preferred Pauline texts: "God's love has been poured into our hearts through the Holy Spirit that has been given to us."
23. Ibid., 5.36.

how the Spirit is God. "So he [the Spirit] is the gift of God insofar as he is given to those he is given to. But in himself he is God even if he is not given to anyone, because he was God, co-eternal with the Father and the Son, even before he was given to anyone. Nor is he less than they because they give and he is given. He is given as God's gift in such a way that as God he also gives himself."[24] We confess that the Spirit is given in God. Because the Spirit is God in this relation of givenness, the Spirit is gift among us. The latter rests upon the former. Sight of and love for this mystery is the fruit of regeneration. Father and Son "give," to be sure, and what is given is the Spirit. Because the Spirit is given in God, the Spirit is given as gift to us. The Spirit "is given" in God and therefore among us as gift.

The mystery after which Augustine quests is how the Spirit can be said to be common to Father and Son and yet not subordinate to them. It is intellectual sight of this mystery that Augustine is after. Father and Son are charity, but charity is also what the Spirit "is called distinctively."[25] All three are love, but the Spirit is love in a distinct sense. That the Spirit is love (charity) in God is because the Spirit *proceeds* as love from the Father. The Spirit cannot author anything other than love, for that is what the Spirit *is*. However, unlike the Son, who is eternally born of the Father, the Spirit proceeds eternally from the Father and/ through the Son. Accordingly, the Spirit "is not a Son though he (the Spirit) proceeds from the Father."[26] The Spirit proceeds from the Son too, but the Son has this only from the Father. The Spirit has a different originating relation with respect to the Father than the Son does— proceeding rather than begetting—and so is love in a different way. Only the Spirit is "given as God's gift."[27]

A regenerate vision glimpses—however obliquely—things as they are. It contemplates how the Spirit originates in God, the mystery of the Holy Spirit's proceeding "simultaneously from" Father and Son as their love.[28] The new birth enables sight of this mystery. Sight, however, is frail. If one cannot see the Spirit due to "infirmities," Augustine does not recommend despair.[29] Instead, he encourages prayer. Jesus heals us

---

24. Ibid.
25. Ibid.
26. Ibid., 5.45.
27. Ibid., 5.36.
28. Ibid., 5.48.
29. Ibid., 5.50.

of our infirmities, enabling us by his Spirit to pray with Augustine: "I have sought and desired to *see* intellectually what I have believed ... Let me remember you, let me understand you, let me love you."[30] Seeing is the fruit, the concomitant, of regeneration. Augustine encourages us to see intellectually what the scriptural word teaches regarding the Spirit's origin in God.

God is love, and the Spirit is love, "both God and from God."[31] In an arresting quote, Augustine relates the gaze of faith to Christ's cross, a gaze that can be extended to the Spirit. Augustine writes, "Christ is never going to be seen on the cross again; but unless we believe that he was once so to be seen, in a manner in which there would be no expectation of seeing him again, we shall not come to see Christ as he is to be seen forever."[32] To see Christ forever is to see him as he was once seen—crucified. To see him "as he is to be seen forever" is to see him as one who died for our salvation. In a pneumatological register, to see the Holy Spirit is to see the Spirit as the love of God and from God, and thus the love by which we love God. One can only appreciate the Spirit's ministry by the Spirit's shedding the love of God abroad in our hearts (Rom 5:5).

In sum, I think sight is an important dimension of regeneration. It reminds us of the intellectual character of regeneration, the renewal of the mind in accord with the truth of God. If we follow Augustine in these matters, as I think we should, love of God is not so much a consequence of sight but simultaneous with it. We are reborn from above through the Spirit in the waters of baptism to see and love. Hence the language of sight serves a useful purpose in Augustine's hands. Augustine encourages us to see that the love with which we love God originates in God. We get a glimpse of this as we ask where the love that the Spirit sheds abroad in our hearts comes from.

REGENERATION AND PERFECTION

John 21:15–19 is a remarkable portion of Scripture with which to conclude the treatment of regenerated sight. In this passage, love and martyrdom are connected. Christ calls Peter to perfect love for him,

---

30. Ibid., 5.51.
31. Ibid., 5.37.
32. Ibid., 5.49.

love that will eventuate in a death that Peter would not wish. The source of that love is the Spirit. The Spirit from whom regeneration comes makes sinners perfect. Although the Spirit is not named in the text, reading it in a pneumatological register goes with its grain. I will attempt to show this by noting the extent to which the kind of sight that we discussed via Augustine in the previous section, simultaneous as it is with love, is costly. Augustine and Thomas have helpful comments to make on the costliness of love's perfection and what its source is in God.

The story's tenor is that of refreshment. Thomas writes of Jesus' provision of breakfast to the seven disciples that "it is appropriate that the one who is raised to this office [of shepherd] be already refreshed with his joyous meal."[33] Jesus' encounter with those gathered on the beach is couched from the outset in grace. We see this grace manifested in Jesus' physical care for them. Jesus' stern words to Peter about his death are preceded by the provision of food. The fact that Jesus prepares a meal, that he meets with refreshment those who only a few days before absconded from him, is but a reminder of the far greater thing: that Jesus died and was raised for them. Indeed, the mission Jesus gives to Peter—"feed my sheep"—rests on Jesus' death and his provision of all things necessary. So Augustine: "For the needful order was that Christ should first die for Peter's salvation, and then that Peter should die for the preaching of Christ."[34]

Jesus knows that Peter is scared and fearful, even though in Jesus' death, death and the fear of death itself have died. So before Jesus tells Peter of the death that awaits him, he feeds him after having died for him, and then and only then asks of him, "Do you love me?" A three-fold confession of love follows. Of this Augustine writes, "Let it be the office of love to feed the Lord's flock, if it was the signal of death to deny the Shepherd."[35] Peter's denial of Christ, rooted as it was in his fear of death, is overcome: "Why should he be afraid, since he now realized that death had died?"[36] Why should Peter be afraid to display the Lord's love by feeding his people? Augustine asks.

---

33. Aquinas, *Commentary on John*, 2616, 3:294.
34. Augustine, Tractate 113.4.
35. Ibid., 5.
36. Aquinas, *Commentary on John*, 2617, 3:295. It is worth noting, as does Thomas, following Augustine, that "Peter does not answer with the same word, but says **I love *(amo)* you**, as if they were the same. And they are the same in reality, but there is some difference in meaning: Love *(amor)* is a movement of appetitive power, and if this is regulated by our reason it is the will's act of love, which is called 'direction' *(delectio)*." See ibid., 297.

Sheep are fed, Thomas avers, in three ways. First, "by being taught"; second, "by example"; and third, "by being offered temporal help."[37] Thomas follows this up with a winsome comment on "three types of people in the Church: beginners, those who have made some progress, and the perfect."[38] Who are the perfect? The perfect are those who love. It is love for Jesus that is to structure Peter's feeding of the sheep, even though it will result in his death. In Thomas's words, "'You shall love the Lord your God with all your heart,' so that you will direct your entire intention to God, 'and with all your soul,' so that your entire will might rest in God through love, 'and with all your might,' so that the performance of all your actions will serve God."[39] To teach the sheep, to lead by example, and to help the sheep in a material sense is what the perfect do. Love for Christ has that shape. It is that love to which Peter is called.

The perfect, the third type of person in the church, is the one whom Jesus would desire Peter to become. Before Christ conquered death, Peter "had a desire for eternal life apart from the grievousness of death."[40] Christ, having already breathed the Spirit, elicits from Peter a confession of "love that ought, in one who feedeth His sheep, to grow up into so great a spiritual fervor as to overcome even the natural fear of death, that makes us willing to die even when we wish to live with Christ."[41] Jesus knows that Peter will suffer death, "shalt be crucified."[42] The confession of love, the desire for eternal life that Peter has, will not be negated by "the grievousness of death."[43] What has changed for Peter and for us too in the light of Christ's destruction of death is that death's grievousness has lost its sting: "It ought to be overcome by the power of that love which is felt to Him who, being our life, was willing to endure even death in our behalf."[44] All of one's intentions, will, and actions are to evidence love for him who endured "even death on our behalf."[45]

Left to his own devices, Peter would continue to disown Christ. In

---

37. Ibid.
38. Ibid., 298.
39. Ibid.
40. Augustine, Tractate 113.5.
41. Ibid.
42. Ibid.
43. Ibid.
44. Ibid.
45. Ibid.

Barth's words, "Neither in the community nor the world is there anyone who is not shamed by Him as Peter is when measured by Jesus."[46] Shame, the fear of death, and death's grievousness are all too much to bear for Peter. Peter, as we do, wants to be a disciple apart from death's grievousness. Fortunately, his (and our) fear is not the last word when confronted with the imperative "Feed my sheep" and what is to become of him in fidelity to that mission: "You will stretch out your hands, and someone else will fasten a belt around you and take you where you do not wish to go" (John 21:18). Fear is not the last word because the one who breathed the Spirit on them continues to breathe the Spirit on him (and us).[47] The shepherds ought to "imitate the Shepherd" and can do so only by the powerful working of the Spirit.[48] So Hoskyns: "Peter's destiny is the complete *imitatio Christi*."[49]

The pneumatological register of this passage although implicit is nonetheless profound. Love for Jesus as reflected in the charge to Peter is love that is of the Holy Spirit. "I am coming to you," says Jesus (John 14:18). Christ comes to us in his Spirit, the Spirit who is love and from God. It is in the Spirit that we see, that we love because the Spirit *is* the love whereby Jesus is loved. The love by which we love Jesus is the Spirit. Such love comes from God, and such love is God as the gift of the love of the Father for the Son and the Son for the Father. Peter will be led to that place where he stretches out his arms because love for Jesus—the Spirit's love for Jesus—propels him. This is again the love whereby Peter loves the one who has conquered death and so his own fear of death. "He will glorify me, because he will take what is mine and declare it to you" (John 16:14). It is by the Spirit that Peter "would glorify God" (John 21:19) in death, because the Spirit sheds love abroad in his heart.

In sum, all of the immanent talk, especially on Augustine's and Thomas's part, of the Spirit as "the gift of God who is love" makes sense of this text, whose central theme is love.[50] The love by which Peter will love Christ unto death is the Holy Spirit. It is the Spirit who will enable Peter and the rest of the apostles and us in them to direct our entire intentions, our will, and all of our actions toward God, to

---

46. Barth, *CD* IV/2, 388.
47. See John 20:19–23.
48. Augustine, Tractate 113.5.
49. E. C. Hoskyns, *The Fourth Gospel* (London: Faber and Faber, 1942), 2:665.
50. Augustine, *Trinity*, 15.31.

imitate Christ to death.[51] This is what the regenerate heart does. It seeks the perfection of its love for Christ in one who is that love, the Spirit.

CONCLUSION

The aim of this chapter has been to show how a corollary theme—regeneration—does not take us far from first principles. Quite the contrary, our brief discussion of regenerative sight not only traded on the Spirit's procession in God but also saw how the Spirit's mission accomplishes love. Thomas's commentary on John 3:5 helped us to see regeneration's eschatological dimension and the Spirit's use of water in bringing the Spirit's regeneration home to us. Moreover, by revisiting some of Augustine's deepest pneumatological writings, we saw how matters that seem, scripturally speaking, oblique are nonetheless to be dragged out of obscurity to be seen. What Augustine sees is the fruit of a regenerated intelligence. Augustine sees the Spirit as given in God as God, and therefore given to us by God as the gift of God poured out into our hearts. Jesus' encounter with Peter, his commission of Peter to an absolute imitation of him even unto death, is a mission rooted in love. We asked, Where does this love come from? It comes from the Spirit. Although the Spirit is not named in the discourse in John 21, Augustine's reflections on the Spirit help us to see that the love with which Peter is to love Jesus is the Spirit. By the Spirit do we love Jesus. Such love is but the fruit of sight, the very perfection of love.

Having discussed the contours of a regenerate vision, we now turn to other correlates, church and tradition. It is fitting and right to do so. The Spirit in whom we believe in Christ takes us to church to hear Christ speak through the proclaimed Word and to feed on him in the sacred Supper. I think pneumatology must indeed talk about the church, the "earthly historical form" of Christ's existence, because in leading us to Christ, the Spirit leads us to Christ's people, his body.[52] By the Christian community, the body of Christ, are we kept by Christ in eternal life. Moreover, intrinsic to an account of the church is tradition. We will distinguish between Tradition and tradition(s). I argue that we are faithful to the latter only to the extent that it encourages fidelity to

---

51. See again Aquinas, *Commentary on John*, 2626, 3:298.
52. This is again Barth's preferred description for the Christian community. See, e.g., *CD* IV/2, 60.

the former. Tradition is used by God to lead us afresh to the apostolic testimony. The relationship between the two is instrumental but not accidental. In unfolding the church and tradition, we will see a similar dynamic take place as in this chapter. The who and how of the Spirit in God not only inform what is said about the church and tradition, but talk about church and tradition is derivative of them. The church and tradition are best explained in relationship to the first principles that Augustine, Thomas, and Barth have helped us articulate.

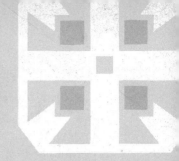

CHAPTER 9

CHURCH AND TRADITION

INTRODUCTION

A good friend of mine says we live "in an age of inflated talk about the church."[1] I think he is right. In the strange world that is the province of Aotearoa, New Zealand, and Polynesia, where I minister, expressions like "doing church" abound. Such expressions indicate a basic level of confusion about what the church is. They suggest the church is something that happens because of our efforts. This is a thoroughly unhelpful and indeed Pelagian way of thinking, dependent as it is upon our efforts to realize a purported ideal: church.[2] There is, I argue in this chapter, a much more profitable way of thinking about the church. Such thinking has its source in who the Spirit is in God and what the Spirit does. Church and tradition are derivative teachings. What we say about them will be true to the extent we depend on the first principles to unfold them. In what follows, I will cast a vision of the church and tradition as derivative of God's life.

The church is a theological reality, gathered, upbuilt, and sent in relationship to Christ and the Spirit he breathes. Likewise, tradition—

---

1. My friend is Joseph L. Mangina, a former teacher, and the quote comes from a book proposal of Mangina's titled *The Vine: A Johannine Experiment in Ecclesiology.*

2. Historically speaking, Pelagius was one who did theological battle with Augustine over the nature of grace, over the extent to which the will was able to respond in and of its own accord to God's grace. For Pelagius, the human is capable of willing what God requires of him or her. Quite the opposite for Augustine: the will is bound. Apart from the working of grace, it will remain enamored with sin and death. Analytically speaking, Pelagianism denotes a way of thinking about Christian teaching that assumes an inflated account of the person, or the community's capacities, to live in harmony with Jesus Christ.

understood as a "living theology ... the living environment that forms the body of the church"—is not separable from the Spirit's revelation of knowledge and truth.[3] Accordingly, tradition works to aid the church in hearing the Word and calling on the Holy Spirit. The church is not founded on itself but on the perfect life of the Holy Trinity as the church's principle of intelligibility. God's self-communication is "of its essence generative of history."[4] This is true not only of the created order but of the church and the tradition that arises in the church whereby the mystery of Christ is continually professed.

As with the previous chapter on regenerated sight, I continue to mine motifs in John's gospel. The pointers I offer regarding church and tradition extend Augustine's, Thomas's, and Barth's insights regarding some of the ecclesial images predominant in the Fourth Gospel, namely, the temple, the sheepfold, and the vine.[5] John's gospel continues to serve as a medium not only to strengthen the deepest insights arrived at thus far regarding the life of the Spirit in God and among us but also to say a few things about what the church is and about what the church does. In the pages that follow, I will talk about the church as a creature of not just the Son and Spirit but of the three, how Jesus' body is said to create a body, and why the church as Christ's body cannot be conflated with its head. After that, I will say a few words about what I think the church must do, if indeed its life is to point to and to contemplate the life by which it arises. Last, I will briefly reflect on tradition. I hope to show that what is said about tradition could not be said were it not for talk of the Spirit's procession in God and among us.

THE CHURCH AS THE WORK OF THE THREE

The famous first article of the *Theological Declaration* of the Synod of Barmen, May 31, 1934, begins by appealing to two scriptural references, John 14:6 and John 10:1, 9. The commentary that follows reads, "Jesus Christ, as He is attested to us in Holy Scripture, is the one Word

---

3. Boris Bobrinskoy, *The Mystery of the Trinity* (Crestwood, NY: St. Vladimir's Seminary Press, 1999), 7.

4. Yves Congar, *Tradition and Traditions: An Historical and a Theological Essay* (London: Burns and Oates, 1966), 264, quoted in John Webster's review essay of the same, "Purity and Plenitude: Evangelical Reflections on Congar's *Tradition and Traditions*," in *Yves Congar: Theologian of the Church*, ed. Gabriel Flynn (Leuven: Peeters, 2005), 54.

5. While this is the order of treatment in John's gospel (John 2, 10, 14), note that I do not treat these images in that order.

of God, whom we have to hear and whom we have to trust and obey in life and in death."

By way of background, briefly, Adolf Hitler was elected chancellor of Germany only a year before, in 1933. The Evangelical (Protestant) Church in Germany was, in Barth's words, forced "to recognise in the political events of the year 1933, and especially in the form of God-sent Adolf Hitler, a source of specific new revelation of God, which, demanding obedience and trust, took its place beside the revelation attested in Holy Scripture, claiming that it should be acknowledged by Christian proclamation and theology as equally binding and obligatory."[6] In other words, the church in this frightening new situation must recognize not only the voice of Jesus as binding but also other voices, namely, Hitler's.

Barth, the principal author of the Barmen Declaration, knew all too well that "God's revelation in Jesus Christ and faith and obedience to Him are 'also' not actually to be reduced to silence and oblivion."[7] God's revelation in Jesus Christ is radically exclusive, demanding a hearing that must not be supplemented or interpreted with other voices. The issue then (as now) was that of other voices besides the voice of the living Word having their way in the church.

What prevents voices such as those of "nature, reason and history" from aligning with Jesus Christ and thus having their way in the church?[8] In short, Jesus Christ as attested to us in the Bible. So Barth: "The fact is that, when nothing else was left for the Church, the one Word of God who is called Jesus Christ remained ... The Word of God still remained, in spite of everything, in the same Church in which it has been so often denied and betrayed."[9] Despite the fact that very few in the Evangelical Church in Germany abided in the Word (those who did forming the somewhat fractious Confessing Church), the Word remained faithful, preserving a remnant "against all expectation ... When it [the church] had lost all its counselors and helpers, in the one Word of God, who is called Jesus Christ, it still had God for its comfort."[10]

Note that the first article of Barmen (as with the others) does not

---

6. Barth, *CD* II/1, 173.
7. Ibid.
8. Ibid., 174.
9. Ibid., 176.
10. Ibid.

stand on its own: the text of the Declaration stands on Scripture. Indeed, one must understand "everything" from the vantage point of John 14 and John 10: "The emphasis of everything said previously lies in the fact that Jesus Christ has said something, and, what is more, has said it about Himself ... I myself am the door. The Church lives by the fact that it hears the voice of this 'I' and lays hold of the promise which, according to this voice, is contained in this 'I' alone; that therefore it chooses the way, knows the truth, lives the life, goes through the door, which is Jesus Christ Himself alone."[11] An evangelical account of the church lies here: "The Church lives by the fact that it hears the Word of God to which it can give entire trust and obedience."[12] The Word, Jesus Christ, who is "the gate" by which the sheep enter the sheepfold (John 10:1), "has founded ... upholds and renews and rules, and continually saves the Church."[13] The church is a theological reality. Jesus constitutes the church, saves it from itself, and in so doing saves it for himself, for a life of love for and service to his gospel. That is the first point to be made.

What about the Spirit? The church exists in relationship to the gate. Apart from the Lord Jesus Christ, the church cannot be. That much is clear. In making this point, we must also say that the church, in preaching the Word by which it lives, proclaims "the Lord who is the Spirit" (2 Cor 3:17). The Word is heard by the Spirit he gives "without measure" (John 3:34). It is the Spirit who draws us to "the gate" by which we enter "the sheepfold" (John 10:1). The Spirit opens Christ to us, and in so doing the church comes to be. The Spirit is the one by whom we enter the community of the sheep. Indeed, the Spirit's voice informs the sheep of their true identity as sheep. "He [the gatekeeper] calls his own sheep by name and leads them out," yet always remains "ahead of them" (John 10:3–4). Interestingly, John refers to Jesus' discourse as "this figure of speech" (John 10:6). Even though Jesus' disciples "did not understand what he was saying to them," we can hear Jesus' discourse as a kind of Trinitarian "figure of speech" that helps us gain a better sense of what the church is (John 10:6).

The sheep live by the gate and are sustained by the voice of the gatekeeper. The one who enters by the gate "will be saved" (John

---

11. Ibid., 177.
12. Ibid.
13. Ibid., 178.

10:9), and whoever continues to listen to the voice of the gatekeeper "will not follow a stranger" (John 10:5). "Through the Gospels," Boris Bobrinskoy notes, "what unfolds in the life of Christ is the Trinitarian Revelation. Thus, to speak of Christ is to speak of the Holy Spirit and of the Father (and vice versa) ... the life of Christ and the presence of the Spirit coincide totally and perfectly. The Spirit in Jesus and Jesus in the Spirit, in a total transparency and reciprocity."[14] We see this on display in John 10:1–10. We have "the gate" and "the gatekeeper." Both keep the sheep, as is the case with Christ and the Spirit "in a total transparency and reciprocity."[15] The Spirit gives the eyes with which to see, the ears with which to hear. With such eyes and ears is a group of witnesses to Christ formed. Bobrinskoy helps us to see that the formation of that witness is due to the agency of the three. Again, "to speak of Christ is to speak of the Holy Spirit and of the Father (and vice versa)."[16] To speak of the church is to speak of its coming to be in relation to Christ *and* his Spirit.

The church is derivative of the acts of the three. Father, Son, and Spirit each contribute—uniquely—to the church being the church. Although the focal point of an account of the church is Christ—the church is Christ's body, not the Spirit's body or the Father's—the church is also a work of the Father and Spirit. We see this Trinitarian logic at work as we continue to read the New Testament. Jesus commands his followers to "abide" in him "in whom we have to abide like the branches in a vine if we are to bear fruit."[17] The abiding to which we are summoned, Barth argues, has "a possibility in what is given them in Jesus Christ and through life with Him and in His church."[18] The possibility given to us of abiding in Christ and in his church is realized in the Spirit. In abiding in Christ, we bear the fruit of the Spirit; the vine is fecund, for the vine gives the Spirit "without measure" (John 3:34). Following 1 John 4:13, "By this we know that we abide in him and he in us, because he has given us of his Spirit": God (the Father) is said to abide in us by his Spirit. By the Father's Spirit, moreover, do we abide in Christ and bear fruit. The 1 John 4 reference is helpful because the language of abiding, the same language we find in John

---

14. Bobrinskoy, *Mystery of the Trinity*, 11.
15. Ibid.
16. Ibid.
17. Barth, *CD* II/2, 600.
18. Ibid.

10, refers to the Father. This is not really an inconsistency but rather a demonstration of the oneness of Father and Son. Just as Father and Spirit are said by Paul to raise Jesus, so too in John's mind does abiding language refer us to Father and Son.

To sum up this section, in sketching an account of the church follow-ing Barth's comments on John 10 and 14, we have glimpsed the extent to which it is a creature of the Trinity. Of the Son only is it said that he has a body, the church. But that is not to detract from the work of the Father and Spirit in giving rise to the Son's body. Barth, moreover, helped us to see that the Spirit by which we abide in Christ is neither our Spirit nor the church's Spirit but rather the Spirit of the Father, whom he pours out upon his people through Christ. In a moment, we will look at some of the profitable things that Augustine and Thomas have to say about what the Spirit's flowing forth from Christ's body teaches us about the church. We will work with Thomas's and Augustine's recep-tion of Johannine imagery in order to better understand this dimension of the relationship between Christ's body and the Spirit.

"THE TEMPLE OF HIS BODY": AUGUSTINE ON THE BODY THAT CREATES A BODY

Augustine's homily on John 2:12–21 has, on many levels, serious affinities with Barth's reflections on John 10 and 14. Both Augustine and Barth are cognizant of how cunning and pervasive are our attempts to domesticate the Word and Spirit. Let me explain. John 2:16 refers to those "who were selling the doves," and records Jesus as responding with "Take these things out of here! Stop making my Father's house a marketplace!" Commenting on this verse and also Mark 1:10, where the Spirit appeared in the form of a dove at Jesus' baptism, Augustine states that "the Dove is not for sale; he is given *gratis*, because he is called grace."[19] Zeal for the house of God is incompatible with its being thought of as a marketplace where doves, among other things, are for sale. Furthermore, the doves being sold in the precincts of the temple point, on Augustine's reading, to *the* dove, the Holy Spirit. In expound-ing the passage, Augustine refers, interestingly, to Simon's attempt to sell the Holy Spirit in Acts 8:18–19. According to Augustine, this

---

19. Saint Augustine, *Homilies on the Gospel of John 1–40*, vol. 12, *The Works of Saint Augustine*, ed. Boniface Ramsey (Hyde Park, NY: New City, 2009), 10, 202.

passage is to be read together with the baptism of Jesus in Mark 1:10 and parallels to draw attention to the pervasiveness of our attempts to own and domesticate the Spirit.

In reading this way, Augustine reminds us that the Spirit is not ours to manage or control, as is the case with the parallel, the temple. The Spirit is not ours to manipulate or give because the Spirit from eternity is the Love that proceeds from the Father through the Son. To unfold this point, we look to John 2:19. We see that Jesus not only identifies himself with the temple but also says that he will raise it up. This Augustine takes to be a sign of Christ's divinity, of "how he too was God: *Pull down this temple, and in three days I will raise it up.* Did he ever say, 'Pull down the temple for the Father to raise it up on the third day'?"[20] Jesus is the agent of his own resurrection. He raises his own body. This he does because he is God. The same is true of his body, the church—Jesus raises it from the dead. The latter exists because Jesus raised himself. The New Testament in other places speaks as we have seen of the Father and the Spirit's role in raising Jesus. But in John 2:19, Jesus raises himself. He raises his own body, and from his body does the Spirit flow, and all this because he is God.

The body of our Lord Jesus Christ derived "from Adam without contracting sin from Adam ... He [Jesus] took from that source the temple of his body, not the iniquity which is to be driven from this temple."[21] By Christ's body is iniquity driven from Adam's body. Through his own body, Jesus Christ removes sin from our bodies. He does this because he is God. Iniquity must be driven away, and that is what Christ's body does in relationship to our bodies. The cleansing miracle that flows from the temple of his crucified body (which he raises) is the Spirit. The Spirit raises our bodies, rendering them within the context of Christ's body (the church) temples of his Spirit, wherein the Spirit is not manipulated but freely received. Christ's body cleanses our bodies of the desire to do with them what we will. He transforms our bodies into his body. He does all this because he is God.[22]

---

20. Ibid., 208. Thomas, too, understands "the sign of his future resurrection" to show "most strikingly the power of his divinity." Saint Thomas Aquinas, *Commentary on the Gospel of John* (Washington, D.C.: Catholic University of America Press, 2010), 397, 1:153.

21. Augustine, *Homilies on John*, 10, 209.

22. For further reading on this theme, see Yves Congar, *The Mystery of the Temple, or The Manner of God's Presence to His Creatures from Genesis to the Apocalypse*, trans. Reginald F. Trevett (London: Burns & Oates, 1962).

Jesus' body creates a body, the church. As does Barth, Augustine teaches that the church is a creature of Jesus Christ—it is *his* body. Where Augustine is helpful is in his appreciation of the extent to which Christ's raising of his own body is a function of his divinity. Augustine's reading of John 2:1–12 gives us a glimpse of how Trinitarian first principles inform an account of the church. The church is one of the primary fruits that Jesus' divinity bears. In him is the church a supernatural reality derived from his divine person and the Spirit. Moreover, I think that an account of the church must take its cues from Augustine in being mindful of how Jesus remains sovereign, indeed the head of his body, the church. Jesus freely presents his body to bodies from which iniquity has not yet been wholly driven out. The church as the Lord's body still, of course, succumbs to being the body it once was: Adam's. Although we try to domesticate the Spirit into our spirit, its source among us and in God is Christ. The Spirit has this source because this is how things are in God. In presenting an account of the church, it is important to be aware of how Christ, because he is God, remains sovereign over the giving of his own Spirit. The irreversibility of the relations of the three in God is on display in what these divine persons do among us.

ON WHY THE CHURCH CANNOT BE CONFLATED WITH CHRIST

If the church is derived from the Trinity, then it follows that the church cannot be conflated or confused with Jesus Christ. The body is not the head. The body, rather, is entirely dependent on the head for its existence. Thomas helps us to appreciate the extent to which the church cannot be considered coextensive with Christ or the Spirit. With Thomas's help, we see why the church is always a second-order affair. Thomas writes, commenting on John 2:21, "For Christ calls his body a temple, because a temple is something in which God dwells, according to 'The Lord is in his holy temple' (Ps 10:5) ... But he [God] dwells in Christ according to a union in the person; and this union includes not only the soul, but the body as well. And so the very body of Christ is God's temple."[23] What the Trinitarian reference secures, Thomas argues, is an account of the church wherein the church is

---

23. Aquinas, *Commentary on John*, 399, 1:154.

not conflated with Christ, where the asymmetry between the two is acknowledged. The church, Thomas explains, is Christ's body by grace; but the temple of Christ's body "is God's temple" according "to a union in the person."[24] God does not indwell Christ in a manner akin to God's indwelling of God's people, for God "dwells in Christ according to a union in the person."[25] In other words, Father, Son, and Spirit are consubstantial; the church and Christ are not. The mystical body of Christ, the church, is what it is by grace; its life always resides in another, that other being Christ and his "Breath."[26]

The Church and Christ are of two substances.

The full force of Thomas's arguments regarding the basic distinction between Christ and the church occur in his comments on Jesus' words, "and in three days I will raise it up" (John 2:19). So Thomas: "And as the divinity dwells in the body of Christ through the grace of union, so too he dwells in the Church through the grace of adoption."[27] Divinity dwells in the church, making it what it is; however, divinity, meaning the Father, dwells in the church in a quite different way than in Christ. The Father dwells in the church "through the grace of adoption."[28] By the Spirit are we united to Christ, and thereby adopted as sons and daughters of the Father. Not so with Christ, for he is indwelt by the Father "through the grace of union."[29] Jesus, and not the church, is consubstantial with the Father.

Thomas, as is the case with Augustine and Barth, is all too aware of the frailty of "the temple of his [Christ's] body ... Although that body [Christ's] may seem to be destroyed mystically by the adversities of persecutions with which it is afflicted, nevertheless it is raised up in 'three days.'"[30] "The temple of Christ's body," despite the gross afflictions to which it is subject, is raised on the third day because it is a *spiritual* body (John 2:21). It is a body that, because it is united with the Father "through the grace of union," shares with the Father in the Spirit from all eternity. The Spirit is Christ's by nature, whereas the Spirit is ours by grace. This point secures the distinction between Christ and the church. The Spirit upholds us in Christ by grace, whereas the Spirit is

Basic distinction between Christ & the Church is his consubstantiality with the Spirit (and Father).

24. Ibid.
25. Ibid.
26. The language of "Breath" is Bobrinskoy's. See his *Mystery of the Trinity*, 29.
27. Aquinas, *Commentary on John*, 404, 1:156.
28. Ibid.
29. Ibid.
30. Ibid.

of Christ by nature. Jesus' whole ministry rests on and is transparent to this sublime truth regarding "the grace of union."[31]

The Spirit continues to raise and to sanctify Jesus' body, to make it over in order that it might be what it is: his body. The church lives, as Barth reminds us, inasmuch as it receives and hears the Word, whom it has to obey in life and in death. In Augustine and Thomas, we note that "the temple of his [Christ's] body" is marked by a receiving of the Spirit whom he gives "without measure" (John 3:34), thereby making our bodies over into a "temple of the Holy Spirit" (1 Cor 6:19). The people of God are those in whom the Spirit dwells "through the grace of adoption."[32] Such emphases are able to resist the kind of thinking that would reduce the church to something we "do" rather than as the fruit of the Father's dwelling in the Son "through the grace of union" in the Spirit. The Trinitarian referent reminds us that the church is summoned by Christ in the Spirit and all that to the glory of the Father.

THE CHURCH EXISTS FOR THEOLOGY

The church is where persons are instructed in such a way that they might learn to see. We learn to see by what we hear. The instrument whereby we are given ears to hear is the prophetic and apostolic testimony. What is more, Christ's summons of us through the biblical testimony takes the form of proclamation. In this section, I reflect on how one of the distinctive marks of the Christian church—"the Word of God purely preached"—is informed by pneumatological teaching.[33]

---

31. Ibid.

32. Ibid.

33. I use the language of "marks" for a purpose. First, it is prominent language in the works of the magisterial Protestant Reformers. Calvin famously speaks of "the marks of the church" as follows in *Institutes* 3.1.9: "Wherever we see the Word of God purely preached and heard, and the sacraments administered according to Christ's institution, there, it is not to be doubted, a church of God exists [cf. Eph. 2:20]. For his promise cannot fail: 'Wherever two or three are gathered in my name, there I am in the midst of them' [Matt. 18:20]." Luther, similarly, identifies seven marks of the church in his treatise *On the Councils and the Church*. They are: the holy word of God; the holy sacrament of baptism; the holy sacrament of the altar; the office of keys exercised publicly; the consecration or calling of ministers; prayer, public praise, and thanksgiving; and the holy possession of the cross of Christ. For an abbreviated version of Luther's treatise and a helpful collection of essays commenting on the same, see *Marks of the Body of Christ*, ed. Carl E. Braaten and Robert W. Jenson (Grand Rapids: Eerdmans, 1999). Furthermore, the language of marks is to be distinguished from what Torrance calls the "attributes" of the church, the classical creedal identifiers of one, holy, catholic, and apostolic. Torrance speaks of them as not denoting "independent qualities inhering in the church," but rather as "affirmations of the nature of the church as it participates in Jesus Christ and are strictly discernable only to faith." See Thomas F. Torrance, *Atonement: The Person and Work of Christ* (Downers Grove, IL: IVP Academic, 2009), 380ff.

Teaching on the acts of the Spirit in God and among us not only shapes what we say the church is but also what the church does. Accordingly, I want to think with Gregory for a short while about how seeing and preaching relate to one another, how God uses preaching as a mark of the church to capacitate spiritual sight. Preaching functions as an explanation of what we have been given to see.

What the pure preaching of the Word must aim at is what Gregory, following the Psalms of David, calls "ascents." Gregory describes "ascents" in his Oration 31 *On the Holy Spirit* as "piecemeal additions," that is, "progress and advance from glory to glory, that the light of the Trinity should shine upon more illustrious souls. This was, I believe, the motive for the Spirit's making his home in the disciples in gradual stages proportionate to their capacity to receive him."[34] Preaching has a catechetical function inasmuch as we are raised by it to higher truth, indeed to what Gregory calls "the **Godhead** of the Spirit."[35] The preached Word generates hearers who "by progress and advance from glory to glory" learn to see the Spirit's divinity.[36] That said, there is something of a reversible relationship between preaching and sight. Referring to Psalm 36:9, "in your light we see light," Gregory says that seeing precedes preaching: "We receive the Son's light from the Father's light in the light of the Spirit: that is what we ourselves have seen and what we now proclaim—it is the plain and simple explanation of the Trinity."[37] Pure preaching also rests, in Gregory's mind, upon seeing, which in turn is given over to pure preaching.

While "there is something especially difficult in the doctrine of the Holy Spirit," a plain explanation is nonetheless possible.[38] What renders it difficult, indeed what is so demanding about a "theology" of the Holy Spirit, is that many in Gregory's day—as in our own—do not think that the Godhead of the Spirit is reflective of biblical teaching: "time and time again you repeat the argument about *not being in the Bible*."[39] What is not in the Bible, so his opponents argue, is "theology," the "theology" of the Holy Spirit.[40] By this, Gregory means deep talk of how the Spirit originates in God. Rather than being "either

---

34. Gregory, *Holy Spirit*, 31.26.
35. Ibid., 27.
36. Ibid., 26.
37. Ibid., 3.
38. Bobrinskoy, *Mystery of the Trinity*, 191.
39. Gregory, *Holy Spirit*, 31.21.
40. Ibid., 7.

begotten from the Father or from the Son," which would result in either the Father having two sons or the Son himself having a son— "what could be odder than that?"—Gregory argues that "to the extent that procession is the mean between ingeneracy and generacy, he [the Spirit] is God."[41] This is what the Bible teaches regarding how the Spirit originates in God. The Spirit is not like the other two because of the Spirit's procession "within the single nature and quality of the Godhead."[42] It is these truths that are to be preached.

Theology of the Spirit as proceeding is what pure hearing receives on the basis of pure preaching. As with Augustine's reading of John 2:12–21 in regard to doves being sold as representative of the Holy Spirit, the Spirit's proceeding is not written on the surface of the scriptural text. Gregory thinks that Scripture must be read by Scripture "with penetration" so that we would *see* "inside the written text to its inner meaning."[43] Preaching unfolds this "inner meaning." Gregory argues that those who deny the biblical basis for the Spirit's Godhead cannot see Scripture's "inner meaning" regarding the Spirit's procession because their eyes are "yet too feeble for it."[44] And because they cannot see, they cannot proclaim. Pure proclamation and hearing are preceded by the sight that the indwelling Spirit makes possible.

Where Gregory's argument is most idiosyncratic is that the Spirit's Godhead is only now made clear. Famously, he writes,

> In this way: the old covenant made clear proclamation of the Father, a less definite one of the Son. The new [covenant] made the Son manifest and gave us a glimpse of the Spirit's Godhead. At the present time the Spirit resides amongst us, giving us a clearer manifestation of himself than before. It was dangerous, too, for the Holy Spirit to be made (and here I use a rather rash expression) an extra burden, when the Son had not been received.[45]

Taking up John 14:26 and 16:13, Gregory argues that reception of the Spirit's Godhead is "gradual," dependent on the Spirit's "dwelling in us."[46] But for the Spirit to dwell, Christ had to first ascend to his Father.

---

41. Ibid., 7, 8.
42. Ibid., 9, 16.
43. Ibid., 21.
44. Ibid., 21, 26.
45. Ibid., 26. All of the biblical references in this paragraph are from John.
46. Ibid., 27.

The Bible enables us to make sense of its inner meaning retrospectively, in a way conditional on the *sight* that the Spirit's actual indwelling gradually capacitates.

By indwelling us, the Spirit enables us to see the Spirit as the Spirit really is. The plain sense of Scripture encourages us to express what we see. By contemplating the Spirit's acts toward us, we see that the Spirit is divine. "Were the Spirit not to be worshipped, how could he deify me through baptism? If he is to be worshipped, why not adored? And if to be adored, how can he fail to be God? One links with the other, a truly golden chain of salvation."[47] The task of a *theology* of the Spirit is to give an account of the identity in God of the one who acts thus.[48] The preaching of the prophetic and apostolic testimony has a similar aim: that we might see who the Spirit is in God. Accordingly, preaching must be sensitive to what distinguishes the Spirit from the other two. The Spirit in the life of the Trinity is only distinguished from Father and Son by a title, namely, "proceeding." "Ingenerate" belongs to the Father, "begotten" to the Son, and "proceeding" to the Spirit.[49] The spiritual recognize that the originating relations by which the three are do not compromise their unity. Instead, the spiritual "worship Father, Son, and Holy Spirit as the single Godhead and power."[50]

While Gregory does not develop an account of subsistent relations as does Thomas or articulate as fulsomely as does Augustine the processions of Son and Spirit as the ground of the missions, Gregory nonetheless recognizes that preaching cannot retreat from "theology."[51] To the extent that it does so, it blinds itself to the light by which it sees. Sight of "the **Godhead** of the Spirit" is the ground of its proclamation.[52]

Before turning to an account of the tradition of the church whereby we are taught to see in this way, let us take a moment to restate the insights arrived at thus far in our sketch of the church. Following Barth, we talked about what the church is as a creature of the Word. Just as Christ is the agent of his resurrection in John 2, so too does he raise up

---

47. Ibid., 28.
48. I do not concur with Frederick Norris's assessment that "the fullest revelation of the Spirit outside the Scriptures" functions, for Gregory, "as a necessary and fulfilling inference for what had gone before." It would seem, rather, that the Spirit fully reveals over time what exactly is said about the Spirit in the very Scripture that the Spirit illuminates. See "Commentary on Oration 31" in Gregory, *Holy Spirit*, 206.
49. Gregory, *Holy Spirit*, 31.7.
50. Ibid., 29, 33.
51. Ibid., 7; Bobrinskoy, *Mystery of the Trinity*, 278.
52. Gregory, *Holy Spirit*, 27.

a body for himself. Following Augustine, we talked about the church as a fruit of the Spirit's flowing from the temple of Christ's body. The Spirit generates a body for Christ, namely, the church. The church does not possess the Spirit, but ever only receives the Spirit from the one on whom the Spirit rests. We noted, moreover, the Trinitarian rationale for why the body cannot be confused or conflated with its head, and why the head always remains sovereign. Following Thomas, we noticed that the basis for this difference is that the Spirit is proper to Christ by nature, whereas the Spirit indwells the church by grace. The Spirit enables the church to be what it is declared to be: Christ's body. Last, and following Gregory, we talked about one of the chief activities of the church—preaching—as a fruit of spiritual sight. But sight, as we noted, comes about by preaching. The Spirit renders us into those who can read, hear, and proclaim Scripture's message so as to *see* its inner meaning regarding the Spirit's Godhead. Pure preaching enables us to see—in a spiritual sense—Scripture's plain sense.

LIVING TRADITION: THE FRUIT OF THE "PERMANENT PENTECOST" OF THE SPIRIT

Tradition is a difficult word for some Protestants. It either smacks of a letter deprived of the Spirit or it signifies lifeless rituals, inventions of the carnal mind rather than a mind illuminated by the Word and Spirit. It is unfortunate that the word has negative connotations for so many Protestants. Quite the opposite should be the case, I argue in this last section. Tradition is a promising theological category, a necessary derivative of church as we continue to develop an account of the Spirit in Trinitarian dimension. Tradition, rightly understood, is a fruit of the Spirit's continually being breathed upon his people by the glorified Christ. Tradition is about the ongoing illumination of the Spirit, who places the church in a "permanent epiclesis."[53]

The account of "tradition" I offer is fairly modest, derivative of the Spirit's proceeding in God and among us. Specifically, I would like to reflect on tradition as a fruit of the Spirit resting "fully in the

---

53. Bobrinskoy, *Mystery of the Trinity*, 159. By "epiclesis," Bobrinskoy means the moment in the Orthodox liturgy when the priest calls on the Holy Spirit to transfigure the bread and wine in such a way that they become the body and blood of Christ.

Church."[54] Christ has not left us alone, for upon him rests the Spirit, and that same Spirit rests upon his body, the church, in the mode of promise. Tradition is something of a heralding of this resting. In the next section, we will expand this thought.

Tradition indicates those instruments that promote attention to the Scriptures. In a primary sense, I mean the ecumenical creeds and, in a secondary sense, those documents in the history of the church—for example, the Barmen Declaration—that point us to the Christ to be confessed in life and in death. Again, that we have creeds, imperfect as they are, and that we have declarations such as Barmen, is because Christ promises that "the gates of Hades will not prevail against" the church (Matt 16:18). Following Bobrinskoy, "The Spirit, in a permanent Pentecost, ensures the presence of Christ in the Church."[55] Put differently, the Spirit who rests on Christ and is breathed by him testifies to him among his people. The Spirit's testimony is no less valid even if it has only a remnant to show for itself.

The "permanent Pentecost" of the Spirit is what makes it possible to speak of tradition.[56] This is tradition's principle of intelligibility. Christ is never without his witnesses, his faithful, his remnant, for by the Spirit is his promise to create a people guaranteed. Tradition, and again I am thinking primarily of the "Rule of Faith" as encapsulated in the ecumenical creeds and secondarily of those instruments by which knowledge of the rule is promoted, is a function of the Spirit's working. Christ never ceases to come to us in the Spirit, thereby ensuring his presence in the church, even to the extent of declaring the church to be a false church.[57]

Christ bears and breathes the Spirit. His body, the church, therefore bears the Spirit in a derivative sense, although it cannot be said to breathe him, as that is Christ's task alone as true God and true man. The Spirit whom Christ bears, the Spirit who rests on his body, the church, is "the Giver of life in the time of the Church."[58] The Spirit gives life; this the church does not do. But the glory of Christ rests on his body—the church—by grace, just as it does on him by nature. To

---

54. Ibid., 71.
55. Ibid., 72.
56. Ibid. Note that this term does not mean Pentecost is paradigmatic and repeatable.
57. I am thinking here of what might be said to differentiate the Confessing Church from the false church of the German Christians in the 1930s.
58. Bobrinskoy, *Mystery of the Trinity*, 73.

talk about tradition in light of the Spirit's proceeding in God and among us is to say that the Spirit who fills the Son also rests on his ecclesial body. The Spirit resting generates a tradition, a faithful hearing, really most basically the communion of the saints, visible and invisible. The communion of the saints is identified by the faithful proclamation and reception of the gospel by which they live. Tradition is the fruit of faithful proclamation. It is the river that such proclamation sources, and in turn that which the Spirit uses to bind us to what is to be proclaimed.

The Spirit is the promise of life whose breathing is never without effect. Talk of tradition as *living* is talk of one of the primary instruments whereby Christ teaches us to remember him and his promises. The ecumenical creeds (primarily) and catechetical documents (secondarily)—like the Heidelberg Catechism, the Roman Catholic Initiation for Adults, or the liturgical documents like the Book of Common Prayer—have indeed been used in quite profound ways by the Spirit.[59] This instrumentality is what John Webster calls "the plenitude of the Christian faith."[60] But that plenitude must be understood always with reference to Trinitarian and pneumatological teaching. Tradition's principle of intelligibility is supplied by pneumatology, more precisely by "the eternal rest of the Spirit on the Son" manifested in the "baptismal descent of the Spirit on the Incarnate Word in Jesus" and promised in turn to the life of the church as the body of the incarnate Word.[61] In other words, the Spirit who rests on the Word's body, the church, generates a history marked by a tradition that witnesses Christ. Revelation has, therefore, "a social and public nature."[62] Revelation takes up space through the summons to conversion, the prophetic and apostolic testimony as mediated by Scripture.[63]

The reason I have engaged three of the church's greatest teachers in this volume—Augustine, Thomas, and Barth—is to demonstrate (in part) theology's service to the church. *Theology* is a churchly undertaking. It tests what the church proclaims by the Word and the extent to which what is proclaimed is faithful to the Word. Accordingly, theology's task is not to simply repeat the Word but to assist the church's proclamation

---

59. See Galatians 5:22–23.

60. See Webster, "Purity and Plenitude," in *Yves Congar*, 44.

61. Bobrinskoy, *Mystery of the Trinity*, 94.

62. Congar, *Tradition and Traditions*, 338, quoted in Webster, "Purity and Plenitude," in *Yves Congar*, 58.

63. The danger of "assimilating the apostolic testimony too thoroughly into the life of the church, lest its summons to conversion be in some way muted," is noted by Webster in ibid., 60.

of it. To do so, it needs help in the form of gifted and perspicuous hearers. If Jesus' promise in John 14:28 is true, then an account of the church must include an account of tradition as a fruit of Jesus' promise. So Bobrinskoy: "Jesus sends the Spirit who proceeds from the Father, just as He rested on Jesus, so does the Spirit rest on the Church. He constitutes the believers as temples of the divine Presence."[64] The Spirit constitutes the body. By the Scriptures, Jesus speaks so as to create a people who are "temples of the divine presence."[65] We read Augustine, Thomas, and Barth, among others, because they help the church to hear. The Lord Jesus promises not to leave his people alone. Rather, by his Spirit he continues to raise up gifted teachers who help God's people hear. It is their hearing that constitutes the church's tradition.

Believers do not make the church: it is the Spirit's work. Because the Word of Christ never goes forth without the Spirit, it will bring forth a people. Until he comes again, Christ's promise to create a people through whom he testifies to his wonderful works in the power of his Spirit remains effective. The Spirit, however much he may be grieved by the church, preserves a remnant over which the gates of hell shall not prevail. Tradition is used by the same Spirit to encourage clear hearing of the apostolic testimony. The church's tradition, then, is rightly described as (hu)man-made. It is not inspired in the same sense as the canonical writings. Of the Nicene Creed, for example, it cannot be said, "the Word of the Lord"; so too with confessional documents like Barmen. And yet that Declaration was used and is still used to draw attention to "the Gate," by whom we always must enter into the "sheepfold" and whose voice we must hear in life and in death.

In sum, tradition is a salutary theological category. It is the fruit of the Spirit, who evokes instruments by which knowledge of the being and works of the Trinity is promoted. On God's beloved Son, the Spirit rests from all eternity; and on the body of his Son, the church, his promised Spirit rests by grace, drawing us to him and supplying us with the means by which we call on him.

---

64. Bobrinskoy, *Mystery of the Trinity*, 104.
65. Ibid.

CONCLUSION

The church is subject to a "permanent Pentecost."[66] By the Spirit, the church utters the cry toward which it lives: "Come, Lord Jesus" (Rev 22:20). Unfortunately, however, the church does not often join in the Spirit's sigh. The church is often comfortable in its captivity. With Barth, we noted the extent to which the Word and Spirit disrupt our captivity. The Word is loquacious: he persists in gathering, upholding, and sending a people forth in the Spirit. "The gate" is never isolated from the voice of "the gatekeeper" (John 10:2–3). The Word is never detached from the Spirit. One of the first principles of an account of the church is to remember, with Barth, that the church is the fruit of "the gate" and "the gatekeeper" (John 10:2–3).

We turned thereafter to Augustine, who helps us to see that the Spirit, who flows forth from the temple of Christ's body, is never the church's to possess but only the church's to receive. The church receives its life in the Spirit. The church's life is extrinsic to it and can therefore never be manipulated or controlled. Christ's body is a spiritual body, the body of one who gives the Spirit "without measure" (John 3:34). It is Christ who raises a people from the dead, just as he raised himself from the dead.

With Thomas, we investigated a further dimension of an account of the church that trades on first principles regarding who and how the Spirit is in God. The church receives Christ in the Spirit by grace, whereas the Spirit is Christ's by virtue of his union with the Father. The Spirit indwells the church, not as a kind of gift or possession, but rather as "the promise of the Father" poured out (Acts 1:4). Without the resources supplied by the doctrine of the Trinity, it is hard to see the distinction between Christ's relationship to the Spirit and the Spirit's relationship to the church.

Having discussed the being of the church in relationship to the Spirit, we looked to Gregory Nazianzen in order to say a few words about how preaching functions to help us *see* "the Godhead of the Spirit."[67] Proclamation, one of the constitutive marks of the church, rests upon sight of the Spirit's Godhead. Within the church, it is hoped, we become mature, able to begin to see by the Spirit in the Trinity.

---

66. Ibid., 192.
67. Gregory, *Holy Spirit*, 31.27.

Proclamation of what is seen is the means by which unspiritual people become spiritual so as to truly see.

We concluded the chapter with a modest account of tradition as a function of the Spirit's "permanent Pentecost."[68] The Spirit rests on the body of the Son in the mode of promise, not possession. Accordingly, the Spirit generates "the plenitude of Christian faith."[69] Tradition is intrinsic to that plenitude. The Spirit poured out bears an instrument by which we are equipped to hear the claims of Christ, and that instrument is tradition. Tradition points to Christ, drawing attention to the one Word by which the church lives and which it must hear. That Word generates, in the Spirit poured out, a body of tradition that witnesses to the promise that "the gates of Hades will not prevail against it" (Matt 16:18).

---

68. Bobrinskoy, *Mystery of the Trinity*, 192.
69. Webster, "Purity and Plenitude," in *Yves Congar*, 44.

CHAPTER 10

ON THEOLOGICAL VISION

INTRODUCTION

In this book, I have sought to offer a descriptive portrait of the third of the three persons of the Trinity, who is incomprehensibly one with the other two. I have done so in reliance upon three of the doctors of the church, specifically their engagement with the Fourth Gospel in conversation with their relevant synthetic works. Each contributes something different. That said, they have much in common. What is held in common is God's prevenience. I first learned to appreciate this dimension of the doctrine of God via Barth. My doctoral research was in part on the divine glory as the sum of God's perfections, and the theological work that an account of the perfections of God undertakes within the doctrine of God. What I have come to see is that Augustine and Thomas in their own ways deepen the rationale for emphasizing the plenitude of God's life. Indeed, I think you need to say the kinds of things Thomas says (as he advances Augustine), if Barth's point about God's aseity is to register fully.

As a result of this study, I have come to appreciate the extent to which Augustinian and Thomistic talk of origins advances Barth's point regarding prevenience. Discussion of divine persons as three relations who are distinguished by their differing origins is precisely what you need to attend to if you are to understand why God remains God in all that God does for the life of the world. God remains God because what God does comes from God. God's acts toward the inside are revealed in God's acts toward the outside. The missions of Son and Spirit are revelatory of their processions in God.

The doctrine of the Spirit is a doctrine that is housed in the Trinity. Pneumatology is a facet of Trinitarian theology. Pneumatology is concerned with asking why the Spirit acts as the Spirit does. In this text, I have argued that the Spirit acts as the Spirit does because of who the Spirit is in God (love), and how the Spirit originates in God in relation to Father and Son (love proceeding). Contemplation of the Spirit's work encourages us to ask where that work comes from. In this book, I have shown that the Spirit's acts unfold their source with respect to the Spirit's identity in God.

As a result of this study, I have also come to see that the economy exhibits something utterly irreducible. It exhibits three who possess the fullness of divine life in a manner appropriate to the relations of origin by which each comes to be. God's work toward the outside is revelatory of the acts that constitute God's life. The burden of this study has been to present Augustine and Thomas as metaphysicians of the highest order—precisely because of their engagements with Scripture—whose insights deepen and extend one of Barth's best insights. Augustine goes further than any of his predecessors (Latin or Greek) in indicating how the missions of Son and Spirit reveal their eternal processions; Thomas modifies and extends—among other things—Augustine's account along the lines of persons as relations. With respect to Augustine and Thomas, Barth promotes the extent to which God acts in a manner utterly consistent with himself in all that God does.

THE PURPOSE OF THE CONTEMPLATIVE DIMENSION

In this last chapter, I want to press the contemplative dimension of pneumatological teaching in a way that does not isolate movement and repose.[1] We rest in the Spirit, who celebrates "the love of the Father and the Son," and we share in the draw of the Spirit among us to the Father through the Son.[2] The draw of the Spirit encourages "the

---

1. In God's being, movement and repose are one, as Vladimir Lossky argues in *The Vision of God*, trans. Ashleigh Moorhouse (Clayton, WI: American Orthodox Press, 1963), 102.
2. Eugene F. Rogers Jr. "Thomas Aquinas on Knowing and Coming to Know: The Beatific Vision and Learning from Contingency," in *Creation and the God of Abraham*, ed. David B. Burrell et al. (Cambridge: Cambridge University Press, 2010), 258.

sense of an invited intellectual gazing towards the rim of what may be grasped by the human intellect."[3] Revelation invites contemplation of the "unfathomable reality of the divine Processions," the "eternal realities by which we live, in time."[4] We live in and by these realities (movement), and we rest in them by gazing upon them.

Why has Trinitarian thinking, at least in many modern Protestant iterations, been hesitant to embrace contemplation? I suspect that the reason for this is a deep fear that Trinitarian *theology* lacks "real existential perspective."[5] I think that a focus on contemplation goes some way toward assuaging such fears. Talk about where the Spirit comes from involves us in Trinitarian *theology*. Through the Spirit's acts of binding us to the Father through the Son, we do get a glimpse of how things are in God. But more than that, we are invited to gaze, in an intellectual sense, upon the one who acts thus and in whom we are given to act. This gaze is not "exalted above the way of action" but is intrinsic to our action.[6] In living by the Spirit we come to gaze upon or see the Spirit—"in a mirror, dimly"—as the Spirit is in God (1 Cor 13:12).

The contemplative life is a *theological* life. The *telos* of contemplation is theology. Contemplation of God the Holy Trinity is how we come to know and speak of God as God truly is. So Bobrinskoy: "To have access to theology, we contemplate: the Father, source of the Divinity, and, for us, source of all grace; the Son, heir to the fullness of the divine Life, of which He is the spokesman in the world; and the Spirit, who accompanies the Son in His eternal radiance and who permeates the world, and hence is poured out into the life of the Church."[7] Contemplation is intrinsic to discipleship. The life of obedience is a contemplative life that comes to see things as they are; such is a truly theological life.

The motor of pneumatological teaching is the inner or immanent life of God, which is both above us *and* of concern to us. God's life is of concern to us because it is from that life that the acts of God arise.

---

3. Lewis Ayres, "Into the Cloud of Witnesses: Catholic Trinitarian Theology Beyond and Before Its Modern 'Revivals,'" in *Rethinking Trinitarian Theology*, ed. Guilio Maspero and Robert J. Wozniak (London: T&T Clark, 2012), 24.
4. This wonderful way of conceiving the processions as the realities by which we live is Boris Bobrinskoy's (see *The Mystery of the Trinity* [Crestwood, NY: St. Vladimir's Seminary Press, 1999], 275).
5. Ibid., 279.
6. Lossky, *Vision of God*, 84.
7. Bobrinskoy, *Mystery of the Trinity*, 275.

God's life is of material importance for understanding the mission of Son and Spirit. The mission of Son and Spirit is transparent to its source in the generation of the former from the Father and the procession of the latter by the Father through the Son. First principles such as these are not only scientific in the classical sense, insofar as they trace things to their principles, but are also what motivates contemplation. What this means in part is that being in Christ is a matter of being in his vision. To know him as he is, as indeed the Son of the Father, is to know him in the Spirit. Not simply to know but to see him as he is—this is a matter of theology, the vision of God being "all in all" (1 Cor 15:28).

Contemplation of the Son and Spirit in God's life is a concrete matter. If I am to receive Jesus Christ as truly God and truly human and the Spirit as "the promise of the Father" poured out, then talk of their origins is necessary (Acts 1:4). Jesus' mission witnesses his origin; the principle of intelligibility for his ministry is its Trinitarian reference. In Bobrinskoy's words, we see in the New Testament a "total correlation, an intimate appropriateness between the eternal mystery of filial (and paternal) love, and that of Redemption."[8] As with the Son's doings, the Spirit's doings reflect this "intimate appropriateness." A sense of this "appropriateness" is arrived at via contemplation, and contemplation aims at theology. Without theology, the mission of the Spirit and the work it accomplishes cannot in all its Trinitarian density be (well) narrated.

Contemplation serves theology as the means by which we begin to appreciate the Trinitarian density of the economy and the life from which it arises. Without contemplation, it would be all too easy to conflate the order of the three within God with how we come to know the three in God. As we read the New Testament, we see that the Spirit precedes the Son insofar as the Spirit conceives the humanity of the Son in the womb of the virgin. In a temporal sense, then, the Spirit precedes the Son. In God, however, the Spirit is the one breathed by the Father through the Son; the Son precedes—in a logical sense—the Spirit in God. These relations in God are irreversible. Contemplation of the Trinity chastens efforts to argue *from* the order of the economy *to* the order of being. Such arguing is wrongheaded because it reverses relations that in God are irreversible. Why does the Spirit rest on

---

8. Ibid., 269.

Christ? Because Jesus Christ receives the Spirit from the Father. Jesus Christ is "the 'place' of rest, the receptacle of the Spirit's plenitude and perfection."[9] The Spirit is not "exterior to the generation of the Son," just as the Son's generation is not exterior to the Spirit's procession from the Father.[10] If one takes the order of the three in their work and extrapolates backward, it would be easy to assume that in God's life the Spirit precedes the Son rather than the Son preceding—in terms of order and not rank—the Spirit. We learn to appreciate such theological truths by contemplation.

We read in Revelation 22:17 that "the Spirit and the bride say, 'Come.'" The Spirit and the church cry for Jesus to come. But Jesus has not yet come to consummate his kingdom visibly, and so the cry of the Spirit and the bride for him persist. This is the cry of the Spirit from eternity. It exhibits the correlation between Son and Spirit and the redemption they effect.[11] The Spirit's cry for the Son to come is demonstration of the fact that from eternity the Spirit comes from the Son. The Spirit's cry is a window into what has always been. Theology's task is to unfold the rationale for the order demonstrated in the economy. That task is a contemplative one.

In sum, I think that the way to *theological* truth is a contemplative affair. Far from being static, contemplation is a "thinking after," a following of revealed truth. Contemplation is a deeply participatory activity. Inasmuch as the Spirit fills us, are we able to glimpse the truth of who the Spirit is in God. The Spirit encourages theological talk regarding who the Spirit is.

THE CENTRALITY OF THE SON TO THE SPIRIT

New Testament teaching on the Son and Spirit aligns but does not conflate them. Pneumatology explains why, and to explain why involves recourse to theology proper. A theological vision explains why the three act as they do. As we have noted, the New Testament presents the Spirit frequently—but not exclusively—as the Spirit of the Son. The Son is central to the Spirit, not only in God but also

---

9. Ibid., 302.
10. Ibid.
11. Ibid., 269.

among us. Paul, for example, concentrates the offices of priest, king, and prophet in Christ, and not in the Spirit. The Spirit is not said to execute these offices or the work of washing, justification, sanctification, and redemption that flow forth from them. That is the Son's work. But because the Spirit shares in all that the Son is, except for the Son's originating relation with the Father, Paul says "you were washed, you were sanctified, you were justified, in the name of the Lord Jesus Christ and in the Spirit of God" (1 Cor 6:11). Not only does Paul in this text reverse the order in 1 Corinthians 1:30; he also adds washing, and furthermore understands it all to take place in Christ *and* in the Spirit. Christ is parallel with the Spirit. However, as Anthony Thiselton notes, "*Paul is not speaking of identity or ontology. Too many passages treat* Christ and the Holy Spirit as *two distinct persons* for this to be possible."[12] A theological vision elucidates why they are distinct.

There is a kind of asymmetry in the relation between Son and Spirit that must be honoured. Theology helps us understand why the Spirit's ministry is so Son-centric. Theology teaches us that this is because the Spirit originates from the Father (principally) and the Son (secondarily). The origin of the Spirit is glimpsed in the Spirit's working. Accordingly, "the Holy Spirit bears witness not to himself, but *to Christ*; but the revelation of Christ comes about through and *by the Holy Spirit*."[13] Because the Spirit originates from the Son, the Spirit leads back to the Son. The Son—and not the Spirit—is "wisdom from God, and righteousness and sanctification and redemption," becoming these things "for us" (1 Cor 1:30). The Spirit is never said to become these things for us; the Son—and only the Son—is sent "for us." That the Son becomes "wisdom from God" for us has its rationale in *theology*. Without theology's help, we have no recourse as to why it is the Son and not the Spirit who became this for us. Similarly, we do not know why the Spirit is happy to actualize the Son's filial relation to the Father among us and for us. A theological vision chastens any sense of voluntarism within the Godhead. The Son does not, for example, decide to become incarnate in conversation with the Father and the Spirit. The Son and Spirit work as they do because of their origins; their work expresses their origins.

---

12. Anthony C. Thiselton, *The Holy Spirit—in Biblical Teaching, through the Centuries, and Today* (Grand Rapids: Eerdmans, 2013), 79.

13. Ibid., 234. Thiselton attributes this view to "writers as diverse as Karl Barth and Joseph Fison."

It is interesting to note that fewer voices in Protestant modernity have wondered what has happened to the Father. I am not aware of a criticism that suggests in Barth—for example—the sublimation of the Father by the Son. That the Father commands us to "listen" to the Son (Mark 9:7 and parallels), his beloved, is not heard as an overdetermination of the Son at the expense of the Father. The contours of the economy are Son-centric. The Father commands us to listen to Christ, the Spirit declares Christ. And yet the *telos* of the economy cannot be said to be Son-centric in any straightforward way, anyhow. The end of the work of God toward the outside is the Fathers' being "all in all" (1 Cor 15:28). If such is the case, then, we see how not only pneumatology but also Christology is derivative of Trinitarian teaching.

When Jesus comes again, he will "be subjected to the one who put all things to subjection under him, so that God may be all in all" (1 Cor 15:28). Jesus draws us to the Father through the Spirit, a foretaste of the Father's being "all in all." The saving work of God reveals *theology*. The Son is sent and the Spirit is breathed in order to return us to the one from whom we—and they—come. However, unlike Son and Spirit, we are not from the Father from eternity. The Father knows himself to be Father only in the Son; the Son knows himself to be the Father's Son only in the Spirit; for the Spirit is the gift and love proceeding of the Father for the Son and the Son for the Father. A theological vision encourages us to see that God does not know himself in relation to us: God's self-knowledge is entirely God's. In sum, it is the office of theology that explains why and encourages the transformation that the knowledge of the Holy Trinity demands.

ON LEARNING TO SEE WITH THE GRAIN OF THE UNIVERSE

The sublime truths of the Spirit's Godhead must be seen; but you and I cannot see of our own accord. We need the Spirit to see how things really are. Theology is the fruit of a renewed vision, of contemplation of who the Spirit is in God and among us. In this section, we will explore what we in the Spirit are given to see.

God cannot be seen in any immediate sense. Sight is subject to the purified vision that the Holy Spirit supplies. Such sight is theological sight. Inasmuch as we receive sight do we learn to see "all things *as related to God*."[14] The burden of this text has been to unfold the object of the contemplative life, the Holy Trinity, and to begin to conceive how God transforms us in such a way that we might see not only God but all things in relation to God. To be sure, God cannot be seen in this life, but he can be known and loved in this life in the one who comes from his bosom in the Spirit. Knowledge of the God that Jesus makes known is knowledge that yields love. Such love is coterminous with sight. So Thomas: "And this is the ultimate perfection of the contemplative life, namely that the divine Truth be not only seen but also loved."[15]

To see with the grain is to see theologically. Theological vision begins in this life. It is not the province of the far side of the eschatological consummation of the kingdom. Inasmuch as knowledge of divine things are received in the obedience of love, the beatific vision is realized, albeit provisionally, in the here and now. This vision is our happiness. It is a matter not only of seeing God as God truly is but of seeing all things as related to God. As Thomas says, "Final and perfect happiness can consist in nothing but the vision of the divine essence," and, we might add, of all things as related to that essence.[16] Of course, this essence, as Barth remarks following John 1:18, "is not seen."[17] What Barth means is that the essence of God is not seen in the way we see other things. Rather, with respect to the essence of God, we behold. "Behold" is in Barth's mind, following John 1:18, a better way to depict the kind of sight the self-revelation of the Trinity brings about. Barth writes, "*Horan* [seeing], as distinct from intuitional *theasthai* [gaze at or behold], means simple, direct, objective seeing. In John this cannot be limited to physical seeing, although we have to start out with this basic sense ... Such *horan theon* in the narrower or broader sense is not given to any human, says the verse."[18] What is given to the human is something better. This is a beholding in Jesus Christ of the divine essence. When he comes again, we shall see him as he is, and our beholding will give way to sight.

In the left margin, handwritten: *Fulfilment of intellect and will*

---

14. Eugene F. Rogers Jr., *Aquinas and the Supreme Court: Biblical Narratives of Jews, Gentiles and Gender* (Malden, MA: Wiley-Blackwell, 2013), 87. The consequences of this move on Thomas's part regarding the nature/grace relationship are significant. As Rogers notes, they are not to be distinguished "from the vantage of their divine integration." (88)

15. Thomas, *ST* II-II, q. 180, a. 7, ad 1, quoted in Rogers, *Aquinas and the Supreme Court*, 94.

16. Thomas, *ST* I-II, q. 3, a. 8., quoted in Phillip Blond, "The Beatific Vision of St Thomas Aquinas," in *Encounter between Eastern Orthodoxy and Radical Orthodoxy: Transfiguring the World through the Word*, ed. Adrian Pabst and Christopher Schneider (Farnham: Ashgate, 2009), 192.

17. Karl Barth, *Witness to the Word: A Commentary on John 1: Lectures at Münster in 1925 and at Bonn in 1933*, trans. Geoffrey W. Bromiley (Grand Rapids: Eerdmans, 1996), 126.

18. Ibid., 127.

The question, it would seem, is the directness of the vision of God's essence. "Medieval theology," writes Barth, "denied this and ascribed to the blessed in heaven, in distinction even from the angels, an immediate vision of the divine essence (*ST* III, 92, a.1) ... And this is the issue in the present passage [John 1:17–18]."[19] Barth, as does Cyril in his comments on the same verse, points us to Exodus 33:18–23, a passage "which is normative for an understanding of this whole section."[20] Accordingly, "the obvious meaning is that because we are humans we can none of us see God's face."[21] We cannot see God as he is in this life. Jesus Christ, whose name first appears in John 1:17, is "the same *theos* without the article as in v.1c and v.18a. The only begotten is God by nature. He shares the divine essence which no one without exception either sees or knows."[22] This Jesus shares the divine essence. In him do we see the Father, and it is by him that we love the Father in the Spirit. Jesus Christ is "the exegete, the communicator, the one with whom we have to do, he who is the *monogenes*, whose information about himself is original, primary, and authentic revelation."[23] This Jesus by whom we know God, love God, is the same one by whom we will see God immediately in the new heavens and earth. In him we see things as they are and God as God truly is. The vision of God is ours in Christ, who shares the divine essence, together with the Father and their Spirit. With the full receipt of the Spirit in the eschaton we see Christ spiritually, that is, no longer "from a human point of view," but rather as he is, and so the divine essence as it is.

God is beautiful. Beauty is, as the rest of God's perfections, intrinsic to who God is. Moreover, God's beauty is the cause of our happiness. Happiness is the fruit that the revelation of God's beauty in Jesus Christ effects. Beatitude is a matter of our natures being elevated by the Spirit, indeed of their being remade by "the knowledge of the glory of God in the face of Jesus Christ" (2 Cor 4:6). Our healing is a matter of our nature's perfection in God. Beatitude describes a union whereby we see all things, including ourselves, as related to God. The key word is

---

19. Ibid., 127–28.
20. Ibid., 128. Cyril's comments are instructive as they occasion reflection on what distinguishes Father and Son, namely, the latter being "distinguished by the characteristic of the one who begat him, and he ascends in his essence to equal dignity because he is by nature God." See *Commentary on John*, vol. 1: *Cyril of Alexandria*, ed. Joel C. Elowsky, trans. David R. Maxwell (Downers Grove, IL: IVP Academic, 2013), 10, 71.
21. Barth, *Witness to the Word*, 128.
22. Ibid., 130.
23. Ibid., 131.

"related." In the case of ourselves as creatures of God, we become "gods by grace."[24] We do not become God. The Father, his Word, and their Spirit are God by nature, whereas we are ever only "gods by grace."[25]

Our sharing in God's nature as beatified creatures is, of course, a sharing proper to creatures. Even in the life to come, we do "not view Him [God] in the same proportion as He does Himself, totally, adequately, and with perfect penetration."[26] We do not know the Father as the Son does—with perfect penetration, a knowing by nature—although we will "see him as he is" (1 John 3:2). As those who are in him, we will indeed see him as he is, but always as redeemed creatures. Redeemed creatures look forward to their being rendered incorruptible by what they see and to their perfect participation in that which they see.

THE VISION OF GOD: ACTIVE OR PASSIVE?

The vision of God is an active and living vision because its object is life itself, the life of the Trinity. Opposing the false dichotomy between contemplation and action, the beatitude of the blessed has dynamic form. After all, John's vision in Revelation 21:22–27 is of a city characterized, as all cities are, by exchange, commerce, trade, and the like. But of course, the city of God radically differs from our earthly cities insofar as it is a city shorn of sin and death. Until that city comes down, however, prayer marks the vision of God. Vladimir Lossky, commenting on Origen, writes, "Action and contemplation, practice and gnosis are united in a single act—in prayers."[27] The vision is nourished in the act of prayer, sustained in the praises of a pilgrim people the fullness of whose life is yet to come.

Prayer is the means by which the Christian community is rendered transparent to the Trinity. Inasmuch as a people pray are they able to see. Prayer draws us into the life of God. In this life, Christians continually pray and watch; we "struggle for incorruptibility in which the human will heroically resist the cunning onslaughts of demons while striving to follow the commandments of the Gospel, above all the

---

24. Cyril, *Commentary on John*, 1.10. With this turn of phrase, Cyril means we come to share in the divine nature; he is not thereby confusing the Creator and the creatures. See 2 Peter 1:14.
25. Ibid.
26. Lossky, *Vision of God*, 16.
27. Ibid., 56.

commandment to love God and one's neighbour."[28] Prayer is the means by which we contemplate; indeed, prayer is contemplation.[29] In this life, contemplation is primarily ascetic in nature. Through prayer is the flesh mortified. When the Lord Jesus comes again to judge the living and the dead, we will no longer pray in terms of either confession or supplication but ceaselessly pray in the form of praise and thanksgiving. We will be vivified. We will see him as he is in all that we do.

God's essence will not only be knowable but seeable in the eschatological consummation of the kingdom.[30] Seeing what no one has hitherto seen will be a matter of "complete happiness."[31] We pray in this life in order that we may love and come to see what is our complete happiness. The ascetic character of contemplative prayer has to do with its teaching us to hate what is not in accord with our true happiness. What renders us happy is God, and this we learn through prayer. Beatitude is the state of perfected humanity in a perfected heavens and earth. In such a state will all our activity will be God-directed, and we will "see with God's own vision."[32]

In the beatific vision, the kind of activity that marks contemplation here and now will be no more. Thomas, whom Eugene Rogers memorably describes as "a Dominican who preaches and teaches and begs," will no longer preach, teach, and beg. The reality of God will not be something into which neither we nor Thomas (the Dominican) will need to grow. The begging and preaching, as with the church and the monastery, will be no more. Divine science will be all in all. "What makes us perfect humans, therefore, is to understand completely (which is not to say statically), or to have science."[33] This is the end of human existence: complete understanding of God.

 The fulfilment of the intellect (and therefore the will) is perfection.

In sum, our *telos* is science, "the saturation of the desire to understand, when we come to share God's knowledge in heaven."[34] Heavenly life is a life saturated with God. The vision that will one day be whole is a vision of radically purified understanding. In this life we only glimpse

28. Ibid., 84.
29. For an ascetic like Evagrius, "theology, gnosis of the Trinity [of which contemplation of the Trinity is the beginning] and prayer are therefore synonymous." See ibid., 87.
30. See *Pseudo-Dionysius: The Complete Works*, trans. Colm Luibheid, Classics of Western Spirituality (New York: Paulist, 1987).
31. Rogers, "Beatific Vision," in *Creation*, 238.
32. Ibid., 239.
33. Ibid., 254.
34. Ibid., 257.

this understanding through the act of prayer and contemplation. "The deep Trinitarian principle of the Spirit celebrating the love of the Father and the Son repeats and reflects in creation and therefore in human beings."[35] This principle will be repeated to all eternity. It is what we seek to understand with a view toward "consummated contemplation."[36] The eschatological banquet is the beatific vision. "O taste and see that the LORD is good; happy are those who take refuge in him" (Ps 34:8).

CONCLUSION

In this book, I have made an argument about how I think pneumatological doctrine should proceed and what it should say. In terms of proceeding, pneumatological doctrine has to keep an especially close eye on the biblical material. Pneumatological teaching within a Trinitarian context will want to not only unfold Scripture's testimony to the Spirit's workings but also reflect on the being and identity of the one who acts in these ways. My primary conversation partner in so doing has been the Fourth Gospel, followed by Augustine, Thomas, and Barth. In accord with John 17:26, I have presented the Spirit in largely Augustinian and Thomistic terms as the "love" with which the Father loves the Son and the Son loves the Father. Moreover, I have relied on Augustine's and Thomas's explanations of how the Spirit, who is this love, originates within God's life. Pneumatological doctrine proceeds by way of Scripture in order to describe where the mission we see narrated therein comes from. It is the task of a theology of the Spirit to articulate, however haltingly, where this mission comes from. The question of the Spirit's origin is indeed a matter of material consequence.

In writing this volume, I have come to see more clearly what should orient a doctrine of the Trinity and pneumatology as one of its correlates. Assuming no division within God between God's inner life and the life of God toward the outside, the doctrine describes for us the one from whom salvation comes. In a pneumatological register, we ask who is the "promise of the Father" and where this promise comes from (Acts 1:4). If the answer is God, as it is, then we also ask how this promise originates in God. This is where the language of originating relations is helpful. It supplies us with a glimpse of how the Spirit, who

---

35. Ibid., 258.
36. Ibid., 260.

is consubstantial with Father and Son, originates in God in a manner quite different from Father and Son.

A doctrine of the Spirit is concerned with what qualifies the Spirit to do what the Spirit does. What qualifies the Spirit to act as the Spirit does? Where and how does the Spirit's agency originate? These questions point to the matter of the Spirit's antecedence. The Spirit's procession from the Father through the Son qualifies the Spirit to do what the Spirit does. Put differently, it is the Spirit's mission to reveal his procession. The Spirit reveals who the Spirit *is* from eternity. Pneumatological teaching has its motor on the immanent level. It is who the Spirit is in God that determines what the Spirit does among us. Moreover, it is the particular shape of the Spirit's divinity that interprets the Spirit's work for us. Thus I have moved from person to work in this volume. It is the person of the Spirit in relation to Father and Son that elucidates what the Spirit does among us in relation to them.

In this book, especially in this last chapter, I have been sensitive to the contemplative dimension of pneumatological teaching. The vision that the Spirit achieves is rooted in the ascetics of prayer, wherein we arrive at a glimpse of the one we will one day see as he is. When Christ comes again, the vision will be complete, "the communion of the total man with God making Himself totally present."[37] The completeness of the vision, however, does not detract from its graciousness. It ever only remains a gift. In the Spirit we really commune with the Father and the Son. That we do so now in a provisional sense and will in an immediate sense does not take away from the fact that it remains grace all the way down, and that we never cease to be creatures even as we gaze on the divine essence in a world shorn of death. And we will gaze in the Spirit, who is the Father and Son's love proceeding, the one in whom each comes to the other and in whom we forever come to them.

In sum, one's pneumatology is only as good as one's wider doctrine of the Trinity. The doctrine of the Trinity is the principle of intelligibility for pneumatology: without the Trinity, not only pneumatology but also all other doctrines lose their anchor. With the Trinity at the center, we come to see the Spirit as one who incorporates us into the Son, in whom we are baptized, and so come to the Father, who, in the Son, is our Father. Until Jesus comes again, we join with his Spirit in crying "Abba! Father!" (Gal 4:6).

---

37. Lossky, *Vision of God*, 135.

SUBJECT INDEX

215

SCRIPTURE INDEX

AUTHOR INDEX